BEYOND THE SECULAR WEST

RELIGION, CULTURE, AND PUBLIC LIFE

RELIGION, CULTURE, AND PUBLIC LIFE

Series Editor: Karen Barkey

The resurgence of religion calls for careful analysis and constructive criticism of new forms of intolerance, as well as new approaches to tolerance, respect, mutual understanding, and accommodation. In order to promote serious scholarship and informed debate, the Institute for Religion, Culture, and Public Life and Columbia University Press are sponsoring a book series devoted to the investigation of the role of religion in society and culture today. This series includes works by scholars in religious studies, political science, history, cultural anthropology, economics, social psychology, and other allied fields whose work sustains multidisciplinary and comparative as well as transnational analyses of historical and contemporary issues. The series focuses on issues related to questions of difference, identity, and practice within local, national, and international contexts. Special attention is paid to the ways in which religious traditions encourage conflict, violence, and intolerance and also support human rights, ecumenical values, and mutual understanding. By mediating alternative methodologies and different religious, social, and cultural traditions, books published in this series will open channels of communication that facilitate critical analysis.

For a complete list of the books in this series, see page 279.

BEYOND THE SECULAR WEST

EDITED BY
Akeel Bilgrami

Columbia University Press

New York

Columbia University Press
Publishers Since 1893
New York   Chichester, West Sussex

Copyright © 2016 Columbia University Press
Paperback edition, 2018
All rights reserved

Library of Congress Cataloging-in-Publication Data
Beyond the secular West / Edited by Akeel Bilgrami.
pages cm. — (Religion, culture, and public life)
Includes bibliographical references and index.
ISBN 978-0-231-17080-2 (cloth)—ISBN 978-0-231-17081-9 (pbk.)—
ISBN 978-0-231-54101-5 (ebook)
1. Secularism. 2. Religion and culture. 3. Taylor, Charles, 1931–
Secular age. I. Bilgrami, Akeel, 1950– editor.
BL2747.8.B49 2016
200.9'04—dc23
2015032306

Cover design: Lisa Hamm
Cover image: Composite (*top*) © Raghu Rai/Magnum Photos,
(*bottom*) © Kevin Grant/Shutterstock

CONTENTS

Preface vii
Akeel Bilgrami

1 CAN SECULARISM TRAVEL? • 1
Charles Taylor

2 THE SUFI AND THE STATE • 28
Souleymane Bachir Diagne

3 THE INDIVIDUAL AND COLLECTIVE SELF-LIBERATION MODEL
OF *USTADH* MAHMOUD MOHAMED TAHA • 45
Abdullahi Ahmed An-Na'im

4 CREATING DEMOCRATICALLY FRIENDLY TWIN TOLERATIONS
OUTSIDE OF LATIN CHRISTENDOM: TUNISIA • 76
Alfred Stepan

5 SECULARISM AND THE MEXICAN REVOLUTION • 97
Claudio Lomnitz

6 IS CONFUCIANISM SECULAR? • 117
Peter van der Veer

7 DISENCHANTMENT DEFERRED • 135
Sudipta Kaviraj

8 AN ANCIENT INDIAN SECULAR AGE? • 188
Rajeev Bhargava

9 GANDHI'S RADICALISM: AN INTERPRETATION • 215
Akeel Bilgrami

**10 A SECULAR AGE OUTSIDE LATIN CHRISTENDOM:
CHARLES TAYLOR RESPONDS • 246**
Charles Taylor

List of Contributors 261

Index 265

PREFACE

These essays were conceived among a handful of scholars from a range of disciplines (history, politics, philosophy, anthropology, law) and provoked by the intellectual claims of an impressive book by Charles Taylor published a few years ago, bearing the title *A Secular Age*. The provocation was simply this: Could a work that had analyzed in great historical and analytical detail the emergence of the secular in Latin Christendom carry lessons for other parts of the world?

Though Taylor himself had avowedly restricted himself to a focus on the Latin West, given the intrinsic generality of the concept of the secular as well as the ideological mobilization that European imperial conquest of distant lands had made possible, a question about the reach of the concept was never far from the offing for Taylor himself and for anyone reading his book with an alertness to its widest implications.

The authors of these essays, though they are by no means all restricted to Columbia University, got together several times over three years or more at Columbia University (and at periodic retreats in nearby Tarrytown, New York) to pursue this large question. The discussions proved so fruitful and exciting that we decided to gather our thoughts and deliver them in essays, which Columbia University Press has helpfully agreed to publish as one among its cluster of publications on the themes of secularism and tolerance.

The essays were always intended by us as looking to the interest of the secular in many different parts of the world beyond Christendom, but no group of scholars could possibly aspire to comprehensiveness on this score. Still, when China, India, Latin America, Africa, and the Middle East are all on offer in one or other essay, it is no small spread. Regional range apart, there are also diverse intellectual and methodological angles provided by the different disciplinary locations of the authors, and there is an illuminating balance between observing the points of affinity and departure from the genealogical roots of the secular in Europe, while also elaborating the local flowering of secularity in quite autonomous terms in these distant settings. India, unsurprisingly, gets somewhat more play in the volume than other settings, because secular*ism* (the specifically *political* doctrine that emerges from the ideal of the secular) has been a subject of such intense and prolonged discussion there just prior to and since decolonization, and it raises questions of its own as to why this should be so or comparatively more so than in other regions of the global South. In general, as one would expect, the essays raise as many questions of this sort and others as they answer.

Many of these questions are very usefully and clearly introduced by Taylor himself in an opening chapter. It would be redundant of me, therefore, to do so in this short preface, as it would be for me to present summaries of the essays that follow, because Taylor himself provides them in an equally valuable set of replies in the concluding chapter.

The volume, thus, owes greatly to Taylor's most obliging willingness to participate in these proceedings and to Al Stepan's inspiring enthusiasm for the subject that infected each one of us. I would like to thank them both and all the other contributors to the book for their essays, a thoroughly fitting outcome of some of the most searching and lively discussions one could hope to have with one's academic colleagues. My thanks too to the Institute of Religion, Culture, and Public Life at Columbia University for bringing many of us together frequently and for its various hospitalities over the years, and especially to Melissa Van for her vigilant eye on all matters of organization and her gently prompting presence during the editing of this volume.

Akeel Bilgrami

BEYOND THE SECULAR WEST

1

CAN SECULARISM TRAVEL?

Charles Taylor

1

We live in a world in which ideas, institutions, art styles, and formulae for production and living, circulate among societies and civilizations that are very different in their historical roots and traditional forms. Parliamentary democracy spread outward from England, among other countries, to India. And the practice of nonviolent civil disobedience spread from its origins in Gandhi's practice to many other places, including Martin Luther King Jr.'s civil rights movements, to Manila in 1983, and eventually to the Velvet and Orange revolutions of our time.

But these ideas and forms don't just change place as solid blocks; they are also modified, reinterpreted, given a new spin and meaning in each transfer. This can lead to tremendous confusion when we try to follow these shifts and understand them. One possible course of confusion comes from taking the word too seriously: the name may be the same, but the reality will often be different.

This is evident in the word "secular." We think of "secularization" as a process that can occur anywhere (and for some people, is occurring everywhere). And we think of secularist régimes as options for any country, whether they are adopted or not. And certainly, these words crop up (almost)[1] everywhere. But do they really mean the same thing? Are there not, rather, subtle differences that can bedevil cross-cultural discussions of these matters?

I think there are and that they do make problems for our understanding. Either we stumble through cross-purposes; or else, a rather minimal awareness of the differences can lead us to draw far-reaching conclusions that are very wrong. As when people argue that since the "secular" is an old category of Christian culture, and since Islam doesn't seem to have a corresponding category, including such notions as distinction of church and state, therefore, Islamic societies cannot adopt secular regimes. Obviously, they will not be just like those in Christendom, but maybe the idea here can travel in a more inventive and imaginative way.

One way of tackling this problem is to start by looking inward, into the Western Christian society that generated the term. If we can get a more exact idea of its contours—the issues about whether it applies elsewhere, and if so how easily and with what changes—it can perhaps be more fruitfully addressed. So let's look at some of the features of the "secular" as a category developed within Latin Christendom.

First, it was one term of a dyad. The secular had to do with the "century," that is, with profane time, and contrasted with what related to the eternal, or higher time. Certain times, places, persons, institutions, and actions were seen as closely related to the sacred or higher time, and others as out there in profane time. That's why the same distinction could often be made by use of the dyad "spiritual/temporal" (e.g., the state as the "temporal arm"). Ordinary parish priests are "secular" priests, because they operate out there in the "century," as against in monastic institutions under rules (the "regular" priests).

So there was an obvious meaning for "secularization" that goes pretty far back—to the aftermath of the Reformation. When certain functions, properties, institutions were transferred out of church control and into the hands of laymen, this was "secularization."

These moves were originally made within a system in which the dyad held; things were moved from one niche to another within a standing system of niches. This feature, where it still holds, can make secularization a relatively undramatic affair, a rearrangement of the furniture in a civilization whose basic features remain unchanged.

But from the seventeenth century on, a new possibility arose. A new conception of social life came gradually to be defined in which the "secular" was all there was. Since "secular" originally applied to a kind of time, profane or ordinary time, seen in relation to higher times, what was necessary was to come to understand profane time as all there is; to deny any relation to higher time. The word could go on being used, but the meaning was profoundly changed, because what it contrasted with was quite altered. The contrast was not another time dimension, in which "spiritual" institutions found their niche; rather, the secular was in the new sense opposed to claims on resources or allegiance made in the name of something transcendent to this world and its interests. Needless to say, those who imagined a "secular" world in this sense saw these claims as ultimately unfounded and only to be tolerated to the extent that they didn't challenge the interests of worldly power and well-being.

Because many people went on believing in the transcendent, it could even be necessary that churches continue to have their place. They could in their own way be essential to a well-functioning society. But this good function was to be understood in terms of "this-worldly," that is, "secular," goals and values (peace, prosperity, growth, flourishing, etc.).

This shift required two important changes: the first brought a new conception of good social/political order that was unconnected either to the traditional ethics of perfection and the good life or to specifically Christian notions of perfection (sainthood). This was the new post-Grotian idea of a society formed from and by individuals to meet their needs for protection and for the means to life. The criterion of a good society in this outlook was that of mutual benefit. The criterion was not only emphatically "this-worldly," but also unconcerned with "virtue" in the traditional sense.

But this hiving off of an "earthly" criterion figured within a broader distinction, that which divided "this world," or the immanent, from the transcendent. This very clear-cut distinction is itself a product of the development of Latin Christendom and has become part of our way of seeing things in the West. We tend to apply it universally, even though nothing this hard and fast exists in any other human culture in history. What does seem, indeed, to exist universally is some distinction between higher beings, or spirits, or realms, and the everyday one we see immediately around us. But these are not usually sorted out into two distinct realms, where the lower one can be taken as a system understandable purely in its own terms. Rather, the levels usually interpenetrate, so that the lower can't be understood without the higher. To take an example from the realm of philosophy, for Plato, the existence and development of the things around us can only be understood in terms of the corresponding Ideas, and these exist in a realm outside time. The clear separation of an immanent from a transcendent order is one of the inventions (for better or worse) of Latin Christendom.

We can see in societies that seem closest to the earliest form of religion a kind of intermingling of the two levels that would defy any such separation. In some tribes it would be unthinkable to set out on a hunt, a paradigm of "this-worldly" activity in our modern understanding, without first sacrificing to or communing with the spirit of the deer. In medieval Europe, each guild of artisans would have its chaplain, its rituals, its patron saints. Connections to higher beings were pervasive in these societies. "La religion était partout," as Roger Caillois put it. Already the distinction of the two realms or levels involves some degree of sorting out. But prior to the modern age, this sorting out didn't entail even the notional possibility of a real separation.

This clear separation prepares the ground for an even more radical position. It affirms, in effect, that the "lower," immanent or secular order is all there is; that the "higher," or transcendent is a human invention. Obviously, the prior invention of the clear-cut distinction between the levels prepared the ground for this "declaration of independence" of the immanent.

At first the independence claimed was limited and partial. In an earlier, deist version, widespread in the eighteenth century, God was seen as the artificer of this immanent order. So (1) since he is Creator, the natural order stands as a proof of his existence; (2) since the proper human order of mutual benefit is one that He designs and recommends, we follow His will in building it; and (3) he backs up His law in this regard by the rewards and punishments of the next life.

So a certain piety is necessary to good order. John Locke will exclude from toleration not only Catholics, but also atheists. Some religion is indispensable. This is the positive relation of God to good order. But religion can also have negative effects. Religious authority can enter into competition with (even good) secular rulers. It can demand things of the faithful that go beyond or even against the demands of good order. It can make irrational claims. Society must be purged of "superstition," "fanaticism," and "enthusiasm."

The attempts of eighteenth-century "enlightened" rulers, such as Frederick the Great and Joseph II, to "rationalize" religious institutions, in effect treating the church as a department of the state, belong to this earlier phase. As does, in a quite different fashion, the founding of the American Republic, with its separation of church and state. But the first unambiguous assertion of this self-sufficiency of the secular came with the radical phases of the French Revolution.

This polemic assertion of the secular returns in the Third Republic, whose *laïcité* is founded on these ideas of self-sufficiency and the exclusion of religion. For radical Republicans, the state should be founded on a *morale indépendante*, that is, one free from and a rival to religious morality.

Needless to say, this spirit is still not altogether dead in contemporary France, as one can see in the discussion about banning the Muslim headscarf. The insistence is still that the public spaces in which citizens meet must be purified of any religious reference.

And so the history of this term "secular" in the West is complex and ambiguous. It starts off as a term in a dyad, which distinguishes two dimensions of existence, identifying them by the kind of time essential to each. But then building on the clear immanent/transcendent distinction, it mutates into a term in another dyad, where "secular" refers to what pertains to a self-sufficient immanent sphere, and its contrast term (often identified as "religious") relates to the transcendent realm. This can then undergo a further mutation, via a denial of this transcendent level, into a dyad in which one term refers to the real (the secular), and the other to what is merely invented (the religious); or where "secular" refers to the institutions we really require to live in "this world," and "religious" or "ecclesial" to optional extras that often disturb the course of this-worldly life.

Through this double mutation, the dyad itself has thus profoundly changed; in the first case, both sides are real and indispensable dimensions of life and society. The dyad is "internal," in the sense that each term is impossible of application without its other, like right and left, or up and down. After the mutations, the dyad becomes "external"; secular and religious are opposed as true/false, or necessary/superfluous. The goal of policy is often to abolish one while conserving the other.

A similar development can be traced if we take the other major term in which issues of the secular are discussed in the West, *laïcité* (*laicità*, *laiklik*). This too starts as a term in an internal dyad, that of clergy and laypeople. Each of these categories exists only in relation to the other. But it eventually mutates to an external dyad in which the suppression of the clergy becomes conceivable.[2]

In some ways, the postdeist modes of secularism continue while transposing features of the deist template described above. In the Jacobin outlook, the designer is now Nature, and so the "piety" required is a humanist ideology based on the natural. What is unacceptable, in turn, is any form of "public" religion. Faith must be relegated to the private sphere. Following this view, there must be a coherent *morale indépendante*, a self-sufficient social morality without transcendent reference. This in turn encourages the idea that there is such a thing as "reason alone" (*die blosse Vernunft*), that is, reason unaided by any "extra" premises derived from revelation or any allegedly transcendent source. Variants of these claims resurface often in contemporary discussions in the West.[3]

The deist template helped to define good or acceptable religion for much of the Western discussion of the last centuries. A good or proper religion is a set of beliefs in God or some transcendent power that entails an acceptable (or in some versions, a "rational") morality. It is devoid of superfluous elements that don't contribute to this morality, and thus of "superstition." It is also necessarily against "fanaticism" or "enthusiasm," because these involve by definition a challenge by religious authority to what reason shows to be the proper order of society.[4]

Good religion can thus be an aid to social order, by inculcating the right principles; and it certainly avoids being a hindrance to this order by launching a challenge against it. Thus Locke is ready to tolerate various views about religion, but he excepts from this benign treatment atheists (whose nonbelief in an afterlife undermines their readiness to keep their promises and respect good order) and Catholics (who cannot but challenge the established order).

In both these ways, positive and negative, the essential impact of good religion takes place *in foro interno*: on one hand, it generates the right moral motivation; on the other, by remaining within the mind and soul of the subject, it refrains from challenging the external order. So public ritual is not an essential element of this religion, unless it can help by celebrating the good public order or by stimulating inner moral motivation.

But there is another feature of the Christian sorting of the two levels that played a role in their eventual separation. On the original view, these two coexisted, they were both ineradicable, but they were also in considerable tension. We can follow Augustine and speak of the two cities that Christians belonged to. They were inevitably involved, along with non-Christians, in the societies of this world, be they republics or kingdoms, which were temporal and passing; but they also belonged to the city of God, which not only lasted for all times but was meant to draw its members up into eternal life. In this life the two societies could not be disintricated, but in the end the higher one would stand clear of the lower. The big danger was that living on these two levels, in relation to profane time and to eternity, Christians were constantly tempted to be over-absorbed in the demands of the earthly city, and to give them priority over the call of the heavenly one. Thus the distinction defined two levels, which could not be separated, but where one went on posing a terrible danger for the other. The relation was fraught with an ineradicable tension.

And indeed, the beginning of the long series of reform in the Western church, which issued in Western modernity, can perhaps be dated with the Hildebrandine reforms of the eleventh century. Gregory VII was concerned above all with recovering (as he saw it) the independence of the church, as the guide to the heavenly city, from the power of lay rulers, who had acquired the right to appoint clergy and hence use Church lands and even use bishoprics as instruments to build dynastic power.

This tension-filled internal dyad could never find a stable form but was the site of continuing struggle up to (and even in some places beyond) the moment it mutated into an external one.

Then this constellation of terms, including "secular" and "religion," with all its baggage of ambiguity and its depth assumptions of a clear immanent/transcendent and a sharp public/private distinction, begins to travel. No wonder it causes immense confusion. Westerners are themselves frequently confused about their own history. But a common outlook today embraces the true/false view, while seeing the earlier two-dimensional, internal dyad view as having created the necessary historical preconditions for its arising. One way of stating this is to understand Western secularism as the separation of religion and state, the excision of religion into a "private" zone where it can't interfere with the common life. Then the earlier Western distinction between church and state, which eventually led to a separation of church and state, is seen as the run-up to the finally satisfactory solution, where religion is finally hived off and relegated to the margins of political life.

But these stages are not clearly distinguished. Thus, American secularists often confuse totally separation of church and state from that of religion and state. John Rawls at one point wanted to ban all reference to the grounds of people's "comprehensive views" (these included religious views) from public discourse.

And the whole constellation generates disastrously ethnocentric judgments. If the canonical background for a satisfactory secularist regime is the three-stage history—distinction of church/state, then separation of church/state, then sidelining of religion from state and public life—then obviously Islamic societies can never make it.

Or again, one often hears the judgment that Chinese imperial society was already "secular," totally ignoring the tremendous role played by the immanent/transcendent split in the Western concept, a split that had no analogue in traditional China. One could argue that Confucianism embodies a view in which good order in this society is essentially related to a higher reality, *tian* or "heaven," and thus straddles the secular/religious divide, as does the Platonism I referred to earlier in another way. But it straddles it without a sense of there being two orders, and even less with any hint of a constituent tension between them.

But if we simply declare this centuries-old Chinese outlook "secular," then we can trace what seem to be "religious" challenges to this secular régime in the periods in which Buddhism and Daoism have been seen as threats to state order. And then if we look at the present régime in the People's Republic, which seems at this time to be resurrecting Confucianism in place of Marxism as a state philosophy, and note that it recognizes five "religions": Buddhism, Daoism, Catholicism, Protestantism, and Islam (which together amount to a minority of the Chinese population) we can easily swallow the view that an age-old "secular" society has been managing "religion" for centuries. But this not only follows a contestable classification of Confucianism but also ignores the strength of the maze of popular cults and ritual, which are often branded with the derogatory term "superstition."

In relation to India, Ashis Nandy, in discussing the problems that arise out of the uses of the term "secular," shows up the confusions that are often involved in analogous statements about the Indian case, for example, that the emperor Asoka was "secular," or that the Mughal emperor Akbar established a "secular" form of rule.

But this kind of statement can also reflect a certain wisdom. In fact Nandy distinguishes two quite different notions that consciously or unconsciously inform the Indian discussion. There is on one hand the "scientific-rational" sense of the term, in which secularism is closely identified with modernity, and on the other a variety of "accommodative" meanings that are rooted in indigenous traditions. The first attempts to free public life from religion; the second seek rather to open space "for a continuous dialogue among religious traditions and between the religious and the secular."[5]

The invocation of Akbar's rule as "secular" can then be a way of redefining the term in a creative and productive way. Such redefinitions start from the problems contemporary societies have to solve, defining secularity as an attempt to find fair and harmonious modes of coexistence between religious communities, and leaving the connotations of the word "secular," as these have evolved through Western history quietly to the side. This takes account of the fact that formulae for living together have evolved in many different religious traditions and are not the monopoly of those whose outlook has been formed by the modern, Western dyad, in which the secular lays claims to exclusive reality.[6]

2

The invocation of popular cults in China, which are often forgotten when people discuss "religion" in that civilization, not only reminds us how protean this term is but also leads us to recognize other features of the Western trajectory that are far from universal. Christianity, as well as Islam, emerges from the Axial turn in ancient Hebrew society, combined with some elements of the Greek Axial revolution. But what do I mean here in talking of Axial turn(s)?

Any view about the long-term history of religion turns on an interpretation of the Axial Age. What was the nature of the Axial revolution? This is sometimes spoken of as the coming to be of a new tension "between the transcendental and mundane orders," involving a new conception of the "transcendental."[7] But "transcendental" has more than one meaning; I note five here. It can designate something like a "going beyond" the human world, or the cosmos (1). But it also can mean the discovery or invention of a new standpoint from which the existing order is cosmos or society can be criticized or denounced (2). Moreover, these two meanings can be linked. The place or being beyond the cosmos may yield the new locus from which critique becomes possible. The Hebrew prophets condemning the practices of Israel in the name of God come to mind.

Again, potentially linked to these two is another change: the introduction of second-order thinking (3), in which the formulae we use to describe or operate in the world themselves come under critical examination.

Possibly linked with these three is another change: what Jan Assmann calls "implied globality" (4).[8] The notion here is that the transcendent being, or the principles of criticism, may be seen as of relevance not just to our society but to the whole of humanity.

But the link with our own society may be weakened in another way. Any of the above changes may bring with them a new notion of the philosophical or religious vocation of individuals. Indeed, the changes may themselves be introduced by such individuals, who invent or discover new forms of religious or philosophical life. The Buddha or Socrates comes to mind. This can be the origin point of a process of disembedding (5), a process I would like to deal with in the following discussion.

These five may be seen as rival accounts of what Axiality consists in, but it might be better to see them as potentially linked changes; in which case, the issue between them would be more like this: which of these changes provides the best starting point from which to understand the linkages in the whole set?

Without wanting to challenge any of these readings, I would like to suggest a sixth way of conceiving the change. It was a shift from a mode of religious life that involved "feeding the gods," wherein the understanding of human good was that of prospering or flourishing (as this was understood) and the "gods" or spirits were not necessarily unambiguously on the side of human good, to a mode in which (a) there is notion of a higher, more complete human good, a notion of complete virtue, or even of a salvation beyond human flourishing (Buddha); while at the same time (b) the higher powers on this view are unambiguously on the side of human good. What may survive is a notion of Satan or Mara, spirits that are not ambivalent but rather totally against human good. I make some of the links clear from the outset, because I would like to present this change in our understanding of the good (6) as a facet of the change I call disembedding (5).

Now, crucial to the Hebrew turn were two related features: first, the sense of possessing the only "true religion," and secondly, the struggle to control and eventually ban "idolatry." The second was seen as an entailment of the first.

Post-Axial religions that trace their roots to the Hebrew Bible share a feature not found in the aftermath of other Axial revolutions; a tendency to restrict, even clamp down on pre-Axial forms of ritual. One might argue that Christianity and Islam incorporate elements of the pre-Axial religions they supplanted, but these are given a new form, and other earlier practices are banned. Moreover, both Christian and Muslim societies go through periodic bouts of reform, in which the claim is heard that too many "pagan" practices survive, and these have to be abolished.

Arguably, one of the great sources of Western secularity, the drive to disenchant the world, is a feature of Jewish-Christian-Muslim religions and the civilizations they nourished. It doesn't exist at all in Indian and Chinese civilization, or at least not in the same form. Thus, the great reform of the Buddha, while it implicitly empties Vedic ritual of much of its meaning, never seems to have inspired a movement to put an end to these practices. It is rather similar to the situation in ancient Greece; philosophers may look down on these rituals, but they see no reason in principle to ban them, provided they don't threaten decency and public order.

Now, the great civilizations that made the Axial turn were the sites of a certain tension between the elements of popular religion, which continued with modification (and which included rituals and devotions of all kinds), on one hand, and the demands of whatever the Axial definition of higher good was, on the other. But this tension could be defused by a modus vivendi between a minority of people, monks, *bhikkhus* (what Weber called "religious virtuosi") who tried to live the full Axial good and the mass of the population who remained deeply attached to (transformed modes of) pre-Axial rituals. The basis for this can be a kind of complementarity; such as, for instance, in Thailand, where laity feed the monks, and this confers merit on them; or to take a medieval European idea: the aristocracy fight for everyone, the clergy pray for everyone, and the peasants work for everyone (*bellatores, oratores, laboratores*).

But this kind of equilibrium was undermined in Latin Christendom by a growing movement for reform, which in the end came to demand a total makeover of the religious life to meet the demands of the Axial good, purging all pre-Axial elements that were incompatible with this.

Now, the drive for this came from the form of the Axial turn, which defined ancient Judaism, which Christianity and Islam inherited, and which I have just described, based on the key notion of "true religion" and the contrast notion of "idolatry," which has to be avoided at all cost. Hence the very widespread idea that intolerance is built into the religions that find their origin in Judaic monotheism.

There is, of course, a crucial question that arises from this story: "How much of the difference between the Western path and, say, the Indian one can be accounted for by the different Axial turns?" Just repeating the point about monotheism and intolerance doesn't get us far enough, because (1) this kind of attempt to expunge the pre-Axial doesn't happen in all civilizations that inherit from monotheism (not in Eastern Christendom, for instance, and sometimes in Islam [Wahhabism], but not everywhere), and (2) we need some more positive characterizations of the Indian Axial turn than just that it's "not monotheism."

And on the other side, certain modernizing movements in recent centuries in India and China seem to have envisaged cleaning up traditional rituals, such as the attempt of the Brahmo Samaj to define a purer Hinduism or the movements to "smash temples" in China. But these seem to have been partly inspired by Western examples and are linked to attempts to develop alternative modernities that could resist colonial takeovers. In this, they were already influenced to some degree by Western secularism, and the targeting of pre-Axial rituals is probably derived from the Western model, which continued and intensified the fight against "superstition" originated by the church.

3

But before we rush ahead with a hypothesis of secularisms that are simply derivatives of the Western model, we have to take another look at the Western trajectory in greater detail to determine exactly what traveled and what didn't.

And determining this requires that we identify the whole interactive context created by colonialism (or threatened colonial takeover), in which the desire to imitate the West and the desire not to be ruled and made over by Western powers arise and have to be reconciled.

The context is this: Western forms of secularity are closely related to Western modernity. One feature of this is the development of modes of social organization and the individual and social disciplines essential for them, which confer great power on those who adopt them. These include: the development of modern states served by bureaucracies, of functioning market economies, and of disciplined armies equipped with the latest technology, and, of course, the development of the nation-state, based on a mass mobilization of the population around a common identity based on equal citizenship, which allows the state to command the resources of society in manpower and wealth to an exceptional degree. A dramatic example of this is the famous *levée en masse*, which saved the fate of the French Revolution at the battle of Valmy in 1792.

Some of these, and in particular the latter, have proved essential to the defense, and if colonized, to the liberation of peoples from Western domination. The path to independence in India, for instance, passed through a mass mobilization behind the national movement; and something similar was attempted later elsewhere, even where in the twilight of empire it was not an essential condition of independence.

This kind of mobilization around a national identity already changes the society, if only because it modifies, mitigates, and/or relativizes previously existing markers of identity. But modern nation-states generally aspire to transform themselves further. The goal is usually defined as "development," by which is meant, among other goals, economic change to bring about growth, education, the mitigation of inequalities, and more generally, the reduction of barriers to equal citizenship. Society becomes capable of working on itself, defining and attempting to follow some direction of change. In the term coined by Sudipta Kaviraj, it becomes "reflexive," an analogy with the reflexive individual, who can take a critical stance to his or her own condition and devise ways of transforming it.

In a reflexive society, the changes may not be democratically endorsed. Élites always play a role, but in some cases the coercion by a "vanguard" may be extreme, as was evident in communist régimes. But there is nevertheless some connection between reflexivity and democracy, because transforming régimes can only fully mobilize their human resources and ensure success in the long run by winning the consent of the people. For this reason, and because they claim to act in the name of the people, despotic régimes of mobilization frequently claim the title "democratic," or claim to be "people's republics." The constant repetition of the claim is meant to help make it come true.

I want now to look at the Western trajectory, through which these modern modes of social organization, and in particular the reflexive nation-state, came to be. We can give a rapid sketch of this in terms of the three *D*'s: disenchantment, disciplines, and disembedding.

1. Disenchantment: Everyone can agree that one of the big differences between us and our ancestors of five hundred years ago is that they lived in an "enchanted" world, and we do not, or at the least our world is much less "enchanted." We might think of this as our having "lost" a number of beliefs and the practices they made possible. Essentially we become modern by breaking out of "superstition" and becoming more scientific and technological in our stance toward our world. But I want to accentuate something different. The "enchanted" world was one in which spirits and forces, defined by their meanings (the kind of forces given off by love potions or relics), played a big role. Leaving this kind of world was not just a matter of dropping certain beliefs. One can see this if one reflects that the "beliefs" themselves are rather strange for us, and the spirits not just invisible personal beings but often embodied forces.

But more, the enchanted world was one in which these forces could cross a porous boundary and shape our lives, psychic and physical. One of the big differences between us and them is that we live with a much firmer sense of the boundary between self and other. We are "buffered" selves. We have changed. We sometimes find it hard to be frightened the way they were, and indeed, we tend to invoke the uncanny things they feared with a pleasurable frisson, sitting through films about witches and sorcerers. They would have found this incomprehensible.

It is this sense of loss that underlies many attempts in our day to "re-enchant" the world. This goal is frequently invoked,[9] but it ought to be clear that what would be regained here is not what we have "lost." People are talking of quite other ways of recovering an analogue of the original sensibility: in the sense of the forces moving through nature in the poems of Friedrich Hölderlin or William Wordsworth, or in contact with spirits of the dead.

Disenchantment in my use (and partly in Weber's) really translates Weber's term *Entzauberung*, where the key kernel concept is *Zauber*, magic. In a sense moderns constructed their own concept of magic from and through the process of disenchantment. Carried out first under reforming Christian auspices, all practices involving the use of spiritual force against or at least independently of our relation to God were condemned. The worst examples were things like saying a black mass for the dead to kill off your enemy or using the host as a love charm. But in the more exigent modes of reform, the distinction between white and black magic tended to disappear, and all independent recourse to forces independent of God was seen as culpable. The category "magic" was constituted through this rejection, and this distinction was then handed on the post-Enlightenment anthropology, as with James Frazer in his distinction between "magic" and "religion."[10]

The process of disenchantment, involving a change in us, can be seen as a loss of a certain sensibility that is really an impoverishment (as against simply the shedding of irrational feelings). And there have been frequent attempts to "re-enchant" the world, or at least admonitions and invitations to do so. In a sense, the romantic movement can be seen as engaged in such a project. Think of Novalis's "magic realism"; think of the depiction of the Newtonian universe as a dead one, shorn of the life it used to have (Friedrich Schiller's "The Gods of Greece").

But it is clear that the poetry of Wordsworth, or of Novalis, or that of Rainer Maria Rilke, can't come close to the original experience of porous selves. The experience it evokes is more fragile, often evanescent, subject to doubt. It is also one that draws on an ontology that is highly undetermined and must remain so.[11]

2. Disciplines: Here I am talking about the development of disciplines of the subject, of self-examination and self-control designed to increase our lucidity about the shape of our lives and to increase our power to redesign and control this shape. These were meant to help us to think more rationally (applying "method," as with Descartes) and also to curb merely instinctive but irrational actions—of anger, of immediate self-indulgence—so that we can act more effectively in the world. The hope often extended to controlling or eventually eliminating the feelings underlying these rash responses. The effective agent learns self-control and is able to carry out plans, delay gratification where necessary, and so on.

These disciplines dovetail with those of social coordination, whereby we learn how to fit smoothly into wider social actions: queuing for the bus, arriving on time at work, going to vote on election day, and so on. Together these two dimensions of discipline underpin the new modes of social organization that confer power.

The personal disciplines both are powered by and help define a certain ethic, which puts a premium on what they define as rational freedom. The individual learns to reflect and act on his or her own, to adopt a critical stance toward self and world, to direct and change his or her life in the light of this critical thought. He or she eventually becomes autonomous, the reflexive individual who is the appropriate citizen of a democratic reflexive society.

3. Disembedding: By this I mean the process wherein people acquire an identity that is independent of any particular social order or community. That is, they come to be able to see themselves as remaining themselves even if they broke free from all the social niches that now help define them—state or church, village, or even, in more extreme cases, family.

The first phase of this kind of disembedding involves the undermining of notions of political order that see it as already inscribed in the nature of things. By contrast, the modern social imagery that develops in the West, following more the formulae devised by the modern natural law theories of Hugo Grotius and Locke, understands societies as ultimately constituted by independent and equal individuals who work together to create a society with an agreed constitution.

Two important types of premodern moral order are worth singling out here, because we can see them being gradually taken over, displaced, or marginalized by the Grotian-Lockean strand during the transition to political modernity. One is based on the idea of the law of a people, which has governed this people since time out of mind and in a sense defines it as a people. This idea seems to have been widespread among the Indo-European tribes who at various stages erupted into Europe. It was very powerful in seventeenth-century England, under the guise of the ancient constitution, and became one of the key justifying ideas of the rebellion against the king.[12]

This case should be enough to show that these notions are not always conservative in import; but we should also include in this category the sense of normative order that seems to have been carried on through generations in peasant communities and out of which they developed a picture of the "moral economy" from which they could criticize the burdens laid on them by landlords or the exactions levied on them by state and church.[13] Here again, the recurring idea seems to have been that an original acceptable distribution of burdens had been displaced by usurpation and ought to be rolled back.

The other type is organized around a notion of a hierarchy in society that expresses and corresponds to a hierarchy in the cosmos. These were often theorized in language drawn from the Platonic-Aristotelian concept of Form, but the underlying notion also emerges strongly in theories of correspondence: for example, the king is in his kingdom, as the lion among animals, the eagle among birds, and so on. It is out of this outlook that the idea emerges that disorders in the human realm will resonate in nature, because the very order of things is threatened. The night on which Duncan was murdered was disturbed by "lamentings heard i' the air; strange screams of death," and it remained dark even though day should have started. On the previous Tuesday a falcon had been killed by a mousing owl, and Duncan's horses turned wild in the night, "Contending 'gainst obedience, as they would / Make war with mankind."[14]

In both these cases, and particularly in the second, we have an order that tends to impose itself by the course of things; violations are met with backlash that transcends the merely human realm. This seems to be a very common feature in premodern ideas of moral order. Anaximander likens any deviation from the course of nature to injustice and says that things that resist it must eventually "pay penalty and retribution to each other for their injustice according to the assessment of time."[15] Heraclitus speaks of the order of things in similar terms, when he says that if ever the sun should deviate from its appointed course, the Furies would seize it and drag it back.[16] And of course, the Platonic Forms are active in shaping the things and events in the world of change.

By contrast, the modern notion of order sees this as constructed by humans. Not that we determine what constitutes good order, because this is sometimes seen as determined by God or (what is often thought to be the same) by the natural law. But the actual constitutions have been set up in historic time, ideally in an attempt to realize this law.

Now, the basic point of the new normative order was the mutual respect and mutual service of the individuals who make up society. The actual structures were meant to serve these ends and were judged instrumentally in this light. The difference might be obscured by the fact that the older orders also ensured a kind of mutual service; the clergy prays for the laity, and the laity defend/work for the clergy. But the crucial point was just this division into types in their hierarchical ordering; whereas on the new understanding we start with individuals and their debt of mutual service, and the divisions fall out as they can most effectively discharge this debt.

Thus Plato, in book 2 of *The Republic*, starts out by reasoning from the non self-sufficiency of the individual to the need for an order of mutual service. But quite rapidly it becomes clear that it is the structure of this order that is the basic point. And the last doubt is removed when we see that this order is meant to stand in analogy and interaction with the normative order in the soul. By contrast, in the modern ideal, the whole point is the mutual respect and service, however achieved.

Our primary service to one another was thus (to use the language of a later age) the provision of collective security, to render our lives and property safe under law. But we also serve each other in practicing economic exchange. These two main ends, security and prosperity, are now the principal goals of organized society, which itself can come to be seen as something in the nature of a profitable exchange between its constituent members. The ideal social order is one in which our purposes mesh, and each in furthering himself helps the others.

This ethic of mutual benefit, together with that mentioned above of rational freedom, ends up yielding the main lines of our contemporary understanding of political legitimacy, often inscribed today in charters of rights: the rights of individuals, particularly freedom; the equality of all citizens, excluding all discrimination between them; and democratic modes of governance.

So disenchantment and the disciplines helped produce a fourth D, the disengaged subject; this subject was dedicated to self-transformation, whence comes a fifth D, development; while the disciplines and disembedding helped produce an ethic of rationality, freedom, and equality.

4

In light of the above, we can see how the making of these power-conferring modes of social organization involved the crucial separation I described in the first section, by which the dyad secular/spiritual becomes an external one, in which the secular can exist on its own.

Let's concentrate on the most significant, overarching mode of social power—that of the nation-state. In a (I hope) permissible simplification, we can discern three ways in which this might intersect with the secular split. In the first (1), it might inhibit the split. National mobilization requires a strong common identity. But it will often be the case that this can only, or best, be found through a religious or confessional marker. Our world contains lots of examples of mobilizations that in some way center on religion. These are immensely varied, of course. In some cases, the mobilization focuses around intensely pious modes of faith, as in the Iranian Revolution of 1979 and many Islamist movements; in other cases, the faith, however lived, defines the shared identity, often during some long liberation struggle (i.e., Poland, Ireland). In third cases, again, piety is no longer an issue, the faith is now a historic marker, what matters is that we share a certain past, whatever our spiritual position today (i.e., parts of Northern Ireland, parts of the Balkans during the recent troubles). We have even seen very secular politicians in Europe suddenly discovering their Christian past when the issue of Turkish membership in the EU arises or when it comes to stigmatizing Muslims. As the last example suggests, these "cool" forms of religious identification can be just as chauvinist as the "hot" forms. The Indian Bharatiya Janata Party (BJP) is an excellent example; the founding figure of its ideology, Savarkar, was an atheist, and many of its existing leadership are not more pious, but it makes "Hindutva" into a historic marker that threatens all other religious identities, unless they accept the hegemony of the majority tradition.

(2) On the other side, national mobilization may identify religion as its enemy, for a number of reasons: because religious authority poses as a rival to the republic, or because religious life is bound up with rival identities (parochial, regional), which the national identity must eliminate or subordinate, or because the supposed (and sometimes real)

irrationalities of religious practice constitute an obstacle to national "development." The classic case here is France. But the very acerbity of the struggle, and the motive for republicans to play a strong secularist card, arose from the fact that a rival national identity of type (1) was on offer, a royalist Catholicism, which its proponents believed would alone make France great. (This was the ideology of Maurras's Action Française.)

(3) A third form of intersection arises in a different context. The national identity must be open to all citizens. But what happens when these are religiously diverse? Mode (1) now becomes very difficult to sustain. An established church, if taken really seriously, threatens to create a distinction between first- and second-class citizens. Consequently some kind of separation, either written into law or at least effectively operative even where the law recognizes one church (England, Scandinavia), must be effected. But this doesn't at all need to involve the wrenching battle and antireligious animus that usually accompanies (2).

These three scenarios are distinguishable as ideal types. But this doesn't mean that they exist quite separately from each other in different societies. We already saw how in the French case there was in fact a struggle between (1) and (2). And in addition, something like the spirit of (3) intervened during the debate on the 1904 legislation on separation, when Jaurès and others insisted on the importance of religious freedom.

The history of the United States is similarly complicated. The original American move was on the lines of (3), the separation of church and state. But on another level, many Americans understood their country as an instance of (1), a country held together by Christian faith. Thus, in the 1830s, a judge on the Supreme Court could argue that while the First Amendment forbade the identification of the federal government with any church, since all the churches were Christian (and in effect Protestant), one could invoke the principles of Christianity in interpreting the law.

For Judge Joseph Story, the goal of the first amendment was "to exclude all rivalry among Christian sects," but nevertheless "Christianity ought to receive encouragement from the state." Christianity was essential to the state, because the belief in "a future state of rewards and punishments" is "indispensable to the administration of justice." What is more, "it is impossible for those who believe in the truth of Christianity, as a divine revelation, to doubt that it is a special duty of government to foster, and encourage it among the citizens."[17]

This primacy of Christianity was upheld even later in the nineteenth century. As late as 1890, thirty-seven of the forty-two existing states recognized the authority of God in the preamble or text of their constitutions. A unanimous judgment of the Supreme Court of 1892 declared that if one wanted to describe " American life as expressed by its laws, its business, its customs and its society, we find everywhere a clear recognition of the same truth . . . that this is a Christian nation" (*Church of the Holy Trinity v. United States*, 143 U.S. 457 at 471).

In the latter part of the century, resistance began to build to this conception, but a National Reform Association was founded in 1863 with the following goal:

> The object of this Society shall be to maintain existing Christian features in the American government . . . to secure such an amendment to the Constitution of the United States as will declare the nation's allegiance to Jesus Christ and its acceptance of the moral laws of the Christian religion, and so as to indicate that this is a Christian nation, and place all the Christian laws, institutions, and usages of our government on an undeniable legal basis in the fundamental law of the land.

After 1870, the battle was joined between the supporters of this narrow view, on one hand, and those who wanted a real opening to all other religions and also to nonreligion. These included not only Jews but also Catholics, who (rightly) saw the "Christianity" of the National Reform Association as excluding them. It was in this battle that the word "secular" first appears on the American scene as a key term, and very often in its polemical sense of non- or antireligious.[18]

Something can already be said about the relation between these three dynamics, before we step outside the West. Intersections (1) and (2) both can be very inhospitable to democracy, both because they risk pushing those who don't share the official ideology into a second-class status and, even more, the battle to maintain and enforce this ideology may require repression of various kinds and even at the limit lead to despotism. On the other hand, (3) is often indispensable to create or sustain the kind of equality democracy requires.

5

This being said, let's move outside the West, and observe what travels and what lessons we can draw from this.

I have already mentioned cases of (1): Iran and Islamist movements, as well as certain Islamic countries in which these movements operate, such as (until recently?) Egypt, which apply elements of their program in order to blunt their opposition. It is also clear that cases of (2) are not hard to find: communist régimes in general but also Kemalist Turkey. We can see the full range of motivations in these cases that I mentioned. To take the case of Turkey: Atatürk plainly saw the ulema as a rival authority; he saw the caliphate, an institution of the international Islamic *umma*, as an obstacle to his goal of a national mobilization of Turks; and he believed that religion was the bulwark of backward, unscientific ways that development had to sweep aside.

At the same time, the negative consequences of (2) for democracy are very evident in the Turkish case. Democracy comes to Turkey only through the restraining or dismantling of Kemalist power, in particular the capacity of the army to intervene and seize power in the name of *laiklik*.

But we also saw another kind of religious repression, the crushing of folk religion, pre-Axial rituals, and various practices branded as "magic" or "superstition" in many cases where (2) was adopted: the "smashing" of temples, already under the Nationalists in China and exacerbated under the Communists, especially during the Cultural Revolution; and similar operations occurred in other communist societies. One can argue that this kind of repression took place under the influence of the Western model, where nation-building and development advance in the wake of disenchantment, something initiated by and inherited from Christian reform. In the light of this model, this kind of purge could be seen as essential to "development."

Interesting (negative) lessons can be drawn from this experience, lessons about what to avoid if one wants to build a democratic society or even one that minimizes popular discontent. The People's Republic of China drew these lessons after the Cultural Revolution. Religions and their practices can be savagely repressed (see the Falun Gong), but only if they threaten power. They are then also stigmatized as premodern and unscientific, but everyone understands that this is not the real motive of condemnation.

But interesting lessons can be drawn from the cases where this Western-modeled program was not followed or was not successful. India is an interesting case. Many of the élites who brought about independence shared this sense of the universal applicability of the Western model, although this was tempered by a desire to avoid extreme repression. Perhaps Nehru typified this combination: on one hand, he probably shared the view that democracy and development could not fully succeed without disenchantment, the universal spread of certain disciplines, and disembedding, particularly in relation to caste differences, which he rightly saw as the source of inequalities and oppression; on the other, he early turned his back on a Bolshevik-type solution and put his trust in persuasion and the democratic process.

But when one looks at the situation today, it seems evident that disenchantment hasn't occurred in a meaningful sense for the mass of the Indian population, that the personal disciplines of the Western trajectory have been embraced by certain élites but not by the majority of the population, and that disembedding in relation to caste (in the sense of *jati*) has not really occurred at all. On the contrary, *jati*, in the form of great coalitions (or "monster castes"), has become a central site of political mobilization in Indian democracy.

And yet: (i) a reflexive society, which has tried to come to grips with some of the worst inequalities of Indian society, such as those associated with untouchability, has come into existence. And this society remains democratic in some very meaningful way. Something new has come into existence that requires rethinking. Obviously, whatever one's normative stance, we can no longer believe that the Western trajectory of the three *D*'s is the inescapable road to social reflexivity and "development," however we want to define this (and the evidence shows that we will have to redefine it fast, in order to avoid ecological catastrophe).

And (ii) India has achieved its own version of (3), based perhaps less on Western models of church and state separation and more on long-standing indigenous traditions of religious pluralism. This in spite of the fact that they use the Western word "secularism" for it. We can speculate, as I mentioned in section 1, that certain historic experiences and traditions, associated for instance with Asoka and Akbar, have played a crucial role in sustaining Indian secularism, in spite of and against the threats it faces from "Hindutva" chauvinism.[19]

I might add that some of us in the West have found Indian secularism a source of valuable insights in rethinking our own régimes of secularism/*laïcité*.[20]

The claims I make under (i) and (ii) are of course open to challenge; and they require a great deal more research and reflection. But the Indian experience cannot but put these questions to us.

Let me try to sum up what (I hope) we have learned from this attempt to examine more closely the concept of the secular in its Christian sources, as well as the trajectory of its evolution in the West. I think we can see (A) that the concept has very little application in precolonial or precontact non-Western societies. So that it is very misleading to say, for example, that imperial China or traditional Japan were "secular," and leads us astray in a different way when we apply the term to Akbar's Mughal régime.

(B) The word then crops up outside the West in attempts to re-create an indigenous version of the essential power-conferring modes of social organization, particularly the reflexive state. The word is less misleading the closer one cleaves to the Western trajectory of the three *D*'s. The farther one departs from it, the more misleading it becomes. This seems to be illustrated by the case of India, where indeed, the word survives, but now designates a concept that has in part indigenous roots and sustains a version of (3) based on traditions very foreign to the West (and from which the West could learn).

NOTES

1. Of course, in a number of Western societies, the term used is *laïcité* and its derivatives, and this is not simply a translation of "secular." There are important differences. But *laïcité* follows a course parallel to "secular" as a term in an internal dyad, which then becomes external. See the discussion following, and also note 3.
2. Why did this become the key term in France, spreading thence to other Latin societies and eventually to Turkey? One reason is that the burning issues concerned the power of the clergy. But on another level, one can see the advantages for those challenging the church. When Léon Gambetta announced early in the Third Republic: "Le clericalisme, viola l'ennemi," he was aware that this slogan could gather much more support than a direct attack on the Catholic religion. Many Catholics were aware of and unhappy with the excessive claims of the clergy.
3. I have discussed this at greater length in "Die blosse Vernunft," in *Dilemmas and Connections* (Cambridge: Harvard University Press, 2011).
4. See my *Modern Social Imaginaries* (Durham, N.C.: Duke University Press, 2004) for a fuller discussion of the modern idea of moral order.
5. Ashis Nandy, "The Politics of Secularism and the Recovery of Religious Tolerance," in *Time Warps* (New Brunswick, N.J.: Rutgers University Press, 2002), see esp. 68–69 and 80.
6. Nandy, "The Politics of Secularism," 85. Amartya Sen also makes use of a similar point about Akbar's rule to establish the roots of modes of secularism in Indian history in *The Argumentative Indian*. For an excellent example of such a creative redefinition, see Rajeev Bhargava's chapter in this volume.,
7. S. N. Eisenstadt, ed., *The Origins and Diversity of Axial Age Civilizations* (Albany: State University of New York Press, 1986), 1.
8. See Jan Assmann, *Moses the Egyptian* (Cambridge: Harvard University Press,1997), chap. 1; and his paper in *The Axial Age*, ed. Hans Joas and Robert Bellah (Cambridge: Harvard University Press, forthcoming).
9. See George Levine, ed., *The Joys of Secularism* (Princeton: Princeton University Press, 2011).
10. Peter van der Veer shows how a not-dissimilar category, *wu*, which can be translated as either "shamanism" or "magic," emerging out of a parallel process of rational reform, was developed in modern China, that is, as a category for what was rejected as inferior, not really religion. See his "Secularism's Magic," in Peter van der Veer, *The Modern Spirit of Asia: The Spiritual and the Secular in China and India* (Princeton: Princeton University Press, 2013).
11. See Taylor, *A Secular Age*, chap. 10.

12. See J. G. A. Pocock, *The Ancient Constitution and the Feudal Law*, 2nd ed. (Cambridge: Cambridge University Press, 1987).
13. The term "moral economy" is borrowed from E. P. Thompson, "The Moral Economy of the English Crowd in the Eighteenth Century," *Past and Present* no. 50 (1971): 76–136.
14. *Macbeth*, 2.3.56; 2.4.17–18 (*Sources* 298).
15. Quoted in Louis Dupré, *Passage to Modernity* (New Haven: Yale University Press, 1993), 19.
16. "The sun will not overstep his measures; if he does, the Erinyes, the handmaids of Justice, will find him out." Quoted in George Sabine, *A History of Political Theory*, 3d ed. (New York: Holt, Rinehart and Winston, 1961), 26.
17. Andrew Koppelman, "Rawls and Habermas," 36.
18. Christian Smith, *The Secular Revolution* (Berkeley: University of California Press, 2003). See also Tisa Wenger, "Rewriting the First Amendment: Competing American Secularisms, 1850–1900," in *Public Religion, Secularism, and Democracy*, ed. Linell Cady and Elizabeth Shakman Hurd (London: Routledge, 2010).
19. See Rajeev Bhargava's chapter in this volume. See also Rajeev Bhargava, "Beyond Toleration: Civility and Principled coexistence in Ashokan Edicts," in *The Boundaries of Toleration*, ed. Alfred Stepan and Charles Taylor (New York: Columbia University Press, 2014) 172–203.
20. See, for instance, Jocelyn Maclure and Charles Taylor, *Laïcité et Liberté de Conscience* (Montréal: Boréal, 2010).

2

THE SUFI AND THE STATE

Souleymane Bachir Diagne

Saad ibn Abī Waqqās is one of the *Sahaba*, which in Islamic terminology means the early companions and disciples of the prophet Muhammad, those who were the first to believe in his mission and to follow him at a time when doing so meant persecution, exile, and the possibility of being killed. Saad, who is said to have been the seventeenth person to embrace the new faith, when he was seventeen, holds a particular place among those who wrote the golden legend of the early days of Islam. According to the narratives of those early times, he resisted the moral blackmail of his mother when she threatened to starve herself to death unless he abjured his new faith and returned to the religion of his forefathers. It is also said that he fiercely fought back a mob that attacked a small group of Muslims during the time when the nascent religion was persecuted in Muhammad's home city of Mecca, thus becoming the first Muslim who shed blood defending himself and his fellow believers. Later, during the wars between the Muslims living in the city of Medina and the Meccans, the fine archer he was became a celebrated hero as he stood among the ultimate defenders of the Prophet during a battle that was lost by the Muslims and in which Muhammad was severely wounded and even thought for awhile to be dead. A perfect illustration in the eyes of Muslims of what it means "to fight for God's cause with their property and their persons," Saad stands as a model for Muslims, especially the Sufis among them, when in the last part of his life he became the emblem of a certain attitude vis-à-vis the state. During the times of turmoil and internecine wars that fractured the Muslim community, starting in the last years of the third caliph Uthmān (d. 656) and culminating in the combats between Ali, the fourth caliph, and Muawiyya, who rebelled against him (from 656 to Ali's death in 661), Saad ibn Abī Waqqās simply retreated from the public sphere, refusing to take a side and endorse one position on the political-religious question of the caliphate. When pressured to do so, he is quoted as having declared that he would enter the arena only if presented with a sword which could tell the right from the wrong side. This attitude calls for two remarks, the first apropos the so-called Islamic state, the second concerning what could be called the Sufi attitude of withdrawal.

* * *

It is fair to say that Saad did not feel *internally* compelled to act or to speak one way or another on the issue. So it is also fair to draw from his attitude the conclusion that if his judgment could be suspended in that matter (although, of course, that does not mean he was or could be *indifferent*), it is because he did not feel that his Islamic faith itself was engaged. When the scholar from Al Azhar, Ali Abdel Razik (1888–1966), discusses the crucial question of whether recognizing and proclaiming a caliph has always been (and therefore still is) a religious duty, he recalls that contrary to an established belief, repeated, for example, by Ibn Khaldun (1332–1406), the answer is *no*.[1] One piece of evidence for that, according to Abdel Razik, is the fact that close companions of the prophet of Islam have, on certain occasions, refused to consider that they had to pledge allegiance to an established caliph. Saad ibn Abī Waqqās's attitude is certainly one such evidence, and not just because the circumstances were a civil war over the issue of who should be caliph.

What does that attitude say about the *Islamic* nature of the state that was created as a caliphate after 632 C.E.? One conclusion to be drawn from Ali Abdel Razik's *Islam and the Foundations of Political Power* is that there actually has never been a state that would be called

"Islamic." The importance of that book cannot be overstated. Its translator in French and editor in English, Abdou Filali-Ansari, rightly says that in spite of its modest size, it constitutes "an exceptional intellectual or literary event" as it "signaled an actual historical turning point, one that had a formative, long-lasting impact on the development of Muslim societies during the twentieth century."[2]

The question the book poses is simple: Is there such a thing as an Islamic state? To answer that question is to comment on the following important remark made by Olivier Roy when he writes:

> The history of the Muslim world shows that power was de facto secular and was never sacralized. It is the movement of re-Islamization in the twentieth century that questions the balance between political and religion, in a rereading of Islam (Islamism, neo-fundamentalism) which presents itself of course as a return to the origins, but is in fact an ideologization of the religious. When they insist on the necessity to return to the time of the Prophet, Islamists as well as neo-fundamentalists are the first to say that no political formation that has existed in the Muslim world has corresponded to a true Islamic State."[3]

Such a statement finds an echo in Abdullahi Ahmed An-Na'im's *Islam and the Secular State*, when the author writes: "The fact that the state is a political and not a religious institution is the historical experience and current reality of Islamic societies."[4] For him, too, the perception that "the secular State is a Western imposition" is the result of the propaganda of Islamist groups, generally influenced by Abul A'la Maududi (1903–1979) or Sayyid Qutb (1906–1966) and not based on "the actual history of Islamic societies."[5]

If we call the "true Islamic state" the "caliphate," the first question to be raised would then be "What is the Qur'anic reference for such a state?" And the answer to that question is that there is none. Nothing is said about the caliphate or a state with even minimal description of its functioning mechanisms. Rare, scattered verses quoted here and there from the Qur'an have been evoked to support the idea that the caliphate, if not explicitly mentioned, has been at least alluded to. Verse 4:59 in particular has thus been oversaturated with meaning to make it say that there is a continuous chain of authority from God to the sultan. The verse declares: "O you who believe! Obey God and obey the Messenger, and those charged with authority among you. If you differ in anything among yourselves, refer it to God and his Messenger, if you do believe in God and the last day: that is best and most suitable for final determination."

Commenting on that verse, one of the most authoritative English translators of the Qur'an, Abdullah Yusuf Ali, has the following footnote: The Arabic phrase "*Ulîl amr*," he says, means "those charged with authority or responsibility or decision, or the settlement of affairs. All ultimate authority rests in Allah. Prophets of Allah derive their authority from Him. As Islam makes no sharp division between sacred and secular affairs, it expects governments to be imbued with righteousness. Likewise Islam expects Muslims to respect the authority of such governments for otherwise there can be no order or discipline."[6]

The affirmation that the Prophet himself established the ideal model of an Islamic state is grounded in the historical fact that the hegira from Mecca of the first Muslims who found refuge in the city of Medina, where the local Arab tribes had converted to Islam, created the new situation of an Islamic community in need of organization. The Prophet's response was to call the newcomers "the Immigrants" (*Muhajjirûn*) and their hosts "the Helpers" (*Ansâr*) and then to establish a one-on-one strong relationship of brotherhood among them to replace traditional tribal organization and law by a new community called *umma* obeying new rules. For practical reasons (for example, there were also Jewish tribes living in Medina), religious pluralism and tolerance were proclaimed at first. Does that original community of Medina thus created out of the destruction (or attempted destruction) of traditional tribal law, founded on the religious authority of the Prophet and also on his practice of consultation (*shura*) with his closest companions among the *Muhajjirûn* and the *Ansâr* constitute the complete model that any subsequent state would have to imitate lest it become deviant? Again, if one looks for something like a Qur'anic prescription concerning the principles upon which such a state could be founded, there are these two verses often quoted relative to "consultation": 3:159 and 42:38. The second (42:38) in particular has given its name to the chapter in which it appears and it reads: "[That which is with God is for] those who harken to their Lord and establish regular prayer, who conduct their affairs by mutual consultation." In order to interpret the statement as being (also) about a principle of government, again, Yusuf Ali comments on this verse (the way political Islam does) by evoking the importance of consultation in the Prophet's private and public life, drawing the conclusion that "modern representative government is an attempt—by no means perfect—to apply this principle in State affairs."[7]

The reference to the first *umma* living under the guidance of the Prophet in Medina became in the Islamic imaginary a sort of Platonic ideal state to be imitated as much as possible in our world of generation and decay. Plato considered the ideal republic a utopia that could not exist in a world of becoming and corruption, a city for the philosopher to live in according to its laws. It is acceptable for a philosopher to speak of the ideal city as utopia, but if we speak of the Prophet and if we consider that it was an essential aspect of his religious mission to also establish a functioning and durable state, then the question should be asked: Why is there no institutional mechanism for duration?

A fundamental difference between Shias and Sunnis needs to be emphasized here. Shia political philosophy does consider that the mechanism was actually clearly indicated in some sort of "testament" but that, humans being humans, tribal law took its revenge after 632 and power was seized by those who created this deviation from the continuation of the ideal. Sunnis consider that until the death of Ali, the first four caliphs were rightly guided in the path established by the prophet of Islam.

What happened following prophet Muhammad's death is well known. Abu Bakr stated upon a hadith—a prophetic saying—the principle that the leadership of the newly created community should stay with the tribe of Quraysh to which the Prophet and many of his early companions belonged. Subsequently Abu Bakr himself was chosen as leader after an oath of the companions (*Ansâr* and *Muhajjirûn*). With him the word *khalifa* acquired the meaning of "successor" (understood: "of the Prophet"). And political philosophy became centered on the question of who should be the caliph.

Abu Bakr launched wars during the two years he was caliph; the wars are known as "wars of apostasy," because he fought against tribes that rebelled against the authority of the state after the Prophet's death. One series of such wars was against false prophets who wanted to "replace" Muhammad in his mission; the other was against tribes who decided not to pay taxes to the state, arguing that they were paying them to the prophet of Islam not to his successors who had no prophetic mission. This second form of rebellion was a much more serious threat to the state, because the rebellious tribes did have a point, as was pointed out by two eminent companions of the Prophet, future caliphs themselves: Umar the second caliph and Ali the fourth caliph. But Abu Bakr held the opinion that eventually prevailed and that he forcefully stated, according to Islamic traditions, by saying that the payment of the *zakāt* (here with the meaning of "tax") could not be separated from performing the ritual prayer, *salāt*, adding: "I swear by God if they withheld only a hobbling-cord [of a camel] of what they used to give to the Prophet, I would fight them for it."

The threat, the discussion, and the final decision by Abu Bakr to fight the rebellious tribes and maintain them in the polity are important for the question of the Islamic state. The rebellion was about ending the nascent Islamic state, since the founder of the religion was no longer there to precisely guarantee its Islamic nature. And the fact that prominent and learned companions of the Prophet were perplexed about the issue of taxes (of course taxation is the foundation of the state itself and guarantees its durability) seems to mean that the possibility of ending the very notion of an Islamic state had been envisioned by them. By associating *zakāt* to *salāt* Abu Bakr actually reaffirmed the religious significance of paying taxes to the state, thus maintaining it. His opinion prevailed, but the question that had arisen was a real one and could be formulated more generally as: "What makes the state *Islamic?*"

Sunnis want to think that something of Muhammad's prophethood was somehow prolonged by the first four caliphs, Abu Bakr, Umar, Uthman, and Ali, considered to have been *rāshidūn*, that is rightly guided. But this divine guidance is said to have ended with them and to have been followed by sheer kingdom (*mulk*). So is the Islamic nature of the state then contingent upon the influence of the Muslim scholars on the affairs of the state, especially legislative and judicial matters? It is important to remember here that there is no single sharia and that even under the four rightly guided caliphs, pluralism had already taken place in political and judicial matters. Does this mean the state was de facto secular?

This opinion is sometimes held by progressive Muslims who want to insist on the fact that Islam was secular even before secularism became a defining feature of modernity. But this is like interpreting "Render unto Caesar the things which are Caesar's" as a statement about the separation of church and state. The reality is that the question of Islamic or secular could not be posed and made no sense. In fact, when we interrogate the origins, when we reread the early history of Islam or any religion, we retro-project our questions and preoccupations upon the period, its issues, and debates.

The question could not be posed in those terms, that is, until the moment when the caliphate effectively disappeared, forcing the elites in Muslim societies to face the political question of the institutions they needed to create. This happened in 1923–1924 when Mustapha Kemal Atatürk abolished what was left of the Ottoman Caliphate.

∗ ∗ ∗

The way in which Saad ibn Abī Waqqās withdrew from the public forum, where his presence could have meant answering the loaded question of who should be caliph, had a rich posterity. A certain number of philosophers and Sufis adopted and theorized it. Abu Nasr Al Farābī (870–950), who can be considered the "founder of an Islamic tradition of political philosophy rooted in the teachings of Plato,"[8] was thus followed by a philosopher such as Ibn Bājjah (Avempace, 1085–1138), who considered the main lesson to be drawn from Plato's philosophy was that "the perfect state" was an impossible utopia and therefore rejected the very notion of an intervention of the "lover of wisdom" in the affairs of the state.

Al Farābī, who considered politics a prolongation of cosmology and the "ideal state" to be a worldly reflection of the perfect cosmic order, identified the truly philosophic ruler of that state with a prophet or an imam legislator. Such an *insān kāmil*, the fully accomplished, *perfectus* human being, the one on whom the active intellect has descended, is the one capable of leading people to happiness. Twelve qualities distinguish him,[9] Al Farābī explains, while his successors will retain fewer and fewer of those: the law of becoming and inevitable decay is inescapable. At least the capacity to deduce new laws by analogy with those established by the first imam should be maintained as long as possible in the successive leaders.

The remark is to be made here that Al Farābī's examination of the perfect state does not pay much attention to history in general and more specifically to the history of that "perfect state" created by the prophet of Islam and "continued" by his successors. Al Farābī's is a general reflection on the "ideality that characterizes the best government" as it is "created ex nihilo . . . by a gifted legislator, an accomplished philosopher, an inspired prophet or all of those in one and the same figure."[10] Consequently "it does not matter if such a figure evokes the Greek legislators (Solo, Pericles) or the government of the prophet of Islam. The similarity of the tasks of the legislator, the prophet and the philosopher . . . make, in that respect, historical precisions totally superfluous and irrelevant."[11]

The ideal city may not be of this world; nevertheless, to live a philosophic life means to live as a citizen of such a republic, according to its laws. In the end governance toward the perfect state may come to mean essentially self-education and the education of others toward one's own accomplishment identified with citizenship in the ideal city. Ibn Bājjah, looking at the corrupt cities, wrote:

> If happy people can exist at all in these towns they have only the happiness of the isolated unit, and the just rule is the rule of the isolated individual only, equally whether the isolated individual is one or more than one, so long as neither nation nor city shares their view. They are they whom the Sufis mean when they speak of "strangers," for, they say, even in their own countries and among their fellows and neighbours they are strangers in their opinions and travel in their thoughts to other levels which are as it were their own countries—and so on.[12]

The notion that the philosopher/Sufi lives as a stranger in this world or, as Ibn Bājjah metaphorically puts it, as a "weed," is also at the center of the philosophical novel *Hayy ibn Yaqzān*, authored by another philosopher from Andalusia, Abu Bakr ibn Tufayl (1105–1185). The novel is the tale of a boy, Hayy ibn Yaqzān, raised by a doe, who is able to retrieve by himself all the fundamental techniques and knowledge that define human civilization and, above all, become cognizant of God as the uncaused cause of everything. *Hayy ibn Yaqzān* can be considered a hymn to the power of human reason. It can also be read as a celebration of a retreat from public life: after his experience of living in society and his failure to share with people the intelligible truths he has grasped and tasted in his solitary life, Hayy chooses to go back into retreat and a life of contemplation. He had come to realize that it was impossible for him to simply go along with the people, following the literal meaning of the religion of the ancestors "protected" by the state, represented in the novel by the character Salāmān. Ibn Tufayl writes: "Hayy saw clearly and definitely that to appeal to them publicly and openly was impossible. Any attempt to impose a higher task on them was bound to fail. The sole benefit most people could derive from religion was for this world, in that it helped them lead decent lives without others encroaching on what belonged to them. Hayy now knew that only a few win the true happiness of the man who 'desires the world to come, strives for it and is faithful.'"[13] One can evoke here the words of Charles Taylor speaking of "those who are fully dedicated to the 'higher' forms, [who] can be seen as a standing reproach to those who remain in the earlier forms, supplicating the Powers for human flourishing."[14]

The tradition of valuing retreat the way Saad ibn Abī Waqqās did in reaction to the state of public affairs has been evoked often by modern philosophers. Muhammad Iqbal considered that one the main causes of the state of petrifaction in which the religious thought of Islam found itself after the thirteenth century is the fact that the best minds among Muslim people turned away from the disheartening state of public affairs and chose the path of retreat into a neoplatonic worldview valuing the *vita contemplativa* above all. Thus, Iqbal writes, "[The] spirit of total other-worldliness in later Sufism obscured men's vision of a very important aspect of Islam as a social polity, and offering the prospect of unrestrained thought on its speculative side it attracted and finally absorbed the best minds in Islam. The Muslim State was thus left generally in the hands of intellectual mediocrities, and the unthinking masses of Islam, having no personalities of a higher caliber to guide them, found their security only in blindly following the schools."[15]

***

The question of retreat from state affairs and the public forum was posed during the encounter with colonialism, as Sufi orders had to cope with the reality of European imperialism. Almost everywhere in the Muslim world Sufi orders found themselves in the situation of being de facto vehicles of resistance to imperialism. Which could mean actual armed resistance, often in the name of religious war (*jihad*), or passive resistance and some form of accommodation with the colonial regime, or both as the circumstances changed. Islam in the West African region traditionally known as *Bilād as-Sudān*, "the land of black people," offers an interesting case study.

Islam was already a reality in the valley of the Senegal River when, at the beginning of the eleventh century, in the kingdom of Tekruur, then situated in the northern part of present-day Senegal known as Fuuta Tooro, Wārjābī became the first king to convert to Islam. He adopted Islamic law for Tekruur, which had become a Muslim territory by the time he died in 1040. The Muslim faith then continuously spread toward the southern regions where learning centers disseminating Islamic knowledge and practices were founded and flourished.

A phase of accelerated Islamization occurred at the end of the eighteenth century and throughout the nineteenth century. In northern Senegal a new regime known as *almaamiyya* seized power in 1776 from the traditional aristocracy, whom they considered "pagan." An *almamy* (a local title in Fulani language coming from the Arabic *imam*) would rule the polity after he had been elected from among the members of a new class of religious families known as the *Torodo*. The region of Fuuta Tooro is also the homeland of the Shaykh Umar al Fūtiyu (1794–1864), who led a religious war in the middle of the nineteenth century for the expansion of Islam in the regions east of the Senegal River.

Umar also fought against the French armies. He died in 1864 fighting a war in Bandiagara, a region in present-day Mali.

The massive Islamization of West Africa occurred during the French colonization and, paradoxically, as a consequence of it. The roads and railways constructed by the colonial administration also benefited Muslim traders, who could travel widely and more easily, preaching Islam to local populations. At the same time, the people who had witnessed the collapse of the traditional kingdoms they lived in and the disruption of the social order they were accustomed to in their homelands were willing to stand behind the religious leadership of masters known as *shaykhs* or *marabouts*.[16] The marabouts headed the Sufi orders that provided the new converts some education in the Muslim religion, the social structure of a fraternity organized around a *shaykh* (master), and a religious center where periodical gatherings would take place. This history explains why Islam in West Africa is massively a mystical Islam wherein the role of Sufi orders is so important. As the influence of the marabouts grew rapidly, those leaders became the target of the colonial administration, because they were always suspected of plotting the next jihad against European rule.

Let us here focus on the case of Senegal, as the country is more than any other in sub-Saharan Africa the land of Sufi brotherhoods. Of course Sufi orders or mystical paths are known throughout the whole Islamic world. Thus *Qadiriyya* (or the path of Abd al Qādir Jīlānī who died in the eleventh century in Baghdad) and *Tijaniyya* (the path of Abul Abbass Ahmad al- Tijānī, who died in 1815 in Fez, Morocco) have local leaders called *shaykhs* or *seriñ* or *ceerno* and many followers in Senegal. Two other important orders, known as *Muridiyya* and *Laayeen* can be considered as specific contributions of Senegal to Sufism.

It has been said that the "popularity [of Sufi brotherhoods] on the African continent has much to do with their assimilation of traditional African customs and elements."[17] It is true of Sufism in general and not only of Sufism in Africa that it is more tolerant and open vis-à-vis ancient belief systems predating Islamization than any interpretation of the Muslim religion: its metaphysics predisposes it to perceiving love as the one driving force behind all different forms of religion and spirituality. Consequently, although African traditional religions are fast disappearing today in the face of the advance of Christianity and Islam, their metaphysics of an enchanted world outlives them as it has been incorporated into the Sufi interpretation of the Muslim religion.

That being said, any generalization about Sufism and Sufi orders is always belied by historical facts at this particular place or at that particular time. Uthman Dan Fodio (ca. 1750–1817), who was a Sufi affiliated to the Qadiriyya order, declared the "jihad of the sword" against the sultanate of Gobir, which he accused of encouraging the practice of paganism, and eventually established the Sokoto Caliphate, in northern Nigeria as a "true" Islamic state devoted to creating a "truly 'Islamic' society."[18] Umar al Fūtiyu, who has been already mentioned and who led a jihad against the pagans and their "hypocrite" Muslim protectors but also against French colonialism, was a spiritual heir of the founder of the Tijaniyya: as such and as a scholar, he wrote profound texts on the metaphysics of Sufism and sincerely despised temporal power and violence.

Still the same "anti-sultan"[19] Tijani leader confronted the French as a sultan and a warrior. Because of their experience with the Shaykh Umar al Fūtiyu and with other leaders of the order, Tijaniyya "in West Africa in the late nineteenth century . . . connoted resistance to colonial rule . . . in the minds of the French."[20] For that reason, the founder of the *Muridiyya* was condemned to exile by the colonial administration when the director of political affairs made the following accusation against him:

> Amadu Bamba, pupil of Shaikh Sidiyya, Moorish marabout of the Qadiriyya sect, had professed in the last few years the Tijani doctrine which involves preaching holy war. Anyone with experience in the country and with the preachers of holy war will immediately understand that Amadu Bamba, without seeming to, was preparing very adroitly to act in the near future, almost surely during the next dry season.[21]

The example of the Tijaniyya brotherhood in West Africa manifests two faces of Sufi orders. The first one is of active armed jihad to create a Muslim space and also to resist colonialism and the colonial administration: after colonial rule was established, quite a few Muslims from northern Nigeria or the Macina Empire created by Shaykh Umar decided to flee toward Arabia and Sudan rather than live in a non-Muslim state. The other face is the one embodied in Saad ibn Abī Waqqās's attitude of withdrawal when he had to face the question of the truly Islamic state. Asked by the French colonial governor in Saint-Louis whether he was thinking of waging a holy war against French domination, El Hajj Malick Sy (1854–1922), another Sufi *shaykh* who played an essential role in the spread of Islam and the Tijaniyya brotherhood in Senegal, is reported to have answered: "My only weapon is my rosary."[22] Along the same lines, Shaykh Ahmadu Bamba, the founder of Muridiyya, made a declaration in 1910 praising the *Pax Gallica* brought by French colonial rule as encouraging and favoring the practice of their religion by Muslims. What those declarations of the main founders of Sufi brotherhoods in Senegal meant was that the pursuit of an Islamic state was not their project, that Muslims could live under the rule of "laic" France, and that such a rule might even be the best way for them to achieve the true goal, which was the creation of a Muslim space and a Muslim community. David Robinson has perfectly expressed the significance of that Saad ibn Abī Waqqās type of attitude in the following lines, which deserve to be quoted at length:

> The irony of the years since 1900, of the period of European colonialism and "postcolonialism," is how widely Islam has spread during that time. Sufi orders continued to be important vehicles under colonial rule and demonstrated that islamization did not depend on jihad or an Islamic state. The *hijra*, interpreted to mean getting away from European or infidel rule, was heroic, as in the case of those who fled the British conquest of the Sokoto Caliphate and settled in the Sudan. But it was not practical for most people. Nor was it successful, because European influence was everywhere, even in Mecca and Medina. Nor was it necessary: Islam could survive and flourish, as it always has, in many conditions. Indeed I would argue along with some Sufis that islamization might go further, in terms of numbers of practitioners and quality of practice, if the government were not in Muslim hands. Leaders such as Ahmadu Bamba of Senegal . . . knew that power corrupts . . . Relieved of the burden of ruling, Sufi leaders

could concentrate more effectively on improving faith and practice and the conditions of the people they served. Muslim space did not require Muslim rule.[23]

The encounter between the pragmatism of the colonial administration when it came to realize that it needed acquiescence and collaboration from the *shaykhs* and the indifference of the Sufi orders to an Islamic state (what I have called the Saad ibn Abī Waqqās attitude), seeking instead to establish a Muslim space and community, led to the modus vivendi rightly labeled "accommodation" by Robinson. Accommodation not only defined the relationship between Sufi orders and colonialism; it would later give shape to a specific notion of secularism in the postcolonial state, a notion totally different from French *laïcité*.

So during the very period following the victory in France of the "laic Republic" marked by the 1905 law, it had to adopt, as a colonial power, a politics of accommodation with Islam and thus become de facto a Muslim power! As Jean Baubérot writes, in the colonial context, "The State anti-clericalism was not for exportation."[24] What that means in practice is that after the phase of distrust of the Sufi *shaykhs*, during which time the colonial administration would keep them under tight surveillance or arrest and deport them as a way of preventing the jihads it always feared they were preparing, France had to collaborate with them to maintain colonial rule[25] and even compete with them as a benefactor of Islam! Thus the colonial administration became an organizer of the pilgrimage to Mecca (a politics initiated by French military governor Faidherbe, who wanted to have his own pilgrims from Mecca with the title of "al Hajj" to counter the prestige and influence of the jihadist Shaykh Umar, who was also known as *Al Hajj* Umar), a builder of madrasas, and an appointer of *qadis* (Muslim judges) for Islamic courts of justice.

* * *

The Sufi *shaykhs*' goal of pursuing the path of accommodation appears to have been reached. Today Senegal is a secular state, but also an "Islamic space" where more than 90 percent of the population is

Muslim and where 90 percent of the Muslims would declare that they belong to one or the other of those orders, only a minority presenting themselves as just Muslims with no Sufi affiliation.

The first consequence of that situation is that any realistic policy had and still has to take into account the force of the brotherhoods: the independent nation-state of Senegal had to uphold the politics of accommodation adopted by the French colonial administration. The second consequence is the relevance of the affirmation of the neutrality of the State and of [its] equidistant position relative to the different religious organizations,[26] Christianity and Islam, and within Islam, the different brotherhoods.

Those are precisely the foundations upon which L. S. Senghor has defined the Senegalese notion of secularism, radically different from France's *laïcité*, but again, France itself had to suspend that model in circumstances where it could not be "for exportation." Today, in West Africa, a region such as northern Nigeria where the push of Salafism has successfully marginalized the Qadiriyya and Tijaniyya Sufi orders,[27] the radical Islamism of Boko Haram has developed, demanding Islamic rule identified with strict application of what they consider to be sharia. The situation in northern Mali has called the world's attention to the push of Salafism into the lands of Sufi Islam. Democratic and secular Senegal, where the Sufi orders are quite strong, appears to offer a sharp contrast to northern Nigeria and Mali. Abdou Diouf, the former president of Senegal and former general secretary of "Francophonie," used to say that in Africa, and more specifically in Senegal, Islam was more immunized than elsewhere from the terrorist corruption of that religion, thanks to the strength of the Sufi orders. To illustrate the point that Islam in Senegal is not very likely to produce a significant Islamist political movement, he would recall Senegal's political history: the fact that the first president of the country, Léopold Sédar Senghor, was a practicing Catholic in a country in which more than 90 percent of the population is Muslim and that he had benefited from the continuous support of the different Muslim leaders (of the Sufi orders) from when he led the country to independence in 1960 to when he voluntarily left the power in 1980. Abdou Diouf is certainly right about what constitutes Senegal's social contract. The question now concerns its future: Will the Saad ibn Abī Waqqās attitude upon which it is founded remain its inspiration?

NOTES

1. See Ali Abdel Razik, *Islam and the Foundations of Political Power*, ed. Abdou Filali-Ansary, trans. Maryam Loutfi (Edinburgh: Edinburgh University Press, 2012).
2. Abdel Razik, *Islam and the Foundations of Political Power*, xi.
3. Olivier Roy, *La laïcité face à l'islam* (Paris: Stock), 107–108.
4. Abdullahi Ahmed An-Na'im, *Islam and the Secular State: Negotiating the Future of Sharia* (Cambridge: Harvard University Press, 2010), 1.
5. Ibid., 45.
6. *The Meaning of the Holy Qur'an*, trans. Abdullah Yusuf Ali (Beltsville, Md.: Amana, 2001).
7. Ibid.
8. Steven Harvey, "The Place of the Philosopher in the City According to Ibn Bājjah," in *The Political Aspects of Islamic Philosophy: Essays in Honor of Muhsin S. Mahdi*, ed. Charles E. Butterworth (Cambridge: Harvard University Press, 1992), 199–200.
9. Those qualities ranging from physical integrity to fine diction or purposefulness are enumerated in Abu Nasr al-Farābī, *On the Perfect State*, trans. Richard Walzer (Chicago: Great Books of the Islamic World, 1998), 247–249.
10. Makram Abbès, *Islam et politique à l'âge classique* (Paris: Presses Universitaires de France, 2009), 202.
11. Ibid.
12. Ibn Bājjah, *Tadbiru'l-Mutawahhid* [Rule of the solitary], trans. D. M. Dunlop, *Journal of the Royal Asiatic Society of Great Britain and Ireland* no. 1 (April 1945): 61–81. www.jstor.org/stable/25222001.
13. Abu Bakr ibn Tufayl, *Hayy ibn Yaqzān*, trans. Lenn Evan Goodman (Los Angeles: Gee Tee Bee, 1996), 164. The quote is from the Qur'an (17:20).
14. Charles Taylor, *A Secular Age* (Cambridge: Harvard University Press, 2007).
15. M. Iqbal, *The Reconstruction of the Religious Thought in Islam* (Dubaï: Kitab al-Islamiyyah), 150–151.
16. The French word "*marabout*" comes from the Arabic "*Al murābitūn*," which means "those from the convent" and is also the name of the "*Almoravids*."
17. Khadim Mbacké, *Sufism and Religious Brotherhoods in Senegal*, trans. Eric Ross (Princeton, N.J.: Wiener), 2005.
18. See David Robinson, "Sokoto and Hausaland: Jihad Within the Dar al-Islam," in *Muslim Societies in African History* (Cambridge: Cambridge University Press, 2004), 144–146.

19. The "anti-sultan" is the subtitle of the book Fernand Dumont has devoted to Shaykh Umar: *L'anti-sultan ou al-Hajj Umar du Fouta* (Dakar and Abidjan: Les Nouvelles Editions Africaines), 1974.
20. David Robinson, "Senegal: Bamba and the Murids Under Colonial Rule," in *Muslim Societies in African History*, 186.
21. Quoted by Robinson, "Senegal," 187.
22. David Robinson, *Paths of Accommodation. Muslim Societies and French Colonial Authorities in Senegal and Mauritania, 1880–1920*. (Athens: Ohio University Press, 2000), 316.
23. Robinson, "Senegal," 207.
24. Jean Baubérot, *Les laïcités dans le monde*, 2d ed. (Paris: Presses Universitaires de France, 2009), 58.
25. The best example is the fact that after it twice deported Shaykh Ahmadu Bamba (1853–1927), the founder of the Muridiyya Sufi order, France needed his and his followers' help to develop an economy based on peanut growing in the central regions of Senegal.
26. See Abdoulaye Dièye, *Secularism in Senegal: Withstanding the Challenge of Lcal Realities: A Legal Approach*, Institute for the Study of Islamic Thought in Arica (ISITA) Working Papers (Evanston, Ill. The Roberta Buffet Center for International and Comparative Studies,Northwestern University, 2009), Working paper No 09-006, March 2009.
27. That push and the dominance of the Salafi movement known as Izala has been studied by Ousmane Kane in his *Muslim Modernity in Postcolonial Nigeria: A Study of the Society for the Removal of Innovation and the Reinstatement of Tradition* (Leiden: Brill, 2003).

3

THE INDIVIDUAL AND COLLECTIVE SELF-LIBERATION MODEL OF *USTADH* MAHMOUD MOHAMED TAHA

Abdullahi Ahmed An-Na'im

Being a Muslim is foundational for me, it informs and guides everything I do or say in every aspect of my life. It is therefore inconceivable to me that I can hold any philosophical or ideological position that is inconsistent with my being a Muslim by my understanding of Islam. I have said that frequently regarding human rights, for instance, and affirm it here regarding secularism. It is from this perspective that I support the secular state for the possibility of being a better Muslim, and not secularism as a life philosophy that diminishes the public role of religion. "In order to be a Muslim by conviction and free choice, which is the only way one can be a Muslim, I need a secular state. By a secular state I mean one that is neutral regarding religious doctrine, one that does not claim or pretend to enforce Sharia."[1] As I will explain later, the neutrality of the state regarding religion does not mean the exclusion of religion from politics—the formulation and implementation of social and public policy outside the realm of the state. The challenge is how to maintain religious neutrality of the state without attempting to exclude religion from politics. I say "attempting to exclude," because in my view it is not possible to do so in practice; the political behavior of believers will always be influenced by their religious beliefs, whether that is acknowledged or not.

It is also from this perspective that I am seeking the mediation of the paradox of the inappropriateness of conceptions of the secular defined in terms of European Christianity for Muslims in general, on the one hand, and the entanglement of Muslims with the postcolonial state that is also premised on European Christian conceptions of the secular, on the other. As I will try to explain later, Muslims' comprehension and experience of the secular, in the sense of the material and this-worldly, are not only positive but also integral to the religious. To Muslims, the inherent consistency and complementarity between the secular and the religious precludes thinking of either independent of the other. Life is all at once religious and secular, spiritual and material, and Islam takes each aspect of the human experience, and all of them combined, equally seriously.

Ustadh Mahmoud Mohamed Taha (hereafter Taha) discusses the Islamic synthesis of the material and spiritual dimensions in terms of the dialectic of civilization and material progress. In his view:

> Civilization may be defined as the ability to distinguish values and to observe these values in daily conduct. A civilized man does not confuse ends and means, and does not sacrifice ends for the sake of means. . . .
>
> Material progress, on the other hand, means the enjoyment of certain comforts and benefits of an advanced standard of living. Thus, if a man owns a grand car, a beautiful house, and nice furniture, he enjoys material progress. If he obtained these means at the expense of his freedom, then he is not civilized, even though he is materially advanced. It is thus possible for a person to enjoy material progress without being civilized, or be civilized without enjoying the comfort of material progress. . . . We strive today to achieve both material progress and civilization at one and the same time.[2]

He also argues that "it is time for man to appreciate that the environment in which he lives is a spiritual environment with material manifestations. This conclusion, proved through recent developments in modern science, faces man with a clear challenge—to reconcile himself with both environments as a condition for survival."[3]

The question I will briefly examine in this paper is how to "translate" Taha's view into a practical approach to what might be called "civilized living" in the postcolonial context of Muslims in their communities.

Regarding the question of the secular outside of Latin Christendom in particular, which is the theme of this volume, I will discuss the relationship of sharia, as the normative system of Islam in general, to the postcolonial state.

There is an apparent paradox in the Islamic view of religious authority. On the one hand, being a Muslim is founded on the strict individual responsibility of each and every Muslim to know and comply with what is required of him or her by sharia. This fundamental principle of individual and personal responsibility that can never be abdicated or delegated is one of the recurring themes of the Qur'an, as can be seen in verses 5:105, 4:79–80, 41:46, and 53:36–42. On the other hand, Muslims have always tended to seek and rely on the advice of scholars and religious leaders they trust, which means that both the advisor and the advisee are responsible for the advisee's actions.

Since this is a private relationship based on personal choice, it cannot be institutionalized, except through the completely voluntary association of individual Muslims. But is the notion of institutionalization at all appropriate or coherent when individual Muslims will be free to affiliate with any organization or group or not and remain free to decide whether to seek advice or not in the first place, and when the advice they receive cannot be binding except to the extent believers themselves find it to be persuasive?

The lack of theological support for institutionalized religious authority in Islamic traditions may sometimes lead to problematic outcomes, as when extremist groups challenge the authority of established scholars and institutions of learning to propose a radical mandate for aggressive jihad. This risk is not only unavoidable in view of the nature of Islamic religious authority but is in my view preferable to institutionalizing that authority to certain designated persons or institutions, thereby forfeiting the right of other believers to disagree with their views. Legitimate Islamic religious authority cannot be monopolized or institutionalized, because it is premised on religious knowledge, piety, and interpersonal trust that cannot be quantified or verified to be vested in an institution.

The idea of a church-like hierarchical clerical institution is unknown to Muslims, though collective religious practice and communal affiliation are encouraged. The notion of the unity of the *umma* (global community of Muslims) has always been invoked as an ideal but never realized in political terms or institutional structure. In any case, unlike the church as the representation of the body of Christian believers, there has never been any attempt to construct an institutional organization of the *umma*. This point is obvious for Sunni Muslims, but I believe it is true about Shia Muslims, too, who accept a hierarchy among their religious leaders (with titles like "Ayatollah"), who must earn their status among their followers. The decision to follow a particular religious scholar is made by individual members of a community of believers, not by a collective.

COMPLEXITIES OF COLONIZATION AND DECOLONIZATION

The question for this paper is how can Muslims affirm their own understanding of the secular in relation in their respective postcolonial context? Since the formative influence of inappropriate Christian European conceptions of the secular continues in postcolonial states, the mediation of the paradox noted earlier depends on a level of liberation of constitutional discourse and political practice beyond formal independence. It is about decolonization of the mind and self-perception of the colonial subject. This will cause the colonizer to retreat from claims of epistemological hegemony, which are associated with military conquest and economic exploitation in the colonial relationship. But the primary objective or motivation of the colonized subject should be to render the colonial and postcolonial relationship altogether redundant.

This is what I call indigenous self-liberation, which means *liberation of the self by the self* that transcends any external constraints or limitations. This level of liberation of the self has to be by the self for itself, because no human being can do that for any other human being, although all can cooperate in creating conditions wherein each person can achieve a profound and permanent degree or level of inner liberation. Based on the model experienced and presented by Taha, I believe that that quality or level of indigenous self-liberation can be

3

THE INDIVIDUAL AND COLLECTIVE SELF-LIBERATION MODEL OF *USTADH* MAHMOUD MOHAMED TAHA

Abdullahi Ahmed An-Na'im

Being a Muslim is foundational for me, it informs and guides everything I do or say in every aspect of my life. It is therefore inconceivable to me that I can hold any philosophical or ideological position that is inconsistent with my being a Muslim by my understanding of Islam. I have said that frequently regarding human rights, for instance, and affirm it here regarding secularism. It is from this perspective that I support the secular state for the possibility of being a better Muslim, and not secularism as a life philosophy that diminishes the public role of religion. "In order to be a Muslim by conviction and free choice, which is the only way one can be a Muslim, I need a secular state. By a secular state I mean one that is neutral regarding religious doctrine, one that does not claim or pretend to enforce Sharia."[1] As I will explain later, the neutrality of the state regarding religion does not mean the exclusion of religion from politics—the formulation and implementation of social and public policy outside the realm of the state. The challenge is how to maintain religious neutrality of the state without attempting to exclude religion from politics. I say "attempting to exclude," because in my view it is not possible to do so in practice; the political behavior of believers will always be influenced by their religious beliefs, whether that is acknowledged or not.

It is also from this perspective that I am seeking the mediation of the paradox of the inappropriateness of conceptions of the secular defined in terms of European Christianity for Muslims in general, on the one hand, and the entanglement of Muslims with the postcolonial state that is also premised on European Christian conceptions of the secular, on the other. As I will try to explain later, Muslims' comprehension and experience of the secular, in the sense of the material and this-worldly, are not only positive but also integral to the religious. To Muslims, the inherent consistency and complementarity between the secular and the religious precludes thinking of either independent of the other. Life is all at once religious and secular, spiritual and material, and Islam takes each aspect of the human experience, and all of them combined, equally seriously.

Ustadh Mahmoud Mohamed Taha (hereafter Taha) discusses the Islamic synthesis of the material and spiritual dimensions in terms of the dialectic of civilization and material progress. In his view:

> Civilization may be defined as the ability to distinguish values and to observe these values in daily conduct. A civilized man does not confuse ends and means, and does not sacrifice ends for the sake of means. . . .
>
> Material progress, on the other hand, means the enjoyment of certain comforts and benefits of an advanced standard of living. Thus, if a man owns a grand car, a beautiful house, and nice furniture, he enjoys material progress. If he obtained these means at the expense of his freedom, then he is not civilized, even though he is materially advanced. It is thus possible for a person to enjoy material progress without being civilized, or be civilized without enjoying the comfort of material progress. . . . We strive today to achieve both material progress and civilization at one and the same time.[2]

He also argues that "it is time for man to appreciate that the environment in which he lives is a spiritual environment with material manifestations. This conclusion, proved through recent developments in modern science, faces man with a clear challenge—to reconcile himself with both environments as a condition for survival."[3]

The question I will briefly examine in this paper is how to "translate" Taha's view into a practical approach to what might be called "civilized living" in the postcolonial context of Muslims in their communities.

Regarding the question of the secular outside of Latin Christendom in particular, which is the theme of this volume, I will discuss the relationship of sharia, as the normative system of Islam in general, to the postcolonial state.

There is an apparent paradox in the Islamic view of religious authority. On the one hand, being a Muslim is founded on the strict individual responsibility of each and every Muslim to know and comply with what is required of him or her by sharia. This fundamental principle of individual and personal responsibility that can never be abdicated or delegated is one of the recurring themes of the Qur'an, as can be seen in verses 5:105, 4:79–80, 41:46, and 53:36–42. On the other hand, Muslims have always tended to seek and rely on the advice of scholars and religious leaders they trust, which means that both the advisor and the advisee are responsible for the advisee's actions.

Since this is a private relationship based on personal choice, it cannot be institutionalized, except through the completely voluntary association of individual Muslims. But is the notion of institutionalization at all appropriate or coherent when individual Muslims will be free to affiliate with any organization or group or not and remain free to decide whether to seek advice or not in the first place, and when the advice they receive cannot be binding except to the extent believers themselves find it to be persuasive?

The lack of theological support for institutionalized religious authority in Islamic traditions may sometimes lead to problematic outcomes, as when extremist groups challenge the authority of established scholars and institutions of learning to propose a radical mandate for aggressive jihad. This risk is not only unavoidable in view of the nature of Islamic religious authority but is in my view preferable to institutionalizing that authority to certain designated persons or institutions, thereby forfeiting the right of other believers to disagree with their views. Legitimate Islamic religious authority cannot be monopolized or institutionalized, because it is premised on religious knowledge, piety, and interpersonal trust that cannot be quantified or verified to be vested in an institution.

The idea of a church-like hierarchical clerical institution is unknown to Muslims, though collective religious practice and communal affiliation are encouraged. The notion of the unity of the *umma* (global community of Muslims) has always been invoked as an ideal but never realized in political terms or institutional structure. In any case, unlike the church as the representation of the body of Christian believers, there has never been any attempt to construct an institutional organization of the *umma*. This point is obvious for Sunni Muslims, but I believe it is true about Shia Muslims, too, who accept a hierarchy among their religious leaders (with titles like "Ayatollah"), who must earn their status among their followers. The decision to follow a particular religious scholar is made by individual members of a community of believers, not by a collective.

COMPLEXITIES OF COLONIZATION AND DECOLONIZATION

The question for this paper is how can Muslims affirm their own understanding of the secular in relation in their respective postcolonial context? Since the formative influence of inappropriate Christian European conceptions of the secular continues in postcolonial states, the mediation of the paradox noted earlier depends on a level of liberation of constitutional discourse and political practice beyond formal independence. It is about decolonization of the mind and self-perception of the colonial subject. This will cause the colonizer to retreat from claims of epistemological hegemony, which are associated with military conquest and economic exploitation in the colonial relationship. But the primary objective or motivation of the colonized subject should be to render the colonial and postcolonial relationship altogether redundant.

This is what I call indigenous self-liberation, which means *liberation of the self by the self* that transcends any external constraints or limitations. This level of liberation of the self has to be by the self for itself, because no human being can do that for any other human being, although all can cooperate in creating conditions wherein each person can achieve a profound and permanent degree or level of inner liberation. Based on the model experienced and presented by Taha, I believe that that quality or level of indigenous self-liberation can be achieved by Muslims through an Islamic personal methodology for liberation within the inner sphere of moral consciousness, where freedom can be absolute. I also believe that Gandhi achieved indigenous self-liberation within the Hindu tradition; this goal is not limited to an Islamic methodology.

Extraordinary human beings like Gandhi and Taha can inspire and guide us all by demonstrating the possibility of indigenous self-liberation at the individual level, but the rest of us need effective safeguards for our fundamental rights. Speaking for myself, I know I am unlikely to take the position of Taha, which I will touch upon later. But I am able to struggle to secure fundamental rights for all of us so we can each strive for collective indigenous self-liberation as a means for as much individual self-liberation as we can achieve. Such extraordinary people will not have a broader and enduring impact unless they also provide a vision and pragmatic means for spreading their model among different societies for others to achieve the same goal.

When Taha was criticized for presenting a utopian ideal, he used to respond that was not true, because he was presenting a practical and pragmatic approach to realizing the vision he was proposing for individual enlightenment and social transformation. I will briefly outline in the last section of this essay my understanding of how Taha's approach might work in the context of the postcolonial state. The formula I am proposing for realizing self-liberation in the postcolonial context involves a combination of moral choices, political action, and investment in normative and institutional resources of constitutionalism, citizenship, and human rights.[4]

Constitutionalism is a framework for the mediation of certain unavoidable conflicts in the political, economic, and social fabric of every human society. This proposition assumes that conflict is a normal and permanent feature of human societies and defines constitutionalism in terms of being a framework for mediation rather than permanent or final resolution of such conflicts. But since struggles over power and resources cannot be practically mediated by all members of any society, there has to be some form of delegation from those who, as a practical matter, cannot be part of the daily and detailed processes of administration and adjudication. At the same time, however, those who have to delegate to others also need to ensure that their interests are served by this process by participating in the selection of delegates and ensuring that delegates act according to the terms of delegation. These pragmatic considerations underlie the basic constitutional principles of representative government, including bureaucratic aspects of democratic administration of public affairs, which is fully accountable to its citizens.[5]

For the appropriate processes of constitutional governance to work properly in each setting, the general population must be able and willing to effectively exercise its powers of delegation to and require accountability from public officials, whether elected or appointed. There are many aspects to such ability and willingness, some relating to the population side, while others pertain to the government and its organs or the conditions of the interaction between the two. On the first count, for instance, the population at large must be capable of exercising intelligent, well-informed, and independent judgment about the ability of its representatives and officials to act on its behalf, and to verify that they do in fact act in accordance with the best interests of the population. The public must also have the capacity to challenge and replace those who fail to implement its mandate.

To ensure and facilitate a wide range of operations and functions of democratic government, all citizens must enjoy certain individual and collective rights, like freedom of expression and association, access to information, and effective remedies against excess or abuse of power by official organs. But in the final analysis, the best principles and mechanisms of constitutional governance will not operate properly without sufficiently strong civic engagement by a critical mass of citizens.

The most critical aspect of constitutionalism, I believe, is civic engagement by a critical mass of citizens. This includes the motivation of citizens to keep themselves well-informed about public affairs and to organize themselves in nongovernmental organizations that can act on their behalf in effective and sustainable ways. People are unlikely to assert and pursue avenues of accountability and redress without the material and human resources and the psychological and cultural orientation to do so. Public officials and the agencies and institutions they operate must not only enjoy the confidence of local communities but also be familiar, friendly, and responsive when approached. This is the practical and most foundational meaning of popular sovereignty, whereby a people can govern themselves through their own public officials and elected representatives. Constitutionalism is ultimately concerned with realizing and regulating this ideal in the most sustainable and dynamic manner possible, whereby the combination of theory and practice of this concept is capable of ensuring self-determination now and responding to changing circumstances in the future.[6]

Such strategies and structural safeguards are normally necessary but insufficient for enabling individuals to achieve indigenous self-liberation. Unfortunately, establishing these safeguards at home does not mean the justice or humanity of what polities may do abroad. Secularism in particular has been more associated with colonial domination and exploitation of other people than with striving to respect their dignity and human rights. There is "a plurality of secularisms in different national, cultural, and religious contexts, including non-Western secularisms. . . . [Although] the formations of the secular follow different historical trajectories and have different religious genealogies in different places . . . they are closely interconnected with hegemonic impositions of Western colonialism."[7]

I use the term "colonialism" and its derivatives in this essay, partly because of their prevalence in current discourse, although colonization as displacement of local population by colonizing settlers did not happen to African and Asian Muslims. I also find these terms appropriate because European colonialism displaced the cultural and political self-perception and awareness of the colonized Muslims in Africa and Asia, without displacing the people physically. The indigenous self-liberation I am proposing must therefore seek to reimagine and retrieve the lost self *as if* colonialism never happened, without pretending that it did not happen.[8]

In my view, the notions of the secular and secularism among Muslims have been distorted by the cultural and political impact of European colonialism. To facilitate and perpetuate colonial relations, European powers subjected colonized peoples to the Euro-memory.[9] By imposing European languages, colonial administrations and Christian missionaries simultaneously broke native memory and constructed a new reality through which the colonized had to perceive the world. Colonial strategies also included the construction of an elite class who identified with European instead of African or Islamic heritage, thereby reinforcing the loss of memory and the dominance of European languages and cultures.[10] Colonial education helped create the illusion that colonial subjects had no history or culture of their own and that nothing of their past was worth reclaiming or preserving, thereby conditioning them to see themselves through the hegemonic memory of the colonizer.[11]

For our purposes here, whatever indigenous conception and experience African and Asian Muslim societies had of the secular is no longer accessible to them today, except through the filter of colonial experiences. The postcolonial consciousness of African and Asian Muslims remain conditioned by the colonial, even when they are resisting neocolonial domination. The irony is that "the postcolonial is always reworked by the history of colonialism, and is not available to us in any pristine form that can be neatly separated from the history of colonialism."[12] In this light, I argue that formal decolonization is necessary but insufficient for sustainable cultural and political decolonization. The deeper and more profound level of decolonization I am evoking here can be realized through what I call indigenous self-liberation to break cultural and epistemological dependency on North Atlantic concepts and discourses.

Yet this process of a deeper level of decolonization still has to occur in the context of neocolonial power relations in an economically and politically integrated and interdependent postcolonial world. The European model of the so-called nation-state in its global systems of economic and security integration are part of the structural, normative, and institutional framework within which self-liberation is supposed to evolve. The possibilities and rationale of self-liberation today could not (and should not be expected to) rid us of European colonialism altogether. However, if we can reconceptualize European colonialism and its aftermath in terms of civilizational evolution of global humanity, that can be the framework for indigenous self-liberation for all human beings, colonized and colonizers alike. I say this because the colonizer is as much in need of self-liberation as the colonized.

My *pragmatically optimistic* view of this is to say, since European colonialism is now integral to the history and context of postcolonial societies in irreversible ways, why not just take it all into account as we move on with our own indigenous self-liberation? My focus on European colonialism is not because it invented the strategies and processes of imperialism for the first time in human history. There have been previous cycles of military conquest, political domination, and cultural hegemony within as well as across various regions of the world. That was true, for instance, for the initial Arab-Muslim military conquest from North Africa and southern Spain to northern India and Central Asia in the seventh and eighth centuries. Arab-Muslim colonization in the sense of cultural/religious displacement can also be seen from the perspective of preexisting cultures/religions of sub-Saharan Africa and Southeast Asia through trade, religious conversion, and enculturation of local populations into Islamic values and socioeconomic formations. It is perhaps relevant to our inquiry into the secular/religious dynamics to emphasize that the two were intertwined in what Ira Lapidus calls "the socioeconomic bases of empire."[13]

However, European colonialism is probably different from earlier cycles of human evolution because of the speed and massive scale and intensity of its transformative impact on social, political, and economic structures and relations from the local to the global. European colonialism is also of particular concern for the subject of this chapter because of the paradox of the relativity of secularism, on the one hand, and enduring realities of European state formations for national politics and international relations, on the other. In terms of the argument I will try to develop in this essay, a conception of the secular that is relative to European Christianity is now being applied to other religions and regions of the world that have also been transformed by European colonialism in socioeconomic and political terms. The possibilities of self-liberation for those societies are inextricably embedded in the same colonial and postcolonial framework from which African and Asian Muslims are seeking liberation.

One caveat to speaking of European this or that seems to support the pragmatically optimistic approach I am proposing: "Europeanness" is not uniform or monolithic. As Frederick Cooper explained, it is problematic to assign general concepts of Enlightenment thinking like modernity and liberalism to Europe as a whole. By assigning these concepts to a generalized idea of Europe in the first place, postcolonial discourse is falling victim to the flawed tendency to flatten discourse and history. The post-Enlightenment ideas resulted from struggles within Europe and clashes of competing viewpoints concerning the exact meaning of notions like progress and rationality. To speak of European this or that only reinforces a universalistic notion of Europeanness that seems to concede the colonial logic that postcolonial discourse is supposed to overcome.[14] Here, the point for me is not to take colonial concepts or frameworks for granted but to simply define the terms as I mean them for my own self-liberation project.

TAHA'S MODEL OF SELF-LIBERATION

Ustadh Mahmoud Mohamed Taha was one of the pioneers of the decolonization struggle in Sudan beginning in the 1930s. He was the author of an indigenous Islamic transformative discourse and leader of a "social movement" to promote that discourse until his public execution on political charges on January 18, 1985, and the subsequent suppression of his movement. Sudan was the context of the paradox in which Taha experienced and presented his model of deep decolonization, which sought to transcend the postcolonial mind-set. As noted earlier, the paradox I mean here is that indigenous self-liberation still has to operate through colonial geopolitical structures and institutions of the territorial so-called nation-state in its global economic and security networks.[15]

In the case of Sudan, Islam is both part of the problem and part of the solution. It became part of the problem through the first cycle of colonization of the country by Turco-Egyptian rule from 1821 to 1885. That colonial experience imposed on the country an Ottoman–Middle Eastern conception of a legalistic Islam, contrary to the preceding community-based Sufi Islam of sub-Saharan Africa.[16] The brief, violent, chaotic, and divisive period of the Mahdist state of 1885–1898[17] gave Sudan an early taste of a so-called "Islamic state."[18] Both varieties of state—bureaucratic, legalistic Ottoman–Middle Eastern and Islamic Mahdist—continue to haunt Sudan and threaten many other Muslim-majority countries with a problematic relationship between Islam and the state. Islam should be part of the solution, because it is part of the problem, but that does not mean that it will be easy to agree upon or implement its inclusion. As I see it, the possibility of Islam being part of the solution is in Taha's model of self-liberation, as I will explore later. But first, let me clarify the colonial and postcolonial situation in Sudan as the context of Taha's experience.

European colonial rule came to Sudan in 1898 as the Anglo-Egyptian Condominium, in which Britain helped Egypt recover its former African colony Sudan, at a time when Egypt itself was a "protectorate" of Britain (1882–1922). Anglo-Egyptian colonial rule, which lasted until 1956, not only reinforced legalistic Islam through Egyptian influence but also introduced European cultural dominance through British education and administration. The combination of these two types of influence (Middle Eastern Islam and a European territorial state model) thrust Sudan into a protracted period of political instability and multiple complex civil wars. In particular, the overnight imposition of so-called Islamic sharia as state law by unilateral decree of President Numeiri in September 1983 represented the most drastic break with the possibilities of a pluralistic, democratic state.

These were exactly the dangers that Taha devoted his life to combating, from his agitation against colonial rule in the 1940s to his opposition to the imposition of sharia and resumption of civil war in the south Sudan by the Numeiri regime in the early 1980s. His life and work can be seen in terms of two overlapping phases. The first phase was the establishment of the Republican Party in 1945 to agitate for the independence of Sudan as a republic. During this "political phase," Taha and members of the Republican Party were apparently inspired by the model of the Indian Congress Party and the nonviolent but open and confrontational style of Gandhi in particular. The second phase was the Islamic transformative phase, which started when he came out of three years of self-imposed seclusion (following two years of imprisonment by the British). This "religious phase" extended from 1951 until his execution in 1985.[19]

I summarize here the fundamentally religious basis of Taha's life and work, of which the political was an incidental outcome: Taha called for the evolution of the understanding and practice of Islam by shifting emphasis from what he called the subsidiary level of revelation of the Qur'an in Medina to the primary level of the original universal message of Islam in Mecca. The distinction between parts of the Qur'an revealed to the Prophet in Mecca, his hometown, and parts revealed in Medina, where he took refuge from persecution, is commonly known and accepted among all Muslims. The profound insight of Taha is the significance of that shift in the content of the Qur'an, and not only in the location of revelation.

As Taha explained in his main book, *The Second Message of Islam* (first published in Arabic in 1967), and in other books and public lectures, the level of revelation and understanding based on the Medina phase was a concession to the historical context of humanity in the seventh century. Since humanity as a whole has significantly evolved since that time, he argued, it is now ready to receive, understand, and practice the universal message of Islam based on the revelations of the Mecca phase. The universal message of Islam, which he called the second message of Islam, proclaims equality between men and women, Muslims and non-Muslims. His view of Islam also calls for the repudiation of slavery and political violence (jihad) from an Islamic point of view.

From 1951 until his death in 1985, Taha advocated his views in open and peaceful ways and applied his views in the education and instruction of his students in his own small community. For instance, he called for equality of men and women and practiced that equality in all activities of his movement. He advocated constitutional democratic governance and opposed sectarian politics in Sudan but did not seek political power for himself or his movement. Yet his work was seen as deeply subversive by traditional political parties and Islamist groups, as well as by Numeiri's regime, which took the final drastic step of executing Taha and suppressing his movement.

An effort to try him for apostasy in 1968 failed, because the charge had no basis in the penal system enforced in Sudan at the time. By 1985, however, it was possible to try him under the same September

1983 laws he was criticizing. He was executed on January 18, 1985, for a combination of a political charge of treason under the Sudan penal code and the charge of apostasy; the death penalty was confirmed by a special court of appeal (although Taha did not appeal his conviction), and it was at this time that the charge of apostasy was added. That posttrial charge was the primary reason President Nuemiri gave for his approval of the death penalty.[20]

In his impromptu statement in an specially convened trial court on Monday, January 7, 1985, Taha rejected the authority of any court of the state to try him for his beliefs. He also explained his reasons for opposing the enactment of sharia norms into what he called "the September Laws" of 1983, which he felt violated and grossly distorted sharia and Islam and drastically undermined the peace and unity of Sudan. He also challenged the competence and integrity of the judges applying those laws and concluded: "For all these reasons, I am not prepared to cooperate with any court that has betrayed the independence of the judiciary, and allowed itself to be a tool for humiliating the people, insulting free thought, and persecuting political opponents."[21]

Through the way he lived and died, Taha vindicated his call for absolute individual freedom by living the values of democracy, socialism, and social justice that he had advocated since the 1940s.[22] The twofold key to his model of indigenous self-liberation can be summarized as follows: constantly striving for total consistency between thoughts, speech, and action—to freely think as we wish, say what we are thinking, and act on what we say, as long as we are prepared to accept responsibility for what we say and do. This means living by the values we hold, immediately, here and now, regardless of what else is happening around us. Otherwise, one would not be observing total consistency between his or her thoughts, speech, and action.

In Taha's view and lived experience, what others do, including state authorities, should not determine what one thinks, says, and does, though persuasion and cooperation remain desirable in social and political discourse. He also held that we are responsible only for where we stand and what we say and do. To him, the divinely ordained destiny of humanity is realized whenever we discharge our immediate obligation (*al-wajib al-mubashir*) to the best of our judgment. In his view, however, identifying our immediate obligation and acting accordingly is the object and purpose of our religious worship and reflection, to be constantly refined and investigated, never judged to be self-evident or taken for granted.

This proposed approach draws on our ability to organize social and political life in ways that facilitate our individual pursuit of self-liberation, but this requires constant examination and correction of our view of the relationship of ends and means, the essential quality of a civilized person, as quoted at the beginning of this essay. Political, economic, and social equalities, constitutionalism, and the rule of law, are the collective means to preserve the environment and context within which each of us strives for her or his self-liberation. In the final analysis, as Taha showed through his trial and execution, self-liberation is indigenous to each and every human being, to be realized within, regardless of what others do or fail to do.

In Taha's model, self-liberation happens when a human being liberates herself or himself from fear, which in his view is the cause of all inhibition and source of all moral perversion and behavioral distortion.[23] In Taha's analysis, self-preservation is the universal motivation of all life, but the quality of our humanity depends on the purpose we seek to achieve out of immediate self-preservation. He clarifies this distinction through what he calls "the will to live," unrestrained self-preservation, and "the will to be free," self-preservation subject to normative limitations. "At the level of this interaction [of the two wills] which produces the mind, the will to live is called the memory, while the will to be free is the imagination."[24] Moral choice is therefore integral to the ends we seek to achieve. In term's of Taha's analysis discussed earlier, for instance, the moral choice we all have to make is whether self-preservation be unrestrained will to live regardless of any normative constraints, or should it be qualified by the will to be free?

As I understand it, Taha is saying that a humane and enlightened outcome of the interaction of the will to live and the will to be free is not a product of forgetting the sources of fear that caused our will to live to be obsessed with self-preservation. To be free is not to simply cease to be aware of or care for sources of danger to our self-preservation. Instead, Taha is saying that a humane and enlightened outcome should be the result of the development of our imagination to see that subjecting our will to live to normative limitations in fact enhances rather than diminishes the extent and quality of our self-preservation.

Moreover, this imagination should not be a futile utopia but a realistic vision supported by empirical methods and experience of how normative constraints can in fact support rather than diminish self-preservation. In this process, belief and trust in God is absolutely essential as the ultimate source of guidance and assurance of humane and enlightened outcome for every single human being. A religious lifestyle and discipline are the necessary means to accessing and benefiting from God's guidance and assurance. That is why Taha rejects, and I agree with him, secularism as a life philosophy.

In his books and public lectures, Taha often criticized the lack of or inadequacy of moral or ethical underpinnings in contemporary materialism, what he called material progress without civilization, as quoted at the beginning of this chapter. In the last text in Arabic he wrote during his political detention without charge or trial in 1983–1984,[25] he criticized secularism by name, though the substance of what he said was similar to his earlier views on unethical materialism. In this limited space, it may be best to give an approximate translation of key points in this text:

- The difference between science (knowledge and insightful comprehension) and secularism is that secularism is based on incomplete or inadequate knowledge, as it is described in the Quran (30:6–7.)[26]
- The scientist coordinates between this lower life and the other higher life.
- The scientist is intelligent, while the secularist is clever, and the difference is that the intelligent person upholds the balance of values and applies a just balance, while the clever person is one who does not have this balance. The intelligent person distinguishes the means from the ends, and coordinates between the two.
- Western civilization, in both its socialist and capitalist dimensions, is a materialistic civilization where the value of the human person is diminished, and the value of material possessions is elevated. It is material progress and not civilization. It is the field

- of tremendous technology and machinery, but the human being is not the master of machines.
- This world is the means to the otherworld, and should be organized intelligently, in a scientific manner, so that it leads to that desired end. Secularists do not have this ability, but scientists do.
- Technology has expanded wealth to fantastic degree, but due to the lack of value, there is no justice in the distribution of wealth, whereby the rich are distracted from their humanity by their wealth and the poor are distracted from their humanity by their poverty. The human being is lost in materialistic civilization.
- Science cannot do without secularism, but it puts it in its right place, which is that of the means to the end.
- The present secular and materialistic civilization is a giant, without a spirit, so it needs a new civilization to infuse it with spirit and redirect it to make it the vehicle of the human being for realizing his or her humanity and perfection.

Accordingly, Taha insists that we must organize social and political affairs in ways that are most conducive to enabling each and every human being to liberate herself or himself from fear. As he explains:

> To restore unity to one's being is for an individual to think as he wishes, speak what he thinks, and act according to his speech. This is the objective of Islam: "Oh believers, why do you say what you do not do? It is most hateful to God that you say what you do not do" [61:2–3 of the Qur'an]. This superior state [of being] can only be reached through a two-fold method: first, the good society, and secondly, the scientific educational method to be adopted by the individual in order to liberate himself from inherited fear.[27]

His reference to the good society in this age of intensive and expansive globalization applies at all levels: local, national, and global; by scientific educational method he meant the religious methodology of trial and error in the process of self-transformation.[28]

In this light, I will argue that addressing external causes of fear through the rule of law and protection of human rights is necessary for enabling people to strive to liberate themselves from other forms and sources of fear. Conversely, if we remain moored only to the memory of mutual violent hostility, we remain mired in the fear that enabled and perpetuates the aggression and domination of imperialism. The challenge is to exercise our moral choice to reach out to the liberating vision of peaceful cooperation, while striving to be as persuasive as we can for others to join us in that vision and the struggle for its realization.

In Taha's fundamentally Islamic vision and experience, liberation of the human person from any form of political and social oppression and the satisfaction of her or his material needs is integral to surrender to God to receive and benefit from guidance and assurance of our individual humane and enlightened self-preservation. For example, Taha explains:

> Human dignity is so dear to God that individual freedom is not subject to any [human] guardianship, not even that of the Prophet, irrespective of his impeccable morality . . . God says [in the Qur'an]: "Then remind them, as you are only a reminder. You have no dominion over them" (88:21–22) . . . This indicated that no man is perfect enough to be entrusted with the freedom of others, and that the price of freedom is continuous individual vigilance in safeguarding such freedom.[29]

As I understand it, Taha's vision is that submission to the transcendental, supreme sovereignty of God (*twhid*) is inconsistent with subjugation to oppressive human authority. In other words, it is a form of idolatry (*shirk*) to submit to the oppressive will of other human beings. As noted earlier, extraordinary human beings, like Gandhi and Taha, may be able to repudiate such oppression on their own regardless of the apparently harsh consequences, but the rest of us cannot be expected to resist subjugation on our own. The Gandhis and Tahas of humanity inspire all of us, but they also create pragmatic frameworks for protecting our freedoms and safeguarding our material well-being to enable us to strive for our self-liberation to the extent we can. I will return to this theme in the last part of this chapter. For now, I want to highlight the paradox indicated earlier, within which self-liberation must be realized.

RELATIVITY OF SECULARISM AND PARADOX OF SELF-LIBERATION

Our human tendency to perceive, reflect, and articulate values and concepts in terms of our own historical and cultural context seems to be so deeply ingrained that even our effort to transcend it remains defined by the parameters of our own perspectives. It is therefore to be expected that human beings understand concepts like the secular from our own perspectives. What is problematic is attempting to impose our relativistic understandings and experiences on other human beings as if those concepts *as we know and experience them* are already the universal norm. This is paradoxical when the concept like the secular is admittedly relative yet seems to be unavoidable for non-Western societies that continue to live with the reality of European models of the state in the postcolonial context.

As noted earlier, there is significant controversy surrounding the definition of the term "secular" in the Western context, but the term is often interpreted simply as "nonreligious" or "lacking a religious component"[30] or as "distinct from or separate from religion."[31] However, it is misleading to contrast the religious and secular in binary terms, because they are in fact mutually interdependent, if only in the sense of one signifying the absence of the other.[32] Another approach that also relies on a binary defines the term "secular" as "the assumption that everything material or abstract derives from human endeavor."[33] While this view may be comprehensible to Christians, it seems to me that it may not apply to nonmonotheistic or so-called traditional or indigenous religions. It is also not helpful in understanding the relationship between what is secular and what is religious.

What qualifies as "religious" is a subject of even greater debate. For instance, religion has been defined as "a unified system of beliefs and practices relative to sacred things, that is to say, things set apart and forbidden—beliefs and practices which unite into one single moral community called a Church, all those who adhere to them."[34] But that is an almost exclusively Christian view of religion that demonstrates the relativity of the religious and secular, how what is considered secular depends on the religion against which it is posed. For example, the meaning of what is secular with regard to Christianity is not necessarily the same as the meaning of secular with regard to Islam or Hinduism. In addition, the secular depends on the cultural and territorial context.[35]

The relativity of the secular and the difficulty of escaping it are reflected in problems of the language we use and epistemology we apply to understanding the issues. The secular is often discussed in terms of the etymology of the term in European languages, which immediately forces our analysis into a local or regional paradigm of looking for the etymology of terms in that language and limits our analysis to the historical framework of where the concept indicated by the term prevailed. T. N. Madan, a leading Indian scholar in the field, discussed the word "secularization" in terms of its having been first used in 1648, at the end of the Thirty Years' War in Europe, to refer to the transfer of church properties to the exclusive control of princes. He continued, "When George Jacob Holyoake coined the term 'secularism' in 1851 and led a rationalist movement of protest in England secularization was built into the ideology of progress."[36] Similarly, Himanshu Roy said:

> In ecclesiastical Latin, the word "saecularis " meant the world, the profane, the base, the lowly in opposition to the church that symbolised lofty ideals, the godly, the sacred, the otherworldly and selflessness ... The struggle of classical liberalism against church and critique of religion facilitated the growth of civil society, religious tolerance and secularism, a development that was intertwined with the emergence and expansion of capitalism that created the space for and assisted the growth of individual freedom.[37]

So, here we have it all in the language and its associations. By limiting our discussion to the term in one language in relation to the institutionalized religion of a specific place, we tend to link the concept to other ideas like capitalism and individual freedom, as conceived and practiced in that place within the time frame identified for us by the location of our discourse. For our purposes, several problematic implications seem to follow from this scenario. To begin with, the secular is related to the profane, the base, the lowly *in opposition to* the godly and the sacred. This represents one major hurdle for Muslims to overcome if they are to accept or work with the secular in this sense (which they do not accept).

Moreover, a conception of the secular that is opposed to the religious is not only presented as essential for emergence of constitutional and human rights values but also linked to capitalism. In view of the prevalence of colonial power relations, it is not surprising for these associations to be presented to the Muslim colonial subject in Africa and Asia as causal relationships among these concepts and systems, whereby it is necessary to have one in order to have the other. Thus, to be secular is to be antireligious, and to be democratic is to be capitalist.

The relativity of the term to a particular religion in its specific context is also reflected in the definition of the term "secularization" as implying that "what was previously regarded as religious is now ceasing to be such, and it also implies a process of differentiation which results in the various aspects of society, economic, political, legal and moral, becoming increasingly discrete in relation to each other.' In other words, secularization leads to changes in (a) the beliefs and practices of individuals, and (b) the nature of institutions and their mutual relations."[38]

What was regarded as religious of course depends on the religion in question and its understanding and practice in a specific place and time. Processes of differentiation vary from one society to another under certain political and economic conditions. The beliefs and practices of individuals vary within the same religious tradition (Catholic and Protestant Christians; Sunni and Shia Muslims), let alone from one religion to another. Whether or not there are religious institutions at all, and their nature and relations to other institutions, is again not uniform within the same religion in different places or over time or between different religions like, for example, Buddhism and Islam. But when Islam is represented as having religious institutions, the phenomenon becomes an approximation of equivalence to Christianity. In what can be called "Christianization" of Islam, for instance, the German state is urging Muslims to organize like the Catholic and Protestant churches so that the state can deal with an identifiable "representative" of the Muslim community.[39]

Despite such factors, which I would consider obvious, the reality of colonial and postcolonial discourse continues to be founded on the assumption that European conceptions of secularism are the norm for the rest of the world and a marker of modernity.[40] The colonial and postcolonial doctrine is bound by its own logic of moral superiority of the colonizer over the colonized to relegate Islamic societies to a permanently lower scale of humanity to justify their domination and exploitation.[41] As that mode of power relations continued in the postcolonial world, European conceptions of secularism became the marker of the relationship of religion and the state in "civilized nations."[42] That imperial calculus will not change except through self-liberation by the subjects of colonization.[43]

Yet the fact that Muslims tend to judge the secular and secularism as these concepts have been understood and experienced by Europeans in relation to Christianity indicate how they have internalized a colonial state of mind that requires what I call deep decolonization through indigenous self-liberation beyond formal political self-determination. The issue is not that Europeans seek to perpetuate colonial relations, which is probably true about some of them, but that Muslims are conceding that ambition.[44] The Algerian public intellectual Malek Bennabi (1905–1973) initiated a concept that might be translated as "coloniability" to refer to an inner susceptibility to being colonized. In his view, colonialism is the consequence of the inner moral decline of Muslims, not its cause.[45]

The preceding narrative of the justification of colonialism and the internalization of that rationalization by the colonized is familiar and commonly accepted. The question I wish to raise here is: What is new about the colonial ideology and postcolonial dependency that we can still observe around the world? What is new, I argue, is the growing ability of the postcolonial subject to realize a level or degree of indigenous self-liberation that can transcend the postcolonial mind-set that still persists among both colonizer and colonized. However, the paradox here is in the fact that self-liberation is supposed to materialize and develop in postcolonial situations where the application of European notions of the secular as the universal norm seems to be necessary for working with European models of the nation-state.

This paradox can be mediated because there is some relative progress on both sides—among the subjects of empire as well as the citizens of imperial power—in comparison with previous generations. More subjects of empire are more forcefully refusing to submit than used to be the case, and more citizens of imperial powers are more apologetic about the domination and exploitation of other human beings.[46] I now find it more plausible than used to be the case that human enlightenment can be achieved by individual persons, everywhere, in their own cultural and religious contexts. It is from this perspective that Muslims can now achieve their own enlightenment and sustain its values on their own terms more than they were able to do during the colonial and postcolonial period.[47]

It is not possible to discuss here all the reservations and concerns one may have about the paradox of the postcolonial context in which postcolonial societies must seek self-liberation. Still, I would close the preceding overview by emphasizing the practical value of the secular in this context. One important purpose of the secular is to give everyone a sort of "common ground" from which to begin discussion. Charles Taylor explains the purpose of the secular as a common ground and why it is important:

> Secular reason is a language that everyone speaks, and can argue and be convinced in. Religious languages operate outside of this discourse, by introducing extraneous premises which only believers can accept. So let's all talk the common language.
>
> What underpins this notion is something like an epistemic distinction. There is secular reason, which everyone can use and reach conclusions by—conclusions that is, with which everyone can agree. Then there are special languages, which introduce extra assumptions, which might even contradict those of ordinary secular reason. These are much more epistemically fragile; in fact, you won't be convinced by them unless you already hold them. So religious reason either comes to the same conclusions as secular reason, but then it is superfluous; or it comes to contrary conclusions, and then it is dangerous and disruptive. This is why it needs to be sidelined.[48]

The possibility of what Taylor calls "secular reason" is what underpins the frequently noted and obviously true purpose of secularism as a political doctrine; namely, to avoid discord among believers in different religions and to allow citizens to practice their own faiths freely. By not making any one religion "official," the state avoids isolating members of other faiths. "No one religion can pretend to speak for the rest."[49]

Contrary to an apparent consensus among Muslims and non-Muslims alike, I believe that it should not be difficult for Muslims to accept a secular state in the sense of one that is neutral regarding all religions, provided the connectedness of Islam and politics is acknowledged. A religiously neutral state is fully compatible with Muslim acceptance of the inherent consistency and complementarity between the secular and the religious noted at the beginning of this essay. At the same time, the connectedness of Islam and politics addresses concerns about secularism as a life philosophy, like those raised by Taha that I summarized earlier.

TAHA AND THE SECULAR STATE: AN INTERPRETATION

I am calling my proposal of a secular state an "interpretation" of Taha's views to make it clear that I am speaking here on my own personal responsibility and not on behalf of Taha or any of the members of his movement in general. I do believe that my proposal is consistent with Taha's views, although he did not advance what I am proposing as such. I also believe that his objections to secularism as a life philosophy noted in the preceding section do not apply to what I am proposing. In particular, I believe that what I am proposing is an appropriate approach to the social and political organization Taha advocated as necessary for self-liberation by Muslims in the present realities of the postcolonial state in its global context.

I call for a secular state in order for believers to be good Muslims in society. The secular state is one that does not take a position on any matter of religion and strives to be as neutral as possible regarding various religions. The key quality of the state I intend is that it does not discriminate among the religious beliefs of its citizens—it does not favor one view or disfavor another view of religion. Society, on the other hand, reflects the religious beliefs and practices of its members, who can be of any faith. To me, society is a community of believers not a "believing community," because a collective entity is a metaphor and cannot believe, think, or feel like an individual person.

For Muslims, there is no possibility of new or additional texts, because the prophet Muhammad is believed to be the final prophet and the Qur'an is the conclusive divine revelation, but there is nothing to prevent or invalidate the formation of a new consensus around techniques of interpretation or innovative interpretations of the Qur'an and Sunna. New interpretations would thereby become part of sharia in the same way that existing techniques or principles came to be part of it in the first place.

The separation of Islam from the state and the regulation of its political role through constitutionalism and the protection of human rights that I propose are necessary to ensure freedom and security for Muslims to participate in proposing and debating fresh interpretations of those foundational sources. This is religiously necessary because any understanding of sharia is always the product of juridical reasoning in the general sense of reasoning and reflection by human beings. "Although the law is of divine provenance, the actual construction of the law is a human activity, and its results represent the law of God *as humanly understood*. Since the law does not descend from heaven ready-made, it is the human understanding of the law—the human *fiqh* [lit.: understanding] that must be normative for society."[50]

To briefly explain, since determinations about whether or not any text of the Qur'an or Sunna applies to an issue, and whether or not it is categorical, who can exercise juridical reasoning (*ijtihad*) and how are all matters that can only be decided by human beings, imposing prior censorship on such efforts violates the premise of how sharia principles can be derived from the Qur'an and Sunna. It is illogical to say that *ijtihad* cannot be exercised regarding a specific issue or question because that determination itself is the product of human reasoning and reflection. It is also dangerous to limit the ability to exercise *ijtihad* to a restricted group of Muslims who are supposed to have specific qualifications because that will depend in practice on those human beings who will set and apply the criteria of selecting who is qualified as one who can exercise *ijtihad*. To grant this authority to any institution or organ, whether believed to be official or private, is dangerous because that power will certainly be manipulated for political or other reasons.

Since knowing and upholding sharia is the permanent and inescapable responsibility of every Muslim, no person or institution should control this process for Muslims. Since the power to decide who is qualified to exercise *ijtihad* and how it is to be practiced affects matters of religious belief and obligation for every Muslim, there should not be any censorship of or control over this process. In other words, any restriction of free debate by entrusting human beings or institutions with the authority to decide which views are to be allowed or suppressed is inconsistent with the religious nature of sharia itself.

The objective for me is to protect individual believers' genuine piety in beliefs and practice by controlling the risk of coercion by the state or society. A neutral state and tolerant society is the means to that end. By organizing and regulating social life, keeping the peace, and delivering essential services without discrimination, regardless of religious belief or lack of it, the state encourages society to be tolerant of religious pluralism. The legal neutrality of the state and social tolerance of diversity and dissent enable individual believers to be more honest in their effort to bring their behavior into conformity with their religious beliefs. Coercion by the state or society encourages hypocrisy, while freedom of religion and belief and social tolerance promotes genuine piety in beliefs and practice. As Gandhi argued:

> While it was the obligation of the state to ensure that every religion was free to develop according to its own genius, no religion which depended on state support deserves to survive. In other words, the inseparability of religion and politics in the Indian [Islamic from my perspective] context, and generally, was for Gandhi fundamentally a distinct issue from the separation of the state from the church in Christendom. When he did advocate that "religion and state should be separate," he clarified that this was to limit the role of the state to

"secular welfare" and to allow it no admittance into the religious life of the people.[51]

I make a distinction between the state and politics, to argue that the state should not claim or pretend to enforce or apply sharia as sharia, though sharia principles can influence state policies through politics. This is what I mean by "negotiating" the influence of sharia, as various political forces struggle to present and defend policies through what I call "civic reason." In this way, political actors should try to explain and support their policy choices by giving reasons that all citizens can debate freely and accept or reject without reference to religious beliefs.

For example, if I want to propose prohibition of charging interest on loans (*riba*), I should present economic and social reasons in support of what I am proposing, instead of simply asserting that the state should prohibit charging interest on loans because that is *haram*. At the same time, Muslims should avoid *riba* in their personal dealings, because it is *haram*. This is the religious behavior for which a believer is either rewarded or punished, depending on his action and intention (*niya*). What the state is doing, whether influenced by sharia principles or not, is politics, and what believers do on their own personal responsible is religious.

In practically every society, religious groups are an important policy constituency on fundamental matters of social life, from education to taxation and from issues of public and private morality to charitable social functions. When I speak of negotiations between religions and the state with regard to these issues, I mean arrangements whereby religious groups are acknowledged as an important political constituency that is neither taken over by the state nor allowed to take over the state itself or any of its institutions. The religious neutrality of the state as the principle of separation of state and religion helps achieve this delicate balance by providing a framework for securing the legitimacy of the state among religious communities while regulating how their concerns are reflected in public policy with due regard to the concerns and interests of other communities and citizens at large.

Since citizens who are not religious or do not organize to lobby the state as religious communities are entitled to equal respect for their views and interests, the state and its organs must not fall under the control of one religious community, however large its numbers may be. In fact, the neutrality of the state regarding all religious and nonreligious perspectives is more important in relation to dominant groups, because the risks of state bias in their favor is greater than in the case of minorities.

It should also be noted that perception in such matters can be as important as reality, because the appearance of bias tends to undermine public confidence in the neutrality of the state even where bias does not exist. The religious neutrality of the state provides a basic structure whereby the state is neither partial nor perceived to be partial to any one religious or nonreligious perspective, while giving due regard to all relevant and legitimate perspectives in the formulation and implementation of public policy.

Moreover, the imperatives of certainty, uniformity, and neutrality in national legislation are now stronger than they used to be in the precolonial era. This is not only due to the growing complexity of the role of the state at the domestic or national level but also because of the global interdependence of all peoples and their states. Regardless of the relative weakness or strength of some states in relation to others, the realities of national and global political, economic, security, and other relations remain firmly embedded in the existence of sovereign states that have exclusive jurisdiction over their citizens and territories.

I will now close with a brief reflection on the religious neutrality of the state within the framework of what I call "civic reason," which refers to the means for facilitating and regulating the relationships between state, politics, and religion. My view is that the state should be institutionally separate from Islam while recognizing and regulating the unavoidable connectedness of Islam with politics. Despite their obvious and permanent connections, I take the state to be the more settled, operational side of self-governance, while politics is the dynamic process of making choices among competing policy options.

The state and politics may be seen as two sides of the same coin, but they cannot and should not be completely fused. It is necessary to ensure that the state is not simply a complete reflection of the politics of the day, because it must be able to mediate and adjudicate among

4

CREATING DEMOCRATICALLY FRIENDLY TWIN TOLERATIONS OUTSIDE OF LATIN CHRISTENDOM

TUNISIA

Alfred Stepan

For many of the most influential "modernization" and "secularism" theorists, religion is "traditional and irrational" and associated with authoritarianism; they see it as the binary opposite of "modernization and rationality," which they view as a necessary path to democratization.[1] Indeed, one of the most influential English-language political philosophers in the last half of the twentieth century, John Rawls, in his early work went so far as to argue that, in the name of arriving at an "overlapping consensus," religious arguments should be "taken off the public agenda."[2] Charles Taylor in his book, *A Secular Age*, discusses the complex historical processes in the North Atlantic world by which a relatively religion-free "exclusive humanism" became the hegemonic view as to how public policies should be designed and publicly defended.[3]

My research on actual democratization efforts in countries such as Indonesia, Senegal, Turkey, and India, as well as Spain, Brazil, and Chile, has led me to believe that the "hard secularism" of the French 1905 type or Atatürk's state-imposed secularism in the name of modernity is not only not necessary for democratization but often creates problems for democratization. Elsewhere I have advanced the argument I call the "twin tolerations." From this conceptual viewpoint, two religion–state relationships require tolerant behavior and laws in a democracy. First, religious citizens must be sufficiently tolerant of democratic procedures and powers that democratic officials are accorded the necessary freedoms to make constitutions and laws and manage the democratic polity. Laws in a democracy must be man-made, not God-made. Second, democratic officials and laws, contra early Rawls or French 1905-type *laïcité*, must tolerate the freedom of expression by religious citizens of their values within civil society, as well as their active participation in political society, as long as such religious activists and organizations do not violate other citizens' constitutional rights or violate the law. Religion does not have to be "off the agenda" in a democracy. Indeed, to force it off is a violation of the second component of the twin tolerations.[4]

From the twin tolerations perspective, transitions to democracy in previously nondemocratic polities can be helped by the degree to which they have already become, in at least some of their values, political practices, and public institutions, twin tolerations–friendly.

However, when considering Muslim countries, many commentators concentrate their attention on the "missing factors" they see as necessary for democracy. Much of what they see as "missing" draws from the repertoire of what these observers think, rightly or wrongly, actually existed in Latin Christendom when democracy emerged in particular countries. However, what needs to be done is to expand our imagination by looking carefully for not what is *missing* but for *innovative additions* socially constructed outside of Latin Christendom that have contributed to the emergence of twin tolerations–friendly practices; without a Protestant-type Reformation, without aggressive secularism, without the hegemony of "exclusive humanism," and certainly without authoritarian, military-imposed secularism as in Atatürk's Turkey.

An examination of contemporary Tunisia helps illustrate this point. In this essay I advance three arguments. First, though pre-independence Tunisia was certainly not moving in the direction of French-style, religiously hostile *laïcité*, I show how, in some important ways, it was becoming twin tolerations–friendly, and that recently this legacy been explicitly drawn upon as part of a "usable past" for a future Tunisian democracy.

Second, I illustrate how at independence, Tunisia's first president, Habib Bourguiba, in the name of "modernization," destroyed key parts of this twin tolerations culture by imposing authoritarian secularism from above. Worse, Bourguiba created a constituency that shored up authoritarian rule for fifty-five years; that of Bourguiba himself from 1956–1987 and that of Ben Ali from 1987–2011.

Third, building on my three research trips to Tunisia since the start of the Arab Spring, I show how, as early as 2003, secular and religious oppositional activists I interviewed had agreed on a common program for a post–Ben Ali democratic transition that to some extent drew upon their usable past to imagine a democratic future. A key part of this agreement was that secularists would allow Islamists to participate fully in democratic contestation and that Islamists agreed that the "sovereignty of the people was the sole source of legitimacy."

SOME TWIN TOLERATIONS–FRIENDLY ELEMENTS IN TUNISIA'S USABLE PAST

Without the triumph of "exclusive humanism," some important aspects of Tunisia's pre-independence cultural heritage had become relatively twin tolerations–friendly. Three areas deserve particular attention: Tunisia's rich intellectual and educational tradition, which combined important secular and spiritual elements; its pioneering mid-nineteenth-century role in building constitutional and state structures that were religiously neutral and rights enhancing; and the emergence of a some politically engaged Islamic thinkers who argued for a more rights-based reading of Islam, especially in the area of rights for women.

Ibn Khaldun, a descendant of a family who had been Ottoman rulers in Seville, was born in Tunis in 1332. He is considered by many to be the founder of sociology, due to his rational and systematic comparison of empires and cultures. Indeed, one scholar sees Ibn Khaldun as the best link between Greek rationalism and *Annales* rationalism and comparative historical studies.[5] Only one statue, that of Ibn Khaldun, adorns the long plaza running down Bourguiba Boulevard, the center of Tunis's public, social, and café life. But what made Ibn Khaldun a great thinker, scholar, and Tunisian cultural hero? He was privately educated in Tunis by the greatest scholars of theology, Sufism, philosophy, history, languages, mathematics, physical sciences, and medicine that he and his father could find.⁶ Most analysts of his work fail to mention his appreciation of religious contemplation as an end in itself and also as a way of helping rational thought. Indeed, many assert that Khaldun's way of thinking had little connection to Islam. They tend to ignore his great intellectual and spiritual attention not only to rational analysis but to the study of Sufism, saints, and mystics.

One of the most important aspects of Tunisia's cultural history is its special connection with the Ottoman Empire in Tunisia itself and in Andalucía. The great British historian of Christianity, Diarmaid MacCulloch, in his book *The Reformation*, asserts that "Western Christianity before 1500 must rank as one of the most intolerant religions in world history. Its record in comparison with medieval Islamic civilization is embarrassingly poor."⁷ The more tolerant Islamic civilizations he refers to, of course are the Ottoman Empire based in Turkey, the Mogul Empire in India, especially under Akbar, and the Muslim Empire in Andalucía, Spain.⁸ Khaldun, in his monumental *Muquaddimah*, makes a special point of stressing that Tunis became one of the preferred destinations for Muslim and Jewish emigrants; he estimates that the "bulk of inhabitants of thirteenth-century Tunis were of Andalusían families who had emigrated from the Spanish Levant."⁹ These emigrants, Jews as well as Muslims, brought such extensive high-level experience in governing and administration from Andalucía that many of them, for centuries, filled very high posts in the Hafsid-led kingdom in Tunisia.¹⁰

Educationally, some of Tunisia's most prestigious institutions were religious, and some were secular. The Islamic-based Zeitouna University was founded in Tunis in 734, some 235 years before Al-Azhar university was founded in Cairo. The School of Military Sciences was created in the 1830s to train Tunisian military officers largely in secular sciences. The secular-based Sadiki College was founded in 1875 and rapidly became the most prestigious and competitive school in Tunisia. Sadiki College was religiously mixed and had a particularly strong Jewish student intake; indeed, as late as the 1950s, Sadiki College had 2,593 Tunisian Muslims and 1,293 Tunisian Jews enrolled.

An important part of Tunisia's usable past that is now appealed to by secular and religious democratic activists alike is its mid-nineteenth-century period of constitutional reform and a religiously neutral state. From 1580 until the French Protectorate began in 1881, Tunisia was often a quiet autonomous part of the Ottoman Empire. A case can be made that the most rights-enhancing Arab country in the nineteenth century and the early part of the twentieth century was Tunisia, closely followed by Egypt. In 1846, two years before France, Tunisia abolished slavery after powerful and persuasive arguments and pressures emanating from both religious and secular groups. This abolition was the first in the Muslim world and occurred nineteen years before abolition in the United States (1865), forty-two years before Brazil (1888), and one hundred sixteen years before abolition in Saudi Arabia (1962).[11]

In 1861, Tunisia passed the first constitution in Arab history. The French social scientist, Jean-Pierre Filiu, who lived for four years in Tunisia, argues in a book on the Arab Spring that this constitution "enshrined a political power distinct from religion: Islam was barely mentioned, only to stress that the text was not contradicting its principles, and it was not even explicit that the Bey [the ruler] had to be Muslim."[12] The 1861 Constitution, under the influence of a major statesman and political thinker, Khayr al-Din (often spelled Khéréddine), who later became the grand wizir of the Ottoman Empire, in articles 86–104, again and again insisted that everyone in the kingdom "whatever their religion have the right" to be judged by a tribunal where some of their coreligionists are on the tribunal, to complete physical security, and to engage in all types of commerce. Filiu also notes that this constitution had been preceded by a "Covenant of Social Peace" that emphasized "public interest, equality before the law and freedom of religion."[13] To be sure neither the covenant nor the constitution was ever fully enforced, but at least they introduced into Tunisian discourse the equality of rights of peoples from *all* religions. Indeed, Albert Hourani, in his classic study *Arabic Thought in the Liberal Age: 1798–1939*, writes that this Tunisian "experiment in constitutional government . . . left its mark: it helped to form a new political consciousness in Tunis, and to bring to the front a group of reforming statesman, officials and writers . . . until they were scattered by the French occupation in 1881. This group had two origins: one of them was the Zaytuna Mosque, where the influence of a reforming teacher, Shaykh Muhammad Qubadu, was felt; the other was the new School of Military Sciences."[14] Zeitouna and Saidiki, together with the School of Military Sciences, produced some major political thinkers who argued, *from within Islam*, for the expansion of rights, including women's rights. The most important such work was written by Tahar Haddad, who in 1924 had cofounded the first major free trade union in Tunisia. In 1927 Haddad argued in his *Notre femme dans la Legislation Muselmane et dans la Societé*, that a correct reading of the Koran should lead to women's equality. The cover of this book depicted a stationary and completely veiled woman in the front and, soaring up behind her, a curly-haired young woman basketball player in athletic attire. [15] Haddad was building on the work of the great statesman and constitutional theorist I mentioned above, Khayr al-Din, who Nathan J. Brown argues "advances a powerful argument for a constitutionalist policy, and locates constitutionalism not only in European practice but also in the Islamic tradition."[16] In the 2003 agreement that I argue later was a fundamental building block for cooperation among the secular and Islamic democratic opposition, two of the four Tunisian leaders explicitly mentioned as part of Tunisia's usable past are precisely Haddad, the advocate for women's rights within Islam, and Khayr al-Din, the advocate for constitutionalism within Islam.

Thus, without following a path toward "exclusive humanism" or hard religiously unfriendly secular *laïcité*, Tunisia at independence in 1956 was a country where rational and religious reasoning and insights had a place in public argument in a relatively friendly, twin tolerations–supportive, environment. What happened at independence that set this process back for over fifty years?

AUTHORITARIAN SECULARIST MODERNIZATION: BOURGUIBA AND BEN ALI (1956–2011)

During his leadership of the independence movement, Habib Bourguiba appealed to Muslim sentiments and identities. However, once independence was won in 1956, his emphasis shifted almost exclusively to French- and Turkish-style, state-led "modernization." His post-independence speeches frequently depicted religion as part of "tradition," not "modernity," and thus a major obstacle to be overcome. In one such speech Bourguiba lamented that "a large mass of our population is still entangled in a mass of prejudices and so-called religious belief." In another, Bourguiba's preference for what Taylor calls "exclusive humanism" is clear: "faith and spiritual values are effective only to the extent they are based on reason."[17]

In addition to such negative discourse, Bourguiba rapidly carried out a number of institutional, material, and occupational measures designed to weaken, marginalize, and control Islam.

Institutionally, the oldest Muslim university in the world, Zeitouna, which had been broadening its curriculum to include sciences and comparative history since the reforms of the 1860s, was closed by Bourguiba. Eventually a small part of Zeitouna was reopened as a purely theological department within the newly created, French-inspired, secular state university, the Université de Tunis. The head of this newly marginalized department was appointed by the state and had no significant education in Islamic scholarship.[18]

Materially, the financial base of Islam in Tunisia at independence was its extensive land holdings, which were managed by pious trusts. Such trusts produced revenues in support of the mosques and some Muslim social programs. Bourguiba, as part of his modernization strategy, nationalized the pious trusts and announced a broad program of agrarian reform and the expropriation of unused lands. By far the fastest and most draconian land reforms were those that eroded the material base of Islam in Tunisia by mass nationalization of the lands managed by the pious trusts.

In the name of modernization, Bourguiba reduced the study of religion to one hour a week in public schools and required teachers to be able to teach in French as well as Arabic. The vast majority of imams, most of whom had been teachers and only knew Arabic, became unemployed. In this context, due to the loss of financial support and state pressure, private Koranic schools "all but disappeared in independent Tunisia."[19]

While there were major religious losers under Bourguiba, there were those who made major secular gains, especially women. The Arab world's most progressive family code ever granted to this day was passed by Bourguiba in his first year in office.[20] This code abolished polygamy, allowed women to initiate divorce proceedings and to divide goods relatively equally, forbade unilateral repudiation of the marriage by the husband, and raised the minimum age of marriage for girls. Nine years later, in 1966, the government launched a robust family-planning program and legalized abortion (seven years before *Roe v. Wade* in the United States and forty-six years before Uruguay became the first Latin American country to legalize abortion).[21] Tunisian women also rapidly began to enter universities.

Bourguiba during his thirty-one years of rule never allowed a free election. Part of the reason why his middle-class urban constituency, female and male, did not demand elections was that Bourguiba implicitly raised the following type of questions: "All these modernizing and secularizing reforms I did against traditional Muslims. After me? With free elections? What would happen?"

Bourguiba was removed from power in 1987 by Ben Ali in what is called the "doctor's coup" (because it was alleged that Bourguiba had dementia). A brief thaw under Ben Ali led to the return of some key dissidents and eventually to slightly more competitive legislative elections in 1989. In the context of the 1979 Iranian Revolution, the growth of the Islamic Salvation Front in neighboring Algeria, pent-up resentment by some Tunisian Muslims because of their exclusion as a political force, and the emergence of a Zeitouna and Sadiki graduate, Rachid Ghannouchi, as the leader of a political group, Ennahda (or Renaissance Party), that could mobilize this opposition, more aggressive Muslims challenged Ben Ali. Despite not being legalized and thus allowed to run as a party, Ennahda saw its candidates run as Independents in the 1989 election. In what was certainly not a fair election, even Ben Ali's officials acknowledged that Ennahda Independents still won 15 percent of the overall vote (and 30 percent in the capital of Tunis). In a polarizing atmosphere, two people were killed in explosions, allegedly by Islamists. It is still not clear who carried out the explosions, but Ben Ali charged Ennahda. In the next few years estimates by Ennahda, by a Tunisian human rights group, and by Amnesty International indicate that at least 20,000 Ennahda members were tried for subversion and sent to jail, and about 10,000 went into exile, many after passing through Algeria, like Ghannouchi.[22] The thaw had turned to ice.

The new polarization helped Ben Ali extend his authoritarian rule for two more decades. To Bourguiba's warning that Islamists would reverse the gains of secularism, Ben Ali, helped by the context of the bloody civil war between Islamists and the military in neighboring Algeria, added the fear of Islamic violence, which he argued only he and his regime could prevent.[23]

THE RE-EMERGENCE OF SOME TWIN TOLERATION–FRIENDLY GROUPS AND PROCESSES

The literature on democratic transitions normally makes a basic distinction between the tasks of resistance within "civil society" that help deconstruct an authoritarian regime and the tasks of "political society" that help construct a democratic regime. Some of the distinctive constructive tasks of political society are the forging of agreements and compromises among leaders of the opposition about such things as a common plan for the interim government after the authoritarian regime collapses or yields power and the timing and type of elections that will generate democratically based, constitution-drafting and ruling bodies and powers.

In my judgment, Tunisia and Egypt had some of the most creative and effective civil society resistance movements in the history of democratization movements. However, as of this writing in October 2012, Egypt has done far less to create an effective political society than any other country I know that has made a successful democratic transition. Tunisia, in contrast, has made reasonable advances toward creating a relatively autonomous, democratic, and effective political society. Much of the reason for this comparative Tunisian success is that both Islamic and secular leaders have worked to overcome their mutual fears and distrust by crafting agreements and credible guarantees in political society. In the process they have begun to reconstruct the twin tolerations–friendly secularism destroyed by Tunisia's secularist and modernization fundamentalists between 1956 and 2011.

In what follows, I organize my analysis around three hypotheses. They hardly make up the whole story of Tunisia's transition, but they do draw attention to areas where Tunisia's successes contrast strongly with Egypt's initial failures in its transition.

First, the religious hypothesis: in countries where religious conflict is likely to be salient, the greater the degree to which the major religion-based political parties and the major secular parties have made significant movements toward accepting both of the core requirements of the "twin tolerations" before or soon after the start of an attempted democratic transition, the greater the chance of a successful democratic transition. Empirically, this means that the major religiously based parties do not argue that God-made law is superior to man-made law, which would violate the first major tenet of the "twin tolerations"; it also means that the major secular parties do not deny the right of religiously based citizens to articulate their values democratically in civil and political society, a denial that would violate the second major requirement of the "twin tolerations."

Second, the civil-military hypothesis: from the viewpoint of democratization, in my judgment the most important aspect of the military to study is civil-military relations, not the military itself. Empirically this means that the less civilians abdicate their right to rule to the military, in an "Eighteenth Brumaire" type of exchange for what for they perceive as security from threats from class or religious rivals that might be produced by democracy, the greater the chance of a successful and militarily unconstrained democratic transition.[24]

Third, the political society hypothesis: this states that empirically, the greater the degree to which political actors and parties craft among themselves or agree to rules of the game for contestation for democratic political power, the greater the chance of a successful democratic transition.

In my reading of the first year of the Arab Spring, all three of these mutually reinforcing processes hold for Tunisia on the positive side and for Egypt on the negative side. Indeed, they go a long way toward explaining why Tunisia had met all four of the requirements (discussed in the conclusion) for a completed democratic transition by December 2011, while Egypt had not yet completed one.[25]

THE RELIGIOUS HYPOTHESIS

The largest, best-organized, and most influential party in post–Ben Ali Tunisia is the Islamist-influenced Ennahda. In March 2011, in my interviews in Tunis with some of the members of the newly liberated press and several of the leading secularists, I found many of them extremely frightened by the prospect of free elections. Indeed, some of those I interviewed were, as were their peers in Egypt, toying with "Brumairian" options, namely the option of exchanging the possibility of democratic civilian rule for the secure protection offered by an authoritarian body, in this case the military.

However, it was striking that in my interviews in June and November 2011, Brumairianism, if not fear, had begun to recede in Tunisia. Why?

In 1997 I had interviewed in London and Oxford Ennahda's exiled leader, Rachid Ghannouchi, as part of my twin tolerations article. In February 2011, after Ghannouchi returned to Tunis from two decades of exile, we met again shortly after my interviews with three top Muslim Brotherhood officials in Egypt. I quickly asked Ghannouchi what he thought about the still unrepudiated Muslim Brotherhood platform in Egypt concerning the ineligibility of women or Christians from election as president. He responded immediately: "Democracy means equality of all citizens. Such a platform excludes 60 percent of all the citizens and is unacceptable."[26] Ghannouchi said he had entered into agreements (confirmed in multiple interviews and documents) with a number of political parties in 1988, and persistently since 2003, saying Ennahda would not try to reverse Tunisia's progressive family code.[27] We talked about a proposed sharia council in the Egyptian Muslim Brotherhood's 2007 platform, whose function could possibly have been to review parliamentary legislation, and it was quite clear that he saw this as an unwarranted intrusion of religious authority on democratic authority—a violation of the twin tolerations. He insisted that neither he nor his party would push for such a body.

In a subsequent May 2011 interview with Ghannouchi, I asked if Ennahda was closer to the Egyptian Muslim Brotherhood or to the Turkish Justice and Democracy Party (AKP). The elected secretary general of Ennahda (and later prime minister of Tunisia), Hamadi Jebali, who was also present, chose to answer, saying "We are much closer to the AKP than to the Muslim Brotherhood. We are a civic party emanating from the reality of Tunisia, not a religious party. A religious party believes it has legitimacy not from the people but from God. A religious party believes it has the truth and no one can oppose it because it has the truth." Ghannouchi concurred and added that the goal was a "civic state, not a religious state."[28] As the campaign went on, Ghannouchi and Jebali continued to try to reduce fears of Islamic fundamentalism. Many, if not most, secularists were still not convinced, but at least Ennahda did not have an unrepudiated, anti-twin tolerations platform (as the Muslim Brotherhood did in Egypt) that secularists could denounce.

THE CIVIL-MILITARY RELATIONS HYPOTHESIS

Unlike Egypt, where military officers have held the presidency continuously since the Free Officers' assumption of power on July 22, 1952, in Tunisia, the military have never ruled for a day. Instead, Bourguiba, and particularly Ben Ali, kept the military small and ruled with the support of the hated police and intelligence security forces, which according to some estimates totaled 600,000 members (as against an army of 35,000). Nonetheless, if Tunisian civilians had wanted "Brumairian" protection, they could possibly have abdicated substantial power to the popular chief of staff of the army, Rachid Ammar, who had confronted the demoralized police and ushered Ben Ali out of the country. But, unlike Egypt, they did not. Within less than a month of Ben Ali's flight, civilians in political society, supported by civil-society activists, had demanded and acquired responsibility for crafting the key rules necessary for making a democratic transition.

THE POLITICAL SOCIETY HYPOTHESIS

According to Jean Daniel, the French commentator and founder of *Le Nouvel Observateur*, the November 2011 elections in Tunisia amounted to a counterrevolution, an unfortunate manifestation of "loyalty to tradition" instead of the "triumph of liberty."[29] It would appear from what Daniel writes that the elections could only have counted as an advance of liberty if they had followed the script of a French model of 1905 *laïcité*—that is, the most religiously "unfriendly" form of secularism of any western European democracy. As noted already, such a model, in a more extreme form, was imposed by the state in the authoritarian secularism under Habib Bourguiba and Ben Ali.

In my judgment, a much more appropriate description of the political situation in Tunisia in November and December 2011 would have been to call it the Arab Spring's first completed democratic transition. How was this achieved in Tunisia? There is a complex story here worthy of several monographs. In this short essay I will start such an analysis based on a number of interviews and some of the documents activists have given me. The essence of the story is the gradual construction of political society, anchored in a democratic and relatively consensual opposition, involving both secularists and a religiously based Muslim party that was ready to start crafting a democracy the day Ben Ali left office. To my surprise, and I believe to the surprise of many close observers, this construction had actually begun *eight years before the fall of Ben Ali.* A strikingly similar process of political rapprochement and commitment to nonviolence and democracy began in Chile in the 1980s, involving the secular Socialist Party and the religiously based Christian Democratic Party, roughly eight years before they defeated Augusto Pinochet in an election and formed a successful, post-Pinochet coalition government.

In June 2003, representatives of four of the five largest political parties (which today have the greatest number of seats on Tunisia's just-elected constituent assembly) met in France and negotiated and personally signed the "Call from Tunis" (Appel de Tunis).[30] The preamble called for building upon the work and arguments of the great progressive, constitutional architect of state religious neutrality, Khayr al-Din, and the major advocate for equality of women, Tahar Haddad, both of whom I discussed earlier. The "Call from Tunis" went on to endorse specifically the two fundamental principles of the twin tolerations: (1) any future elected government would be "founded on the sovereignty of the people as the sole source of legitimacy," not on God's law; and (2) the state would "guarantee liberty of beliefs to all and the political neutralization of places of worship." Ennahda, which like AKP in Turkey or the Christian Democratic Party in Germany had its roots in religion, accepted both these fundamental agreements.

Further, as we have seen, one of the accomplishments of Bourguiba was the creation of the Arab world's most egalitarian family code and policies toward women. The "Call from Tunis," which Ennahda signed, demanded "the full equality of women and men."

From 2005 on the four main political parties, together with representatives of some of the other smaller political parties, met to reaffirm and even deepen their commitment to the principles of the "Call from Tunis." One such document, issued under the rubric "The 18 October Coalition for Rights and Freedoms in Tunisia" stresses that as a result of a "three-month dialogue among party leaders" they have come to a consensus on a number of crucial issues. First, concerning women, all the parties, including Ennahda, supported with great detail the policies of the existing very progressive family law. Second, the document states that any future democratic state must be a "civic state . . . drawing its legitimacy from the will of the people." Third, it asserts that "political practice is a human discipline. . . . which therefore denies it any form of sanctity. And fourth, it claims that "there can be no compulsion in religion. This includes the right to adopt a religion or doctrine or not."[31]

I am not arguing that a fully developed political society existed in Tunisia before the fall of Ben Ali, but I am arguing that the four parties that received over 60 percent of the votes in the first free elections in Tunisia in November 2011 had been negotiating and arriving at agreed democratic political principles for a future twin toleration–friendly state for eight years before the fall of Ben Ali.

Within days of Ben Ali's ouster, the interim government, still composed of Ben Ali's appointees, decreed a new organization to craft procedures for a rapid presidential election, presumably of Ben Ali's long-standing prime minister, Mohamed Ghanouchi. However, protests by civil society activists, particularly the Kasbah One demonstrators outside the prime minister's office, were rapidly supported by political society activists and forced the creation of a new body representing all the political parties and civil society, the High Commission for the Fulfillment of Revolutionary Goals, Political Reform, and Democratic Transition, generally called the Ben Achour Commission, after its chairman. This newly structured commission turned out to be one of the most successful and consensual organizations in the history of crafting a democratic transition. Nothing remotely like this was created in Egypt during the first ten months after the fall of Mubarak, when the military, via the Supreme Command of the Armed Forces (SCAF), structured all significant political dialogue through more than 150 unilaterally issued communiqués.

In November of 2011, I talked at length with Ben Achour himself, with some of the members of the commission from political parties and civil society, and with two of the expert (but nonvoting) legal advisors to Ben Achour. I was also given many of the key documents the commission had voted upon. Here are the main points they discussed at length and the decisions they made:

1. The commission recognized that many changes were important for improving Tunisia and consolidating democracy. However, they correctly agreed to concentrate as a body only on decisions that were *indispensable* for creating a democratic government to make these reforms (e.g., voting rules, free and fair elections).
2. What office, or organization, should be elected first? They decided that the first election to be held would be to create a constituent assembly, one of whose central tasks would be to produce a new constitution which itself would have the sovereignty to decide on whether to have a presidential, semipresidential, or parliamentary system. This was a crucial decision; if a president had been directly elected first, this sitting president would have great capacity to structure the constitution. Further, the decision to have direct elections for a powerful presidency might have created disincentives for party building, because many of the most prominent political figures, as in Egypt, might have decided to run as independent, nonparty, presidential candidates.
3. It was agreed that the constituent assembly, based on the legitimacy of its election, would select a government that would responsible to

the constituent assembly and subject (as in the Spanish and Indian transitions) to a vote of no confidence.
4. It was agreed that the electoral system would be one of pure proportional representation. This decision was correctly understood to have crucial, antimajoritarian, democracy-facilitating, coalition-encouraging implications. If an English "first-past-the-post, single-member district" electoral system had been chosen, Ennahda, which had the first plurality in almost 90 percent of the electoral districts, would have won near 90 percent of the seats, instead of the 41 percent it now has due to the pure proportional representation system.
5. To help ensure strong participation of women in the constitution-writing process, it was agreed to aim for male-female parity in candidates by having every other name on the candidates' lists be a woman.[32] By all accounts the first party to accept this gender parity provision was the Muslim-inspired Ennahda.
6. To ensure that all the contesting parties would have confidence in the fairness of the electoral results, it was decided to create Tunisia's first independent electoral commission and to invite many international electoral observers and give them extensive monitoring prerogatives. In sharp contrast, in Egypt, SCAF initially unilaterally denied the entry of international observers on the grounds that their presence would be a violation of Egypt's sovereignty. Eventually SCAF allowed into the country some election "followers," whose number and prerogatives were substantially less than in Tunisia.
7. On the issue of what to do with Ben Ali's official party, the commission decided to ban the party and some of its most important leaders from being candidates for the first election. However, in order not to exclude a large group of citizens from participating in the first free elections, the assembly declared that former Ben Ali party members and/or supporters were free to form new parties.

On April 11, 2011, approximately 155 members of the Ben Achour Commission voted on this package of measures to create a democratic transition. There were two walkouts and two abstentions; all the other members voted for the package. Solidaristic jubilation ensued.

CONCLUSION

In our book *Problems of Democratic Transition and Consolidation: Southern Europe, South America, and Post-Communist Europe*, Juan J. Linz and I spell out what we believe is required for a successful democratic transition to be completed. The first requirement is that "sufficient agreement has been reached about political procedures to produce an elected government." The second is that "a government comes to power that is the direct result of a free and popular vote." The third is that "this government *de facto* has the authority to generate new policies." And the fourth requirement is that "the executive, legislative and judicial power generated by the new democracy does not have to share power with other bodies *de jure*" (such as military or religious leaders).[33]

According to these requirements, Tunisia may be said to have completed a transition to democracy when the prime minister and all government nominated ministers were approved by the parliament and commenced their duties on December 23, 2011.

Such a completed democratic transition does not, of course, mean that democracy is successfully consolidated. Many socioeconomic reforms are needed, and democracy is always only "government pro tem" and politically always has some dangers that must be guarded against by a nonmajoritarian constitution, a vigilant independent judiciary, a robust and critical civil society, and a free press.

But as of this writing, October 2012, Tunisia's fledgling democracy, building upon the consensually agreed decisions of April 11, 2011, and the electors' decisions, had a number of credible constraints in place.

A crucial democratic constraint was that Ennahda won only 41 percent of the seats in the constituent assembly and thus had to form a coalition with two secular parties to get the necessary 50 percent plus 1 majority to form a government. If Ennahda were ever to succumb to pressures from Islamist militants in its base during the constitution-making process, the two secular parties in the coalition would have incentives to withdraw from the ruling coalition. Ennahda, in the de facto parliamentary setting created by the April 11 laws, could even lose its control of the constituent assembly.

Another major constraint was that is that there is agreement among virtually all the opposition and the government party leaders I talked to—including Ahmed Nejib El Chebbi, the leader of the most important secular opposition party, the Progressive Democratic Party, which polled less well than predicted—that elections were in fact free and fair. Crucially, Chebbi went on to say he was certain that free and fair elections would actually be held again in 12 to 18 months after the constituent assembly has completed its work. When I asked Chebbi why he did so poorly in the constituent assembly elections, he said he made the mistake of following the advice of his U.S. election consultants, who urged him to concentrate on television ads. He told me that in the next election he will spend more time and effort on grassroots organization. He predicts that given the problems of the world economy and the great pressure on Ennahda to deliver on their economic promises, a broader coalition of opposition parties will have a serious chance to form a government after the next round of elections.[34]

Chebbi, and indeed virtually all the party leaders I talked to, now see elections as "the only game in town" for acquiring political power. This politically incentive-based assumption, in itself, is one of the things Linz and I argued long ago is necessary for a democracy. The vast majority of political party leaders I talked to praised the work of the independent electoral commission and the role of international election observers and want and expect them to play an important role in the next elections.

Tunisia is not Algeria in 1992, nor is it France in 1905. Nor is it a counterrevolution, but rather a democratic transition, in which secular party leaders, and Islamic-influenced leaders in Ennahda have a chance to add to the world's repertoire of existing patterns of religion/state/society democratic relations. Too often, analysts tend to downplay the importance of Tunisia, because it is much less populous and less important strategically than Egypt. But since it is the only Arab country to have met the four requirements of a democratic transition, analysts and activists of democratization might pay more attention to the Tunisian case, especially to how potentially conflicting secularists and religious political actors negotiated the democratic rules of the game and crafted important coalitions.

NOTES

1. Alfred Stepan, "Multiple Secularisms of Modern Democratic and Nondemocratic Regimes," in *Rethinking Secularism*, ed. Craig Calhoun, Mark Juergensmeyer, and Jonathan Van Antwerpen (New York: Oxford University Press, 2011), 114–144.
2. See John Rawls, *Political Liberalism* (New York: Columbia University Press, 1993), 151–154.
3. See Charles Taylor, *A Secular Age* (Cambridge: Belknap, 2007), esp. 19–21, 26–28, 642, and 674.
4. See Alfred Stepan, "The World's Religious Systems and Democracy: Crafting the 'Twin Tolerations,'" in *Arguing Comparative Politics* (Oxford: Oxford University Press, 2001), 213–253. All further citations in this chapter will refer to this article. A shorter, relatively undocumented version of this article appeared as "Religion, Democracy and the 'Twin Tolerations,'" *Journal of Democracy* 11 (October 2000): 37–57.
5. See Stephen Frederic Dale, "Ibn Khaldun: The Last Greek and the First *Annaliste* Historian," *International Journal of Middle East Studies* 38 (2006): 431–451.
6. Ibn Khaldun meticulously discusses the exact name and specialties of these Tunis-based scholars in a chapter entitled "Mon education, mes maîtres" in his autobiographical work, Ibn Khaldun, *Le voyage d'Occident et d'Orient* (Paris: Sindbad, 1980), 45–71.
7. Diarmaid MacCulloch, *The Reformation: A History* (New York: Viking, 2003), 653.
8. For example, see Maria Rose Menocal, *The Ornament of the World: How Muslims, Jews and Christians Created a Culture of Tolerance in Medieval Spain* (New York: Little, Brown, 2002). For the role of interreligious toleration in the Ottoman Empire, see Karen Barkey's award-winning *An Empire of Difference: The Ottomans in Comparative Perspective* (Cambridge: Cambridge University Press, 2008). For Akbar and toleration in medieval India see the essay in this volume by Sudipta Kaviraj.
9. For this estimate by Khaldun, see John D. Latham, "Towards a Study of Andalusian Immigration and Its Place in Tunisian History," *Les Cahiers de Tunisie* 5 (1957): 203–252.
10. For the exact names of Jewish high officeholders and the posts they held in Tunisia, see Latham, "Towards a Study of Andalusian Immigration," 216–220.
11. See Roger Botte, *Esclavages et abolitions en terres d'islam* (Bruxelles: Versaille, 2010). For the religious and secular reasons behind the early abolition in Tunisia, see 59–92.
12. See Jean-Pierre Filiu, *The Arab Revolution: Ten Lessons from the Democratic Uprising* (London: Hurst, 2011), 142.

13. Ibid.
14. Albert Hourani, *Arabic Thought in the Liberal Age: 1798–1939* (New York: Cambridge University Press, 1983), 65.
15. For the cover, see the book *Pensees de Tahar Haddad* (Tunis: Snipe, 1993), 38. As early as 1904 the influential Sheik Thaalibi argued in his *The Liberal Spirit of the Koran* that a true reading of the Koran would lead to overdue political and social reforms.
16. See Nathan J. Brown, *Constitutions in a Nonconstitutional World: Arab Basic Laws and the Prospects for Accountable Government* (Albany: State University of New York Press, 2002), 19.
17. These and other similar speeches are cited in Mark Tessler, "Political Change and the Religious Revival in Tunisia," *Maghreb Review* 5 (January–February 1980): 8–19. Also see Lotfi Hajji, *Bourguiba et l'islam: Le politique et le religieux* (Tunis: Sud Éditions, 2011).
18. For this attack and its effect on Zeitouna, see Mahmud 'Abd al Moula, "L'Université Zaytounieene et la Société Tunisienne" (PhD diss., l'Université Paris-Sorbonne, 1971), 205–228.
19. Quote from the previously cited work by Tessler, "Political Change and the Religious Revival in Tunisia," 10.
20. "Code du Statut Personnel," Décret du 13 août 1956.
21. See the UN statement on Tunisia's abortion policy from the Population Policy Data Bank maintained by the Population Division of the Department of Economic and Social Affairs of the United Nations, www.un.org/esa/population/publications/abortion/doc/tunisia.doc.
22. Interview with Samir Ben Amor, a defense lawyer who is secretary general of the Ex-Prisoners Association, Tunis, May 29, 2011. Also see Amnesty International, "Tunisia: Prolonged Incommunicado Detention and Torture," March 1992 MDE 30/004/1992.
23. To a significant extent this regime-orchestrated "double fear" worked for Ben Ali. One account, written as late as 2010, concluded: "Many secular democrats have been grudgingly complicit in Ben Ali's authoritarianism. . . . as the lesser of two evils." See Christopher Alexander, *Tunisia: Stability and Reform in the Modern Maghreb* (London: Routledge, 2010), 66.
24. By "Brumairian" abdication to the military, I am referring to the type of tensions during the French Revolution between different revolutionary factions and the compromises with Napoleon Bonaparte that created the opening for him to seize power. See Karl Marx, *The Eighteenth Brumaire of Louis Bonaparte*, numerous editions.
25. For reasons of length, in this essay I will focus on Tunisia, but I present substantial evidence for this assertion about Egypt in my Freedom House posting of January 13, 2012: "The Recurrent Temptation to Abdicate to the Military

in Egypt," http:blog.freedomhouse.org/weblog/2012/01/two-perspectives-on-egypt's transition.html.

26. Interview with Rachid Ghannouchi, Tunis, March 26, 2011.
27. Lisa Anderson, in her article on the brief thaw and pact of 1988, notes that the Islamic representative to the pact agreed to "the retention of the Code of Personal Status." See her "Political Pacts, Liberalism, and Democracy: The Tunisian Pact of 1988," *Government and Opposition* 26, no. 2 (1991), 244–260. Since about 1980 Ghannouchi has stressed the need for much greater equality of men and women inside of Islam; see citations to this effect in Azzam S. Tamimi, *Rachid Ghannouchi: A Democrat Within Islam* (Oxford: Oxford University Press, 2001).
28. Interview with Rachid Ghannouchi and Hamadi Jebali, Tunis, May 30, 2011.
29. Jean Daniel, "Islamism's New Clothes," *New York Review of Books*, December 22, 2011, 72.
30. This was given to me, with the names and affiliations of the signers, by several participants. A French version is now available at www.cprtunisie.net/spip.php?article30. Participants included the current presidents of the CPR, Ettaktol, and PDP parties. Ennahda was represented by the president of its political bureau because its two top leaders were either in jail or denied a visa to France.
31. Given to me in the headquarters of the most secular party in the current ruling coalition, Ettakatol, by one of the drafters, Tunis, November 11. Translation from the Arabic by Mostofa Henfy.
32. The actual outcome of the elections unfortunately did not produce the hoped-for parity, because while all political parties had women as 50 percent of all their candidates, with the exception of Ennahda, almost none of them placed women's names first. In many constituencies, only a single candidate from the party won, and so many more men than women ended up being elected. Nevertheless, about a quarter of the members of the constituent assembly are women.
33. Juan J. Linz and Alfred Stepan, *Problems of Democratic Transition and Consolidation: Southern Europe, South America, and Post-Communist Europe* (Baltimore: Johns Hopkins University Press, 1996), 1.
34. Interview, Tunis, November 8, 2011.

5

SECULARISM AND THE MEXICAN REVOLUTION

Claudio Lomnitz

My object in this essay is to present elements for a study of radical Mexican secularism in a fashion that is in critical dialogue with Charles Taylor's account of secularism. It is a double-edged endeavor that seeks, on one hand, to explore the pertinence of some of Taylor's core concepts for the analysis of secularism in Mexico and Ibero-America and, on the other, to try to place that region in relation to the historical arc that Taylor conceptualizes and explicates. My contribution is offered with the aim of identifying a few general conceptual and historical parameters in the case, and not as an appraisal of an existing bibliography or as a novel empirical exploration.

When I read *The Secular Age*, I felt some unease with regard to the boundaries of its historical subject, "the West," whose secularism Taylor describes as developing dialectically out of a medieval "Latin Christendom." My sense of discomfort may very well be shared by other scholars working in Latin America, a region that was from its inception a kind of "far West," with a religious sphere that was built largely on the efforts of militant "Latin Christians" who were direct participants in the cultural matrix discussed by Taylor. The unease, in short, relates to a question that almost any sensible student of Latin America would rather avoid.

Indeed, the question of whether or not Ibero-America is Western is so politically fraught that any schema that provides it with a clear response is liable to get bogged down in a quagmire. Thus, the politically seminal generation of Latin American intellectuals led by figures such as José Martí, José Enrique Rodó, and later José Vasconcelos viewed "Our America" (Ibero-America) as the true heir of Western culture, as against a materialist United States that had turned its back on its inheritance and, later, during World War I, also as against a Europe that had lost its way. Latin American nationalisms thus have often had a kind of Hellenistic affectation (not unlike German nationalism), or else they identified with French civilization and pan-Latinism, as opposed to English civilization.

Anti-Western views of the nature of the Latin American nations exist as well, certainly. One can even find them enshrined in official documents—as in Bolivia's new constitution, for instance. Last but perhaps not least, there are stock images of these nations as developing (late, of course) along a path similar to that of the United States. These are all readily available modes of identification that can always be adopted at any or all of the region's nationalist carnivals (so to speak).

From a strictly historical perspective, Ibero-America has about as much right to be thought of as Western as the United States, Canada, Australia, or New Zealand, but it also has about as much right to think of itself as non-Western as South Africa or India. It is important to clarify this ambiguity from the start, because the question of the position of this Ibero-America in relation to Taylor's story cannot begin from any prejudice with regard to its position inside or out of the West.

My itinerary will be to offer a few general parameters for thinking historically about the problem of secularization in Spanish America, in order then to focus on the political and cultural dynamics of secularization in the postcolonial history of one of the republics that emerged from the breakup of the Spanish empire, Mexico, and then to supply a brief analysis of the cultural conditions and politics of secularism around the time of the Mexican Revolution (1910).

EARLY BACKGROUND: "SPAIN" AND SPANISH AMERICA

I am by no means a specialist in early modern Spanish or Colonial Latin American history, nevertheless all analyses of secularism in nineteenth- and early twentieth-century Mexico rely, in the end, on some historical presuppositions with regard to these times and places, and it is best to make those explicit, since they are not necessarily shared, even by all specialists.

Politically, the Iberian Peninsula in the twelfth and thirteenth centuries was a ground of coexistence and conflict between Christian and Muslim kingdoms, with a strong Christian pole in the north, a strong Muslim pole in the south, and a patchwork in between. This fact of competition, however, should not distract us from the fact that realms were all multireligious: Muslim kingdoms had Christian minorities, and Christian kingdoms had Muslim minorities. Jews were also prominent and numerically significant in both Muslim and Christian cities.

The complicated history of interfaith relations in the Christian and Muslim kingdoms of Iberia gave rise to two competing stereotypes: late medieval Iberia as a site of radical religious intolerance and anti-Semitism and an early home of ethnoreligious "cleansing," or alternatively, as a site of an unparalleled and relatively harmonious *convivencia* that was wrecked at the end by a few fanatics. These two contrasting views were deeply inflected by their implications for twentieth-century history—Spanish progressive historians of the early twentieth century explored *convivencia* as an image of alternative possibilities for Spain, in the face of both ultramontane Catholicism and the rising tide of fascist-Catholic *sinarquistas*. Emphasis on the deep history of anti-Semitism and of anti-Muslim sentiments and their connection to the expulsion of the Jews, and later of the Moors, was developed by Jewish historians particularly as part of the broader history of ethnic cleansing. And more recent reactions to that view are, again, related to the desire to counter contemporary Islamophobia in Europe or to provide Arab nationalists with a genealogy that promotes a tolerant self-image.

Thanks to much new research, the two key contrasting images of tolerance and intolerance have been superseded, in at least some recent scholarship, by a perspective that understands the Spanish *convivencia* not as a regime of tolerance but rather as a web of policies that were oriented to the carefully calibrated management of intolerance.[1] Conviviality did not mean equality but was, rather, a regime of power and economy that built on religious differences, emphasizing and containing them within a fundamentally hierarchical order. Thus, Iberia was one of Christianity's most intense contact zones with Islam, as well as with Judaism

On the Christian side, the reforms and reformist movements that are key to Taylor's theory of the origin of Western secularism, what he calls "the mother of all revolutions," also had a robust presence in the Iberian Peninsula. The mendicant orders—Franciscans and Dominicans—gained ground there, and a militant Christianity was visible in various dimensions of social life—from religious art, to an emerging militant popular literature, to the legislation of civil life.

On the other hand, Spanish towns were often not the tranquil parishes that Taylor seems to have in mind in his discussion of the enchanted life prior to these reforms, because policies regulating irreconcilable religious differences—what might best be thought of as codes developed for the "regulation of intolerance"—were equally in place in Christian towns that had Muslim and Jewish minorities as in Muslim towns with Christian and Jewish minorities. There was not, in short, the kind of uniformity of belief that is implicit in Taylor's view of the (northern) European parish.

Indeed, Iberia was a land of religious competition, subordination, differentiation, *and* toleration. As a result, there developed in it a peculiar dynamic with regard to the question of reform. The dialectic discussed by Charles Taylor for Latin Christendom concerned the elaboration of distances between elite and popular forms of (Christian) religiosity and the development of a kind of hyper-Christian interiority as a result of the dialectics of distinction between the high and the low.

In Spain, tensions between elite and popular Christianity were complicated by a variety of borders and frontiers between the Christian and the infidel. The emphasis on a variety of interreligious boundaries and interdependencies is important, because Christians related to Muslims in ways that were in some respects distinct from their connections to Jews, for instance. On the other hand, as Christianity expanded and came to dominate the entire peninsula and beyond, the boundaries between external irreconcilable differences (Christian/

infidel) dissolved, insofar as there were no more Muslim kingdoms in the peninsula, and these differences now became useful mainly to give shape to internal boundaries and to formulate new forms of subjectivity as Spain colonized the Americas. In that context, militant attitudes of reform and vigilance developed into a veritable political economy.

One key example is the development of distinctions that were drawn between "Old" and "New" Christians—a process that gained legal recognition in the fourteenth century around the formulation of *limpieza de sangre* (blood purity) and was then re-adapted in the Americas, where it was used to legitimate a new caste system.

THE SPIRIT OF REFORM IN SPANISH AMERICA

Moving on to Spanish America, there is no question that colonization there was subject to the kind of reform dynamics that Charles Taylor discusses. Indeed, the pressure to demonstrate Christian loyalty—noted in shorthand as the distinction between Old and New Christians—became the basis for the organization of political power, status, and class.

This issue has rather subtle implications from the viewpoint of reform. As the Americas entered the imperial fold, the Iberian Peninsula itself was undergoing a process that we today would call ethnic cleansing—the forced assimilation, persecution, or expulsion of the infidels. The Americas, by contrast, were meant to be a space that was being founded without the macula of infidelity. The so-called Indians were regarded as pagans rather than infidels. Contrary to Spain's Jews and Muslims, they had never yet been exposed to the Word. Here was, then, a chance to develop a society that was pure and free of the infidels' influence. For this reason, Jews, Moors, and conversos were not allowed to emigrate to the Americas, and there were efforts to proscribe or regulate the trans-Atlantic movement of New Christians. After the Reformation, of course, Protestants too were most resolutely banned.

On the other hand, the distinction between Old and New Christians that had been used in the Iberian Peninsula in order to justify political and economic prerogatives for Old Christians as against Jewish and

Muslim converts was now found by colonizers to be a useful instrument for framing emerging caste divisions between "Spaniards" (now Old Christians) and natives or "Indians" (now New Christians).

There is a tension here that deserves to be acknowledged. While the Americas were being cast as a novel space of Christian purity, they also were being colonized on the basis of old and invidious distinctions between Old and New Christians, which were now deployed to create a stark and entirely new caste system, wherein the New Christians (i.e., the Indians) owed tribute and political subservience to the Old Christians (i.e., the Spaniards).

These trends implied the formation of at least some versions of what Charles Taylor has called hyper-Christians. The conceptualization of America as a Christian utopia was particularly important to the early missionaries. Friars as different from one another as the Dominican Las Casas and the Franciscan Toribio Benavente ("Motolinía") coincided in their representation of natives as being more sincere Christians than most Spanish colonizers. Las Casas even went as far as to claim that native paganism proved that the Indians were superior material for this Christian utopia—they were, so to speak, all potentially hyper-Christians. So, for instance, Las Casas made the bold argument that even such apparent abominations as human sacrifice were proof of the Indians' superior diligence in following natural law, and therefore of their promise as Christians: "And so, as to the first point, concerning how to prepare the cult and religion of their gods, the people of New Spain proved to exceed all others of the world, and in this they had a better, clearer, less confused intelligence, and a more subtle judgment and clearer reasoning than the rest."[2]

For his part, the Franciscan friar Vasco de Quiroga set up "hospitals" in Michoacan and the Valley of Mexico modeled on Thomas Moore's ideas. Though they eventually failed and foundered, these hospitals could have served admirably for Taylor's (or Michel Foucault's) discussion of Latin Christendom's reform spirit and its connection to modernity. Moreover, despite the failures of some of the early missionizing utopias, the conceit that Spanish America would be a pure Christian space was strengthened after the Council of Trent. Spain's role as the bulwark of Roman Christianity in the Counter-Reformation made axiomatic the notion that Spaniards would make true and worthy tutors of their New Christian wards.

It is certainly true that the various visions of America as a "pure" Christian space were defeated by the pragmatic realities of colonization (including not only the economics of the new colonies but also the very low ratio of clergy to converts); however, the potential of America as a space for the ignition of Christian values remained very much alive and has in fact been a leitmotif in Spanish-American social, political, and intellectual history.

On the other hand, the idea that Indians were New Christians, weak in the faith, who required constant discipline and vigilance, also implied a trend toward reforming the people, albeit within a framework that was more widely tolerant of a "popular Christianity" that was viewed as being laden with error and superstition and prone to various forms of "idolatry."

There was, in short, a twin dynamic that is pertinent to Taylor's arguments regarding the formation of a divide between popular religion and reform militancy: the conceit of being Old Christians justified Spanish tutelage (spiritual and political) and extraction of Indian tribute, but it also required some formal attention to the upper caste's claim to greater religious knowledge and devotion. On the other hand, the image of the Indian as moldable and pure: Indians were not infidels but they were, rather, a childlike and humble people, whose very simplicity, which had once made them Satan's instrument, could now transform them into a peculiarly devout flock.

Spaniards were under pressure to demonstrate regularly and publicly that they were truer Christians than Indians. This pressure was to a large degree alleviated by church policy, which supported those pretensions by demanding the observation of more holy days (via fasting, charity, masses, or suffrages) by Spaniards than by Indians. Thus, the ecclesiastical councils of Mexico and Lima—and the pope himself—legislated differences between Spaniards and Indians by inscribing a differentiated set of ritual demands and expectations on each "caste."

In addition, Spanish settlers in New Spain developed informal mechanisms to patrol the boundary. This is manifested, for instance, in the turn that terms such as "ladino" took. In principle, ladino referred to (neo)Latin, either as a language or as the ability to be conversant in it. The term soon came to refer to Jews and Muslims who were, let us say, acculturated. However, in Spain (and contrary to Pascal's idea) external practice was not enough to make a *true* Christian. Indeed, the distinction between external signs of conversion and true trustworthiness of faith was a litmus test for holding royal office, for membership in guilds, and for noble status. In the American context, María Elena Martínez's research shows that certificates of blood purity, which in Spain itself had become passé by the early sixteenth century, flourished once again in the Americas in the sixteenth and seventeenth centuries.[3] In such a context, the term "ladino" slowly evolved to signify being two-faced, hypocritical, or untrustworthy, a meaning that is still dominant in Mexican Spanish today.

All of this generated a space for reform that was distinct from that of Protestant Europe but not alien to it, and this reformism, in turn, became a referent in recurring waves of Christian renewal. Utopian ideas about reviving the Primitive Christian faith among indigenous peoples, for instance, have been cyclically revived: in eighteenth-century Jesuit missions; in various experiments in religious education, certainly; but especially in nineteenth- and twentieth-century political life. On the other hand, the chasm between elite and popular religion also created ample space for the sort of distinctions between high and low that Taylor represents as the characteristic modality of religiosity in Latin Christendom in the medieval period.

In short, it is difficult to place late medieval Spain and early-modern Spanish America squarely within the reform processes of late medieval Latin Christendom as Taylor understands them (insofar as there were quotidian boundaries with the infidel within Spanish Christianity in the early period and then a routinization of a caste system based on the Christian/hyper-Christian distinction in America). But neither can the Ibero-American experience be placed squarely outside the history he has outlined, suggesting that Taylor's typology may be insufficiently attentive to the problem of reform in border regions, like Iberia, or in areas of militant expansion, like Iberia and America.

THE PROBLEM OF SECULARISM IN THE SPANISH-AMERICAN REPUBLICS

De-colonization in most of Spanish America occurred in the form of republican revolutions. These revolutions changed the playing field for the development of political secularism (which Taylor refers to as "secularism 1") and for the cultural conditions of secular belief (Taylor's "secularism 3").

Some of the key policies of this new playing field had in fact been instituted during the late colonial period in a set of imperial reforms that began during the 1740s and continued through the eighteenth century. I have no space to develop this, so I will be very schematic. The Bourbon monarchs who gained the Spanish succession at the turn of the eighteenth century sought to implement a project of modernization inspired by the model of French absolutism. That involved a range of familiar policies: the substitution of monastic orders with a secular clergy that was squarely in the control of the Crown (a process that began in 1749 and culminated with the expulsion of the Jesuits from the Crown's domains in 1767); reduction in the number of religious holidays; a decisive move away from earlier emphasis on purgatory, hell, and the afterlife; an emphasis on practical education; a rationalization of political-administrative territories; an emphasis on urban hygiene and policing; and (greater) emphasis on enlightenment and public knowledge.

All of this was in play or in place by the early 1800s, but new pressures emerged with independence. The Spanish-American republics needed allies among the great powers, and those allies were either Protestant (England, and later the United States and Germany) or much more deeply secularized than Spain (postrevolutionary France). So, even in cases such as Mexico, where Catholicism was kept as the national religion after independence, at least some practical policies of toleration had to be set in place: British mining concerns were allowed to set up Protestant services and special sections for non-Catholics in at least a few graveyards, for example. Of greater import, secular transnational organizations, Freemasonry in particular, became an indispensable resource for political and merchant classes.

Secularized spaces gained ground only slowly at first, because Mexico stagnated economically in the decades following independence, but they gained importance in the final decades of the nineteenth century, when direct foreign investment intensified and ambitious immigration and colonization projects began to take shape. True, the bulk of the immigrants who arrived to places like Argentina, Uruguay, Brazil, Venezuela, or Cuba were from Catholic countries, but there many non-Catholics as well—Jews, Protestants, Japanese, Chinese, among others. Moreover, even many of the Catholic migrants were anticlerical, or at least secularists: German émigrés from the 1848 revolution and Jacobins, socialists, and anarchists from Spain and Italy or Russia and Germany. In short, openness to foreign capital and labor implied increased toleration in the Lockean tradition, regardless of whether Catholicism was or was not the official religion.

At the same time, the Catholic religion was arguably the only shared basis for the new national identities being built, a point was consistently argued by Conservative politicians. Literacy was very limited in nineteenth-century Mexico; the Spanish language was unevenly spread through the population; regional militias were often more powerful than the new federal army; and transportation was incredibly cumbersome, making regional isolation endemic. So there were strong incentives to avoid the separation between church and state coming both from religious conviction and political expedience. In other words, the position against separation between church and state was upheld by at least some "enlightened" members of the elite, who nonetheless favored urban reform, modernization of church ritual, and clamping down on popular Catholicism.

SECULARISM IN MID- AND LATE NINETEENTH-CENTURY MEXICO

By the middle of the nineteenth century, the Mexican economy and Mexican society had many of the elements that were needed for the development of a robust secular project, including a rich tradition of religious reform; a prolonged experience with the modernizing policies and illusions that stemmed from French absolutism and "enlightenment"; and a set of real economic and political incentives.

In addition to all of this, a set of political developments produced heightened tensions around the relationship between church and state. After bitter defeat in its war with the United States (1848), the Mexican state faced deep fiscal and political difficulties that increased tensions between the Liberal and Conservative parties, leading Liberals to an increasingly radicalized, "Jacobin" position that promoted the expropriation of church property and a decisive shift of control over social reproduction (education, marriage, baptism, and burial) from the hands of the church to those of the state. Tensions culminated in a civil war in the 1850s, which the Liberals momentarily won, but the conflict was prolonged to the following decade, when Conservatives built an alliance with Napoleon III, who sent troops and helped instate an empire led by Maximilian von Hapsburg. That adventure, however, also ended in defeat in 1867.

The triumph of the Liberals in 1867 again enshrined their constitution, the Constitution of 1857, which was radically anticlerical and secularist. All church property was permanently confiscated and convents were outlawed, as were religious schools. A civil registry was instated, and religious weddings, baptisms, and burials no longer had legal standing.

At least on paper, these changes have been long-standing. This is because, after the defeat of the French/Conservative alliance in 1867, the Catholic Party was de facto banned: in a foreign invasion and a foreign monarch, the Conservative Party had dealt in treason and so had forfeited its own legal standing. Although the Catholic Party was again legalized during the fourteen-month presidency of revolutionary leader Francisco I. Madero (1911–1913), it made the mistake of supporting a counterrevolutionary coup. As a result, the 1917 Constitution, which superseded that of 1857, was every bit as anticlerical as its predecessor, and between 1867 and 2000, Mexico was governed either by liberal parties or by heirs of liberal parties.

Nevertheless, banishment of the Catholic Party left Mexico's Liberals in a paradoxical position. Liberalism was now the only acceptable patriotic ideology; as result, it was above democratic debate. The radical separation between church and state and the political ban on the Catholic Party left the Liberals open to the criticism that the state was secular but the society was Catholic. Indeed, the inability of Catholics to organize in a political party fed this very illusion. In Charles Taylor's terms, we had a particularly radical version of political secularism (secularism 1) that created the illusion of an absolute absence of societal secularism (secularism 2). That illusion has, I think, been responsible for the mistaken notion that Mexico is "not secular" in the sense either of secular society (secularism 2) or of having produced cultural conditions for disenchantment (secularism 3).

I believe that the commonly held notion that Mexican society and culture were not secular and that secularism was championed only by the state, against society, is in fact an illusion fostered by the elimination of the Catholic Party from political life after 1867 and the undemocratic practices of Mexican liberalism. But this position requires some elaboration, because I also do not take the contrary position, that is, that Mexican society and culture were in fact secular. Instead, I wish to emphasize that there was a deep history around societal and cultural secularization, with a correspondingly complex repertoire of reform and modernization. Secularism was a state project, but it was not only a state project.

It is not simply not true, for instance, that Mexican elites were secular while the popular classes were Catholic. There was, as we shall see in our discussion of the Mexican Revolution, a robust tradition of "popular liberalism" (as historians have called it), as indeed there were Catholic and Conservative elites. As a result, the secularist trend relied heavily on cross-class alliances as much as on Conservative or Catholic, trends.

There were, moreover, other social implications. Because there was no longer space for the Conservative Party to champion Catholic interests, Liberal governments had to concern themselves with appeasing at least some religious sensibilities. During the Porfirio Díaz dictatorship (1876–1911), this led to a set of informal agreements between the government and the church hierarchy, known colloquially as *las contentas* ("the happy ones"), as well as to gendering of the relationship between state and church, with Porfirio Díaz's wife, Carmelita, assuming her

Catholicism openly, and thus feeding the illusion that politics was to religion what public was to private, what male was to female, and what state was to society.

Although I have no space to make an extended analysis of the significance of this historical development for cultural and political history, I at least wish to point out that this form of gendering secular politics and religious life is also consonant with a broader Ibero-American development that was described a few decades ago by Brazilian anthropologist Roberto DaMatta, who pointed out that in Brazil, possessive individualism and hierarchical complementarity (which correspond roughly to Charles Taylor's "buffered self" and "porous self") are both widely and simultaneously available as discursive *registers*, and the individuals and groups shift from one register to another depending on context. The buffered self is a mask that is as widely available and as widely used as that of the porous self.[4]

In other words, Ibero-American developments generated more space for play in the development of the self than what Taylor has described for Europe. The "individual" and "the person" (to use Marcel Mauss's terminology) are subject positions that can be inhabited by the same individual, sometimes even in the very same contexts. There are, in other words, a performative *choice* and a politics of play and movement between the buffered self and the porous self that makes personhood more intensely existential and less monotonous.

SECULARISM AND THE PEASANT COMMUNITY

The cozy arrangement between the church and the Liberal dictatorship under Porfirio Díaz encouraged a deep transformation of the religious environment and of the various meanings of secularism. Within Catholicism, it led to the formation of a political fringe that was antidictatorship and antihierarchy—that is, a militant Catholicism based principally in urban sectors of artisans and the middle class. These Catholics were adamant in their attack on the dictatorship's corruption, and they were also critical of the corruption of the church hierarchy. They were nationalists and associated the ills of capitalism with American imperialism and often also with Protestantism (which they also nationalized and represented as American influence). The sensibilities of this Catholic wing were distinct from both the pro-accommodation segments of the Catholic elite and from peasant popular Catholicism, and its position was strengthened to some degree by the church's own attempt to counter the rise of socialism with the *Rerum Novarum* encyclical (1891).

Also on the modernizing side, though with a different political philosophy, were two strands of liberal and patriotic groups that were radically secularist and critical of both the church and the accommodationist state: the Protestants, and the Jacobin liberals, some of whom turned to socialism or anarchism as the nineteenth century came to a close. These tendencies were not confined to urban middle classes. There were Protestant associations arising in villages that had conflicts with hacienda owners who were allied to village priests, for instance. Anticlericalism, in other words, was being generated as a reaction against alliances between landowners and village priests.

Perhaps an aside is needed to help clarify this point. During the colonial period, the Crown was interested in mitigating the power of local landowners and merchants in the Americas. This was because distances and the lack of a robust standing army demanded a delicate policy of balance of power. In that context, the Crown used the church as an instrument for defending Indian communities with regard to the Spanish landowning class, thereby putting limits on the latter's autonomy. After independence, though, this policy all but disappeared. There was a marked tendency for republican governments to align themselves with the landowning class and for landowners to build alliances with parish priests, either directly or through the mediation of a bishop. This meant that some peasants—and sometimes entire villages—found themselves in an antagonistic position vis-à-vis the clergy. Some of them turned to Protestantism, others to Jacobin liberalism—the so-called popular liberalism.

The image of the peasant community as an idealized site of popular Catholicism and transcendence that lived with its back turned to cultural secularism was shaped from a variety of diverging positions. One might say that it was an illusion produced by a confluence of many disparate interests. Thus, the positivist intellectuals—who were the Porfirian state's most prominent ideologues—saw peasant villages as a locus of popular ignorance that needed to be eradicated to move resolutely into the positive or scientific era (a position they shared with the "enlightened despots" of the eighteenth century and with many conservative elites of the nineteenth). Similarly, the peasant community was figured by Jacobins and Protestants as the inert and abject by-product of the alliance between the Catholic Church and political power (for them, popular ignorance was the result of a deliberate policy rather than the natural emulsion of an inferior race). Finally, Catholic politicians viewed peasant religiosity as proof that the Liberal state was fundamentally unpopular and undemocratic.

This multiplicity of perspectives about the nature of the same object (the peasant village) provides a cautionary example of the effect of infusing such localities with utopian possibilities—Mexico's peasant communities have too long been overloaded with varying, often contradictory, emancipatory expectations, many of which were and are mutually incompatible and correspond to different dimensions of social reality. But they add up, and present villagers as wrapped in an enchanted veil of either religiosity or ignorance. Or both.

ILLUSTRATIVE DEVELOPMENTS, 1892 AND 1910

The agrarian revolts and upheavals that transpired in Mexico between 1891 and 1893 are a useful place from which to think about the split between secularism and religious community in peasant villages of the period. These upheavals are interesting, because contrary to what happened during the revolution of 1910, these village revolts were very rarely in communication with one another. The Mexican railroad was still very new then, and although economic articulation to markets was being achieved at a rapid pace (which is what accounts for the relative synchronicity of the revolts), means of communication were still insufficiently developed for local revolts to articulate to one another.

The revolts in question—which were geographically scattered and widespread—were nevertheless more or less simultaneous. They were responding to a period of rapid modernization that involved changes in land use, the commercial exploitation of areas that had historically been marginal to world markets (for instance, the Mexican tropics), privatization of village commons, termination of long-term rental and sharecropping agreements between peasants and haciendas, and increased land values and taxes. Moreover, revolts coincided with a world economic recession that caused layoffs in some sectors. Finally, they coincided with the third consecutive reelection of Porfirio Díaz (1892), which was distinctly a moment of transition of that regime into a durable and hardened dictatorship.

The interest of these revolts for our discussion of secularism is that some of them took on a strong "millenarian" turn—casting economic and political developments as demonic departures from a moral economy and an enchanted world—while other revolts were directed at what was perceived as the dictator's betrayal of liberal principles and most particularly a betrayal of the separation between church and state. Both kinds of revolts were popular, though the liberal revolts also tended to incorporate the middle classes.

The millenarian sort of revolt had, I think, two dimensions. One of these was traditional to a certain genre of peasant and Indian upheaval known in Mexico as caste wars (*guerras de castas*). As we have seen, the church played a key role in the legitimation of the caste system in the colonial period. As a result, it was not unusual for indigenous movements to claim direct, unmediated connections to God, casting aside the church and then violently attacking and trying to eliminate the dominant caste. These movements typically centered upon a symbolic figure or object, for instance, an Indian Virgin Mary in the Chiapas revolt of 1712 or the "Talking Cross" that was the fetish and inspiration of the Mayan revolt in Yucatán.

One added dimension of at least some of the millenarian-style revolts of 1891–1893, though, was tuned to the new developments of the late nineteenth century. It involved rejection of *secularization* (rather than a simple reappropriation of the church) and associated the perversion of the local moral economy to that process. So, for instance, in their political "manifesto," peasants of the Guerrero Mountains, whose revolt centered around the cult of an image of *El Señor de las Misericordias*, wrote:

And because we want to know whether there will be help for our King of Heaven, because we have already overburdened the Savior; because today in the fiesta of our Lord, those who go no longer go with a promise, they only go to steal and to make trouble. And may the Lord lend us grace and courage, and for seven years we will not pay a cent, but from to those who help, and so as to get something edible from the rich, because the rich are Freemasons and Protestants.[5]

On the other hand, not all revolts took on this kind of millenarian character: others took up radically anti-Catholic positions. So, for example, the revolt led by Catarino Garza on the Texas-Tamaulipas border adopted the same language that Porfirio Díaz had used in his revolt of 1876 and argued for the restoration of its liberal principles. Thus, Garza denounced "the betrayal of the Revolution of Tuxtepec and our Constitution of 1857, which cost the country so much blood." Similarly, the student riots of Mexico City of 1892, which protested Díaz's reelection, claimed to be following in the footsteps of Benito Juárez and other liberal fathers of anticlerical reform.

These two opposed reactions to Porfirian progressivism suggest that Mexico had been secularized by the late nineteenth century, at least to some degree: the secularization of public space was only incipient or even nonexistent in many places, but it was legally on the books, and there existed clear options of nonreligious identification, as well as infrequent but nevertheless growing possibilities of belonging to another religion (Protestantism). Moreover, the secularist pole of political society felt that it had been betrayed by the accommodationist policies of Porfirian positivist evolutionism, and so a radical Jacobin trend, which had been fundamental in the 1850s and 1860s, reemerged, and came into fully blown expression by the time of the revolutionary outbreak of 1910.

By the time the revolution of 1910 erupted, there was a complex mosaic in place from the viewpoint of secularism. Francisco I. Madero's political platform included the legalization of the Catholic Party, and for a brief period of a about two years, that party came into existence and was a real contender for political power. Nevertheless, the democratic play between political parties during Madero's brief presidency can be said to have furthered the secular trend of consolidation of cultural secularism (secularism 3—the buffered self, the immanent frame), regardless of the fact that Jacobin liberals saw it as a betrayal of the separation between church and state. This was most particularly the case, since the Catholic Party, too, was by and large a party of "modernizers." But even beyond that, the image of religion as a political choice of course implied cultural secularism.

Among the anticlerical leaders of the Mexican Revolution, some were traditional Jacobin liberals (Carranza, Obregón, Calles), others Protestants (Pascual Orozco, Aaron Sáenz), and yet others socialists (Antonio Villarreal, Eulalio Gutiérrez) or anarchists (Ricardo and Enrique Flores Magón). At the same time, many radical agrarian movements had no major conflict with religion or the church. Villismo was not so very opposed to Catholics. Zapatistas often wielded images of the Virgin of Guadalupe in their hats.

In short, the situation during the Mexican Revolution was not unlike that of 1892, but with a difference: broad regional coalitions were now formed. As a result, local millenarian movements were less important, and a true national revolution developed. With it came a moment of radical and violent revolutionary anticlericalism, followed by a second prolonged era of state accommodation with the church.

CONCLUSION

It is possible to argue that, despite the separation of church and state, Mexico remained an "enchanted" region, insofar as liberal conceptions of the autonomous self remained ideals, dear only to one segment of political society. The salience of corporations throughout the nineteenth century—the church, the peasant village, the hacienda, the artisanal guild—is generally understood as standing in the way of the emergence of the modern individual. This, of course, is just as true for early modern Europe, but what is distinct about Ibero-American contexts is that, due to the political crisis wrought by national revolutions and republicanism, capitalist development was slowed down, particularly compared with what was transpiring in northern Europe and in the

United States. Indeed, Spanish America "fell behind" economically at a precipitously rapid rate in the first two-thirds of the nineteenth century. This process of economic stagnation—which occurred alongside the rise of popular politics—strengthened the peasantry considerably, both in landed villages and in convenient tenancy arrangements with the latifundia.

All of that hindered the development of individualism and what Taylor usefully calls the buffered self, insofar as secure individual property matters to that mode of existence. But does that place Spanish America outside the dynamics of secularization that emerged out of Latin Christendom and then developed along with the history of capitalism? By no means. The ideological mechanisms and the economic and political projects that militated for such a development of the self were alive and well, both within the Catholic camp, in the form of modernized secular religion, and under the broad umbrella of liberalism.

Indeed, the strength of this push was such that Spanish-American Conservative parties were never able to wrench themselves away from key aspects of Liberal rhetoric. And this was so not only because of the logical and argumentative consistency of liberalism but also because the economic situation of these nations required clear property laws and openness to globalization, a process that made the future of the buffered self secure or at least supplied it with a viable social base within a fragmented economic sphere.

Indeed, one result of this economic heterogeneity is nineteenth-century Spanish America's obsession with "imagined citizens," as both François Xavier Guerra and Fernando Escalante put it. The obsession with the citizen as a kind of utopian figure has too often been interpreted as proof of the failure of secularizations 1, 2, and 3, that is, as the failure of political secularization, though compromises like *las contentas*, which were just reflections of a deeper failure to secularize society or even to create the cultural conditions of secularism

My position here questions this interpretation. The dynamics of political secularism in Mexico had more of a social basis than is often recognized, underwritten as it was not only by modernized and urban middle classes but also by agrarian class conflict. As a result, cultural conditions for secularization in fact suffused the political landscape, albeit most often either as a fantasy or as a precariously constructed alternative.

Because of this, the peculiarities of Mexican (and Ibero-American) development led to the cultural elaboration of competing codes or *registers* of the self, one of which corresponds squarely with the ideals of the buffered self and the other with those of the porous self. The movement between these registers and modes of identification has become a durable characteristic of everyday life.

NOTES

1. See David Nirenberg, *Communities of Violence: Persecution of Minorities in the Middle Ages* (Princeton: Princeton University Press, 1998); and Nirenberg, "Conversion, Sex and Segregation: Jews and Christians in Late Medieval Spain," in *American Historical Review* 107, no. 4 (2002): 1065–1093.
2. Fr. Bartolomé de las Casas, "Apologética historia sumaria . . . ," in *Los indios de México y Nueva España (antología)*, ed. Edmundo O'Gorman (Álvaro Obregón, Mexico: Editorial Porrúa, 1999), 104.
3. María Elena Martínez, *Genealogical Fictions:* Limpieza de Sangre, *Religion, and Gender in Colonial Mexico* (Stanford: Stanford University Press, 2008).
4. Robert DaMatta, *Carnivals, Rogues and Heroes: An Interpretation of the Brazilian Dilemma* (Notre Dame, Ind.: Notre Dame University Press, 1991); and DaMatta, *A casa e a rua: espaço e cidadania, mulher e morte no Brasil* (Rio de Janeiro: Brasiliense, 1985).
5. "Proclama zona central de Guerrero," in *Porfirio Díaz frente al descontento popular regional (1891–1893)*, ed. Friedrich Katz (Mexico City: Universidad Iberoamericana, 1986), 127–128.

6

IS CONFUCIANISM SECULAR?

Peter van der Veer

My aim in this contribution is to focus on four moments in history that may illuminate the nature of Confucianism from a comparative perspective and in conversation with Charles Taylor's work on the secular age. Establishing a definition of Western secularism and then searching for this object in the societies of China, India, and elsewhere does not make much sense, since it will only establish that "they do not have it" or "they have something that resembles it but is different." Comparing different traditions of transcendence and immanence as well as their political dynamic can help us to move beyond a history of "haves and have-nots" or "lack" to a better understanding of both the situation in Latin Christendom and in China. Especially in the nineteenth century (and to an extent in the sixteenth and seventeenth centuries) this is not merely a matter of comparison but also of global interactions that may prevent us from claiming that these histories are discrete and not entangled. My discussion begins with the Axial Age, a historical period that takes a central place in theories about transcendence and immanence in the work of Taylor and others. It continues with the Jesuit understanding of Confucianism in the sixteenth and seventeenth centuries, a period of important intellectual interaction between Europe and China. The third period I want to discuss is that of imperial interactions of the nineteenth century, when the Qing Empire was forced by Western powers to open up for trade and new ideas about progress and backwardness, as related to religion in China. The final period to be discussed is that of contemporary China, where we find a new Communist project to elevate Confucianism to the status of civil religion.

500 B.C.E.: THE AXIAL AGE

Weber's work on the rationalization of religion in Europe and Asia has been a major influence in the comparative sociology of civilizations. It has inspired a group of scholars around S. N. Eisenstadt to argue that a sharp disjunction between the transcendental and the mundane came up in a number of civilizations in the first millennium before the Christian era.[1] These civilizations include ancient Israel, ancient Greece, early Christianity, Zoroastrian Iran, early imperial China, and the Hindu and Buddhist civilizations. Sociologically this development assumed the emergence of an intellectual elite (e.g., Confucian literati, Brahmins, Buddhist *sangha*) who wanted to shape the world in accordance with their transcendental vision. Eisenstadt and his colleagues included theories by the anthropologists Tambiah and Redfield to point at a concomitant development of a global network of sacred centers and of a great tradition in them. This revolution in civilizational thought that occurred in all these civilizations in a relatively short time span around 500 B.C.E. was called "the Axial Age breakthroughs," using a concept developed by the philosopher Karl Jaspers, who argued that in this period a shared framework for universal historical self-understanding emerged.[2] The central idea in this theory is that in the Axial Age there is the emergence of a new stress on the existence of a higher transcendental moral order and of the problem of salvation and immortality. How this problem is addressed differs from civilization to civilization. Unfortunately, his generalizations lead Eisenstadt to suggest in a totally expected (if not clichéd) manner that Hinduism and Buddhism stand for an entirely transcendental (other-worldly) approach to salvation, while Confucianism stands for an entirely this-worldly approach.[3] Below I will attempt to explicate this understanding of Confucianism, which is also quite popular in China.[4]

Jaspers's and Eisenstadt's Axial framework has deeply influenced Charles Taylor's recent work on the secular age, in which he emphasizes the particularity of the Western development. In an essay on Western secularity Taylor mentions in passing that "one often hears the judgment that Chinese imperial society was already 'secular,' totally ignoring the tremendous role played by the immanent/transcendent split in the Western concept which had no analogue in traditional China."[5] In Taylor's view the Axial dyad of immanent/transcendent (these two belong to each other) was split in European thought from the seventeenth century onward, and that split gave rise to the possibility of seeing the immanent as all there is and to see the transcendent as a human invention. "This-worldly" in the Chinese case, then, does not mean exactly the same as "secular" in the Western case. Such arguments, however, tend to essentialize civilizational unities to compare them without exploring the highly fragmented and contradictory histories of the societies in which civilizational debate takes place. They also tend to underestimate the influence of thought that does not fit easily in the immanent/transcendent dyadic framework, such as, for example, all those religious movements in China that emphasize the unity of being (yin and yang) instead of emphasizing either transcendence or immanence. And on the side of Latin Christendom or Western secularity Taylor's work, in my view, underestimates the popularity of religious thought and spiritual thought after the sixteenth century that does not establish the split between transcendent and immanent. The best examples within Latin Christendom are the evangelical and Pentecostal as well as the Catholic charismatic movements. It seems to me that it is only in parts of contemporary Europe and in intellectual classes all over the world that the secular age has arrived.

A version of the argument that Confucianism is secular states that it is in fact a "philosophy." One needs to understand here that what we call Confucianism is in fact in China called *rujiao*, the "teachings of the *ru* (literati who are followers of Confucius)." It is therefore a "tradition," and it is useful to quote Talal Asad's definition: "A tradition consists essentially of discourses that seek to instruct practitioners regarding the correct form and purpose of a given practice that precisely because it is established, has a history. These discourses relate conceptually to a past (when the practice was instituted, and from which the knowledge of its point and proper performance has been transmitted) and a future (how the point of that practice can best be secured in the short or long term. Or why it should be modified or abandoned), through a present (how it is linked to other practices, institutions, and social conditions)."[6] The question whether Confucianism is a tradition that can be respectfully regarded as a philosophy (and not as a devilish heathendom competing with Christianity) comes up when the Jesuits attempt to find a space in imperial China from which they can expand the Catholic faith.[7]

SIXTEENTH AND SEVENTEENTH CENTURY: THE JESUIT ENCOUNTER

The Axial Age is conceptualized as a historical moment of comparison between mutually independent processes in civilizations. A historical moment of both comparison and interaction comes in the late Ming and early Ching in the sixteenth and seventeenth centuries, when the Jesuits try to accommodate their doctrine of God, the Lord of Heaven with the Confucian worldview, for which (among other texts) we have Matteo Ricci's *Tianzhu Shiyi* (天主實義), "the substantial meaning of the Lord of Heaven," published in 1603. What we have in the Confucian worldview is a cosmology that emphasizes Heaven (*tian*) as a metaphysical force that is impersonal and directs the universe and human society through its Mandate (*tianming*, 天命). This conception of a morally positive universe directed by the Mandate of Heaven had important ritual and political consequences: the emperor was the chief executor of the heavenly mandate in his ritual role as Son of Heaven. He was the performer of the great sacrifices to Heaven and Earth, these being the apex of a ritual-political system that integrated the empire. This system was *zheng* 正 , which one may translate as "orthodoxy," but which is perhaps better translated as "legitimate rule." Everything not in accordance with this political cosmology was *xie* 邪 (heterodox or illegitimate). Besides this political orthodoxy there has been an element of self-cultivation and therefore of spirituality in Confucianism that was probably influenced by Chan-Buddhism but aimed at tranquility and equilibrium. Moreover, there is a denial of the transcendent/immanent dyad to the extent that the ultimate unity of the internal and external, of mind and nature, of self and the world, of being and nonbeing is emphasized.[8]

Confucianism, then, can be seen at the level of the state as a political cosmology. If one accepted this cosmology one could fill in personal spiritual needs with Buddhist devotion or Taoist magic or indeed with the Jesuit doctrine of the Lord of Heaven. This looks syncretistic and tolerant, but it is all under the condition that one accepts the political cosmology. All this points at the important fact that if we compare Confucian China with Christian Europe, we need to look at political formations, the politics of religion, and certainly from the sixteenth century onward, at global interactions. In Charles Taylor's work there is a focus on the history of ideas in the philosophical canon. While he does look, like Weber, at Protestantism, he seems to neglect the Counter-Reformation and, in general, developments in Catholicism. However, it is the Catholic Counter-Reformation that is significant in Sino-European interactions, because of the presence of the Jesuits in China.

The Jesuits brought the latest products of Western science with them, especially to China, but did not have a notion of a clear superiority between Europe and Asia. Certainly, they did think that the belief in Christ as the Savior was the true faith, but one of the most important issues was to introduce the Christian doctrine without emphasizing its difference, rather by emphasizing the extent to which it could be adopted within already existing cultural schemata. This Jesuit policy of accepting the imperial order in which they could give Christianity a place came under increasing pressure from other Catholic missionary orders, such as the Franciscans and Dominicans in the early eighteenth century, and led to the famous Chinese Rites Controversy, in which the Emperor Kangxi expelled those who did not accept his ultimate authority. One needs to remember here that the Qing rulers were Manchu "barbarians" and had adopted the Confucian cosmology in order to establish the legitimacy of their rule. Being outsiders they had to constantly show their orthodoxy in defending the Confucian political cosmology, while keeping their ethnic identity alive. In passing it might be observed how different the Qing strategy of adoption of Confucian political cosmology was from the Mughal strategy of keeping Islam as their faith while creating political alliances with Hindu rulers.

The confrontation between the pope and the emperor (both central in their respective cosmologies) led in 1724 to the banning of Christianity in China. Power and the authority to determine ritual matters, not civilizational superiority, was the issue in this dispute, as indeed it had been in medieval Europe. One cannot say that the split of the transcendent/immanent dyad played any role in this. Chinese intellectuals embraced the empirical science the Jesuits informed them about, while Leibniz was inspired by Chinese ideas that were brought to Europe by the Jesuits.[9] The issue was ritual power and thus a clash between the claim that the emperor had the Mandate of Heaven as Son of Heaven and the claim that the pope had the Mandate of Heaven as Primus Apostolus (the successor of Peter) and Vicarius Christi. The claims of the pope were deeply politico-theological and were disputed in the Reformation, which led to the wars of religion in early modern Europe. One of the ways to solve these conflicts was the emergence of a kind of territorial sovereignty that determined the state religion (*cuius regio, eius religio*). In China also, any mobilization around heterodoxy (*xiejiao*, 邪教) could lead to rebellion against imperial authority and thus had to be repressed violently. In China these heterodoxies often took the form of millenarianism with a promise of an end to injustice and the coming of a just polity, a paradise on Earth with some Buddhist overtones, gesturing to the Maitreya, the Buddha who is to come to Earth at the end of time (the age of lawlessness).

NINETEENTH CENTURY: IMPERIAL INTERACTIONS

The third moment of comparison, in which interaction more than comparison becomes central, is "the long nineteenth century," the age of imperialism and nationalism, of which we today are the heirs. China is "opened up" by imperial power for missionization after the first Opium War (1839–1842). As elsewhere (for example, in India) imperial expansion created a new interest in mapping the world and understanding and ruling its populations and religions. It is this period in which Confucianism makes the transition from being a "philosophy" to being a "religion" in the Western understanding. I want to focus on the construction of Confucianism as a "world religion."

China was not so much "opened up" for the return of the Jesuits (deeply mistrusted as a transnational force by the emerging nation-states in Europe) but for all kinds of missionary societies, primarily the very assertive new Protestant missions. Protestantism has, of course, always been seen as an important historical site of thinking about the reflexive subject, about unmediated access, and about agency. In Protestant conversion, missionaries are concerned with the purification of improper forms of agency, a purification that is seen as liberation from false understandings of nature. These Protestant notions are paradigmatic of a wider Western and ultimately global discourse of the modern self.[10] It is such issues that are also crucial in missionary projects and raise fascinating questions about materiality and transcendence that feed into nineteenth-century constructions of spirituality as opposed to materialism and into constructions of rationality and agency.[11] Directly related is another important issue, namely the tendency to define Christian religion not only as universalistic but also as rational, in line with scientific progress, which becomes central in later Victorian evolutionism. It is the nature of that rationality that needs to be explored further in its Protestant antecedents and secular consequences. It is not only the nature of religion that is under construction but also the nature of secularity and secularism.

In the colonized world the old battle to convert the heathens continues, but an important voice is added as a result of the "secularization of the European mind," namely science of religion. One element of the modern transformation of religion is "the invention of world religions," as Tomoko Masuzawa calls it in her recent book.[12] "World religions" as a category is a product of comparative theology and the science of religion. Comparative theology begins and ends with the singularity of Christianity in comparison with other religions, while science of religion attempts to be a science that deals with all religions evenhandedly. In addition, science of religion derives part of its scientific status from being closely connected to historical linguistics and philology.

The most important figure for translating Chinese traditions into the new category of world religion was James Legge (1815–1897). Friedrich Max Müller (1823–1900) and Legge were colleagues at Oxford University, and Legge produced the Sacred Books of China for Müller's Sacred Books of the East series, which was published in fifty volumes between 1879 and 1902. India was of much greater interest to British scholarship than China, primarily because India had been colonized and secondly because India's cultural and linguistic heritage had been shown to be deeply related to that of Europe, while China was not in the Indo-European family and seemed deeply alien to scholars. Nevertheless, Müller accepted Confucianism and Daoism into the fold of world religion and invited his colleague and friend Legge to make his translations of the classical texts of these religions available for his famous series.

Legge had learned Chinese as a missionary in China for the London Missionary Society and had already begun his monumental work of translating Chinese classics in Hong Kong. When he returned to England he became the first professor of Chinese at Oxford (1876–1897). In Oxford he came more and more under the influence of Müller's science of language and science of religion and turned from a religious missionary into a scientific missionary. A major element of this scientific approach as different from a religious approach is the willingness to see some essential truth shining in all existing religions. This deters the student of a particular religion from attacking the other religion and allows for a liberal, tolerant attitude that is clearly conducive to a scholarly approach to non-Christian religious traditions. This attitude makes the great project of translations contained in the Sacred Books of the East feasible in the first place.

Although Max Müller was not allowed to deal with Judaism and Christianity and publish the Old and New Testament in this universalist series, he was able to make his point in an indirect way that God's truth can be found in all the great traditions ("the Bibles of Humanity" as he called them in a letter to Ernest Renan).[13] It is clear that the orientalist translation of the great traditions of India and China by Müller and Legge was embedded in Christian theological disputes as well as colonial knowledge. The exception granted to Judaism and Christianity was just as political as the ability to deal with the other religions. Nevertheless, as Girardot observes, the spirit of Müller and Legge's enterprise was symbolized by the fact that the earlier gift of the Rig Veda by the prince of Wales to Indian nobles was replicated by the gift of the Sacred Books to Queen Victoria and by the gift of a Chinese New Testament by Wang Tao (1828–1897), Legge's Chinese collaborator in translation projects and a respected intellectual in China, to Cixi, the dowager empress in Peking.[14] At the same time, however, the translation of the Sacred Books of the East also re-created these traditions for the societies from which they came. A Buddhist monastery in Japan sent two pupils to Müller to learn Sanskrit and make the Sanskrit tradition of Buddhism again available in Japan. King Chulalongkorn of Siam (Thailand) gave a grant for the translation of three volumes of Buddhist Sanskrit texts.[15]

Legge was embroiled in a dispute between different Protestant missionary groups concerning the translation of the term *Shangdi* (上帝) in Confucian texts with the term "God." The term *Shangdi* for God is now commonly used by Protestants in China, while Catholics (following the Jesuit Matteo Ricci) widely use the term *Tianzhu* 天主. The old problem of the translation of the Christian message, and specifically the Bible, became connected to the new, liberal, theological ("fulfillment") position that one could also find God in the ancient Chinese texts. The latter was the position that Legge already held when he was still a missionary, but his translations in the Sacred Books would allow him to give it a scientific authority. This struggle for authority meant that Legge's contributions to the Sacred Books did not fail to get an animated response from missionary circles. The issue is, obviously, fascinating: Do the Chinese classical texts have a theology that is recognizable and comparable to Christian theology? Is there an ancient Chinese monotheism? Legge's position is, in that period, a liberal and progressive one in its attempt to draw Chinese traditions into the orbit of comparative religion. His opponents object to it from a conservative perspective that sees the Chinese traditions as immoral and certainly inferior to the Christian tradition to the extent that finding equivalences is a form of blasphemy.

Legge draws on Müller's theory of symbols and metaphors to argue that *Di* (帝, also the word for emperor) and *Shangdi* (上帝) were the original names of the concept of God and that a word denoting Heaven

(*Tian* 天) was used as a concrete metaphor to symbolize the pure concept of God.[16] *Shangdi* is thus not only compared with Indo-European ideas about Heaven as a God but also to the Hebrew and Christian God. This is particularly clear from Legge's publication of 1880, *Religions of China: Confucianism and Taoism Described and Compared with Christianity*. All of these comparisons ultimately lead to the evolutionary view that the religions of mankind share a basic kinship but they are ultimately "fulfilled" in Christianity. It is hardly possible to make a coherent summary of the conflicting arguments that result from the combination of theology and scholarship, but it is precisely their ferment that is so interesting against the backdrop of colonialism, nationalism, and secularism.

While these debates about the nature of Confucianism may seem to be confined to a small group of scholars and missionaries, this is, in fact, not the case. It is instructive to have a look at the World Parliament of Religions in Chicago in 1893, which was part of the Columbian Exhibition and drew wide public attention. Peng Guanyu, the first secretary of the Chinese legation in Washington, D.C., was invited as representative of Confucianism in the World Parliament of Religions. He gave the orthodox view of scholar-officials in the Qing dynasty that Confucianism is not a religion (*zongjiao* 宗教), a modern term that was adopted from Japan at the end of the nineteenth century, but the law and the teaching (*jiao*) of proper human relations by the ruler and his officials. Another notion that had also existed for centuries in China—that there were three teachings (*sanjiao*), namely Buddhism, Daoism, and Confucianism—assumed certain equality between these teachings and was therefore not accepted in the orthodox circles of scholar-officials to which Peng Guanyu belonged. Peng Guangyu argued that the term "religion" could be translated in Chinese not by "teaching" (*jiao*) but by "shamanism" (*wu* 巫). Christianity could thus be seen as a form of shamanism. Shamanism had to be controlled by the state, because in fact it was a primitive set of superstitions, created by a self-interested clergy, and could easily lead to millenarian rebellions. His arguments show an uncanny connection between modern secularism and Confucian thought. In his view religion was something dangerous and primitive that should be, if not overcome, at least controlled by proper government. It is imperial rule based on Confucian principles in the

Qing dynasty that sets the norms according to which religious believers in Buddhism, Daoism, or Christianity have to conform.[17] All those religious teachings have fundamental flaws, but as long as they did not violate the political order they could be tolerated.

What I want to emphasize here is the hidden "third" in discussions of the interaction between religion and secularism, namely what Peng calls *wu* (巫). In the Western scholarly discussion *wu* is mostly translated as "shamanism," a relatively neutral term for spirit-religion, but in Chinese scholarly discussion it refers to an early substratum of truly primitive belief that has been overcome in imperial ritual. In contemporary usage it refers to surviving forms of magic, witchcraft, sorcery, and so on. As such, it is really Chinese popular religion, the religion of the illiterate masses, to which Peng refers and, as such, the very widespread and substantial folk traditions to which both Daoism and Buddhism have close connections.[18] Peng Guanyu's discussion of Chinese traditions relates directly to the opposition between magic and religion that is created in nineteenth- and twentieth-century Western thought. This opposition is an important aspect of secularism. It is central to ideas of science, rationality, and secular progress.

At the end of the nineteenth century (the end of the Qing dynasty) attempts were made to make Confucianism into the national religion (*guojiao* 国教). Kang Youwei (1858–1927), a major intellectual and official of the period, was behind this attempt, and it is important to note that he was also the main protagonist of a campaign to "destroy temples and build schools." Progress was now seen to depend on the destruction of Chinese superstition and the creation of a civil religion that resembled Shinto in Japan. While the transformation of Confucianism as the political religion of the ancien régime into a civil religion of a modern state failed, the destruction of temples and other manifestations of religion continued for a century.

TODAY

After a century of repression of popular religion (*minjian zongjiao* 民间宗教) as well as half a century of Communist repression of Confucianism (as one of China's feudal ideologies), we see a revival of Confucianism today. Chinese intellectuals are in the forefront of this revival. The philosopher Tu Weiming has for a long time sought to influence Chinese authorities with his interpretation of the positive contribution of Confucianism to society and to the world. For a while Singapore adopted some of his ideas in its state ideology, but in general one may conclude that the effects have been limited. The political philosopher Daniel Bell, who teaches at Tsinghua University, relates ideas developed in the context of communitarianism to Confucian traditions and also sees some positive social morality coming out of these traditions for contemporary Chinese society.[19] In short, there is quite a burgeoning effort by intellectuals inside and outside China to promote Confucianism as an alternative to a stagnant Marxist ideology.[20]

This raises the question of what Confucianism is today. Let us look briefly at the idea that China is a Confucian society. President Hu Jintao and other Chinese leaders have reevaluated the Confucian tradition. They now concede that harmony as the central value of Confucian teachings is something to be cherished. Worrying about growing economic disparities amid rapid economic growth, the Chinese Communist Party (CCP) focuses on Confucian harmony as a form of societal consensus and solidarity. For the first time in sixty-six years the Party organized a lavish worship ceremony at Tianjin's Confucius Temple in November 2004. In the town of Qufu, the birth place of Confucius, the official ceremony of commemorating his birthday has since 2004 become an important public ritual, broadcast live on state television.[21] The ministry of education is encouraging numerous courses in Confucian culture by establishing Confucius Institutes all over the world, following the model of the Goethe Institute, the Alliance Française, or the British Council. This is not so much to promote Confucianism, since language courses form the main curriculum, but it does suggest that for the Chinese state Confucianism is the heart of Chinese civilization.

The popularity of the notion that Confucianism is central to or even equivalent with Chinese civilization is also related to the fact that it extols the virtue of filial piety (*xiao*) as a central part of its teaching. The rites of passage (birth, marriage, death) and especially the ancestor cult are fundamental to Chinese religion, and filial piety can be considered a kinship norm that is extended to the wider society and the state. However, to conflate these practices of the household and the wider kinship structure with their ideological expression in Confucian teachings would be a mistake. One could argue that filial piety is part of any patrilineal system that gives the older men of the clan authority over younger men and can be found in different parts of the world without Confucian connections. Moreover, ancestor worship is fundamental to other forms of Chinese religion. Buddhism is deeply connected to the rituals of death, while Daoism emphasizes all kinds of rituals that connect to the choosing of the grave and the worship of the ancestors. All of this has changed thoroughly during Communist rule. Not only were the old family structures seen as feudal, but the costly death rituals and burials and ancestor worship were all repressed. In the Cultural Revolution children were either set up to denounce their parents or were brought up outside parental control. The CCP attempted to replace filial piety and kinship structures with party loyalty or national loyalty.

In important ways kinship structures and their religious expression have been transformed under Communist rule. Not only the patrilineal clan has lost most of its significance in most parts of mainland China, but the household has also been deeply affected by the one-child policy implemented in Chinese cities. The single son has become the "emperor" of the household. References to filial piety as a fundamental value of Confucian civilization do not make much sense under modern conditions. This is not to say that some of the old views and practices concerning the dead and the blessings of the ancestors have not returned in an altered form. An indication of this is the declaration of Qingmingjie (清明节, the grave sweeping festival) as a public holiday in 2008. This is especially interesting in relation to the successful promotion of cremations in China, which would in principle make the cleaning of graves superfluous. Graves, however, have been replaced by urns that can still be ritually approached.

What remains central in the use of Confucian conceptions of national civilization is a state authoritarianism that enforces social harmony. It is not so much that people have shared values but that a social cohesion and consensus is produced by economy and politics, as is well-illustrated by Singapore's so-called Confucian state. The economic liberalization of China from 1978 onward has brought a liberalization of the religious field in its wake. It is very hard to assess the direction of developments today, since they take place at different levels: local, regional, and national. Local authorities are constantly negotiating the extent to which they will allow (or even stimulate) the rebuilding of temples, ancestral halls, and the reinstatement of local festivals and rituals.[22] They have to deal not only with regional political developments but also with new national policies. This is a volatile field that cannot be easily put into a single interpretive frame in a society as big as China. It seems, however, that the volatility of economic development, with its interaction between political authorities and economic entrepreneurs as well as the involvement of the central state in big developments, may be a good blueprint for our understanding of what is happening in the religious arena.[23] At the same time, it is important to realize that a century of persecution has severed the chains of oral and ritual transmission in many parts of the country and destroyed the lives and livelihood of clergy and therefore much of the infrastructure of religion. A crucial element in this destruction has been the land reforms that took away the economic base of religious establishments. This cannot be built up again in contemporary China, and thus economic support has to come from other sources, mainly from tourism, since many of the shrines are in places of touristic interest. The rebuilding of religious infrastructure is thus related to new forms of consumption and will be closely dependent on them. This leads also to a revitalization of old claims that religion is not really spiritual but materialistic and consumerist.[24] In this sense the market is, obviously, an important aspect of religious change in China. However, this market has to be analyzed in direct relation to political power. Since local governments depend more and more on their ability to develop economic growth without central state support, they will more and more negotiate with entrepreneurial elites who may want to express their economic desires and feelings of uncertainty and expectation in a religious idiom.[25] A Confucian-Communist state ideology of harmony and filial piety is far removed from these realities on the ground but does provide a language of national unity and historical continuity that can be convenient for Party control. The revitalization of Confucianism is part of Chinese religion today, but its complex relation to central state power should make us question any attempt to make it into the essence of Chinese civilization.

CONCLUSION

In early modern Europe one should not only look at Protestantism, but also at Catholicism and especially at the Counter-Reformation. The Jesuits (as well as their Dominican and Franciscan counterparts) are a socio-religious movement that connects Latin Christendom with Latin America, India, and China. Charles Taylor's discussion of the early modern period in the West could be fruitfully connected to a discussion of that period in the rest of the world by examining this movement. For the nineteenth century it is the relation between religion-nationalism-imperialism that seems to form the triad that produces forms of secularism. In the Chinese case there is an emphasis on "secular progress" produced by science and on popular religion ("superstition") as an obstacle to progress. In this period it is modern Christian (especially Protestant but also Catholic) missions, which carry both modern education and Christianity, that are crucial for the connection between West and Rest.

Among Chinese intellectuals it is a popular concept that Chinese religions are tolerant and syncretistic, as in C. K. Yang's description of Chinese religion as "diffused religion," while European Christianity is aggressive and intolerant, because early modern Europe is split up by religious wars and Christian missionaries go all over the world to convert people to the "true faith."[26] However, Chinese religions are only tolerated as long as they fit the heavenly mandate of the imperial ritual. China has many millenarian rebellions, but they are not called religious wars, because China is not split up in many different states with different languages and cultures.

The old Chinese distinction between politically correct teachings and politically incorrect teachings is in the nineteenth century mapped onto the distinction between magic and religion. It is the Western scientific debate about the evolution from magic to religion or the "disembedding" of popular beliefs that has provided a legitimation for progressivist attacks on Chinese religious beliefs. Rather than a secularization (in Charles Taylor's interpretation of Western Christianity, a gradual disembedding) it is an aggressive secularism (carried by intellectuals and the state) that one can find in China. It is the conceptual tension between religion and magic that provides most of the dynamic in Chinese attempts to produce a secular age.

Today's attempt to make Confucianism again an element of political culture resembles the attempt made by Kang Youwei and others to make it a national religion (*guojiao*), which failed, partly because it was not accompanied by an attempt to elevate Buddhism and Daoism as a part of that national religion. The difference is, obviously, that the Communist Party has, after half a century, not succeeded in taking control of the religious imagination of the Chinese people. Confucianism can be part of Chinese nationalism, but it will not bring in a "secular age" in China.

NOTES

I want to thank Joseph Adler, Mary Evelynn Tucker, and Peng Guoxiang for helpful comments on this paper.

1. S. N. Eisenstadt, ed., *The Origins and Diversity of Axial Age Civilizations* (Albany: State University of New York Press, 1986).
2. Karl Jaspers, *Von Ursprug und Ziel der Geschichte* [About the origin and goal of history] (Frankfurt: Fischer, 1955), 14.
3. S. N. Eistenstadt, Introduction to *The Origins and Diversity of Axial Age Civilizations*, Frankfurt: Fischer, 1955, 16.
4. Rodney Taylor, *The Religious Dimensions of Confucianism* (Albany: State University of New York Press, 1990). For a wonderful discussion of the issues involved: Joseph A. Adler, "Confucianism as Religion/Religious Tradition/Neither: Still Hazy After All These Years" (lecture given at Minzu University of China, June 23, 2010).
5. Charles Taylor, "Western Secularity," in *Rethinking Secularism*, ed. Craig Calhoun, Mark Juergensmeyer, and Jonathan Van Antwerpen (New York: Oxford University Press, 2011), 36.
6. Talal Asad, "The Idea of an Anthropology of Islam" (Occasional Paper Series, Georgetown University Center for Contemporary Arab Studies, Washington, D.C., 1986).

7. Voltaire agreed with the Jesuits in seeing Confucianism as a philosophy in the last chapter of his *Siecle de Louis XIV* (1751): "Disputes sur les cérémonies chinoises. Comment ces querelles contribuèrent à faire proscrire le christianisme à la Chine," but of course he went beyond the Jesuit strategy by using the Confucian example to attack Christianity.
8. See Chung-Ying Cheng and Nicholas Bunnin, eds., *Contemporary Chinese Philosophy* (Oxford: Blackwell, 2002).
9. David Mungello, *Leibniz and Confucianism: The Search for Accord* (Honolulu: University of Hawaii Press, 1977).
10. Webb Keane, *Christian Moderns* (Berkeley: University of California Press, 2007).
11. Peter van der Veer, "Material Religion: The Journal of Objects, Art and Belief," *Spirit* 7, no. 1 (March 2011): 124–130.
12. Tomoko Masuzawa, *The Invention of World Religions* (Chicago: University of Chicago Press, 2005).
13. Quoted in Lourens van den Bosch, *Friedrich Max Müller* (Leiden: Brill, 2002), 134.
14. Norman Girardot, *The Victorian Translation of China: James Legge's Oriental Pilgrimage* (Berkeley: University of California Press, 2002), 351.
15. Van den Bosch, *Friedrich Max Müller*, 133ff.
16. Girardot, *Victorian Translation*, 281.
17. Hsi-yuan Chen, "At the Threshold of the Pantheon of Religions: Confucianism and the Emerging Religious Discourse at the Turn of the Twentieth Century" (paper given at the Conference on Chinese Religiosities, Santa Barbara, California, 2005).
18. Kristofer Schipper even goes so far as to argue that Daoism is the textual tradition of these folk religions in *The Taoist Body* (Berkeley: University of California Press, 1993), 6.
19. Daniel Bell, *China's New Confucianism: Politics and Everyday Life in a Changing Society* (Princeton: Princeton University Press, 2007).
20. See John Makeham, *Lost Soul: "Confucianism" in Contemporary Chinese Academic Discourse* (Cambridge: Harvard University Asia Center, 2008).
21. For ethnographic accounts of these state ceremonies as well as for alternative (nonstate) forms of Confucianism, see a special issue of *China Perspectives* 80, no. 4 (2009).
22. Mayfair Yang, "Spatial Struggles: Postcolonial Complex, State Disenchantment, and Popular Reappropriation of Space in Rural Southeast Asia," *Journal of Asian Studies* 63 (2004): 719–755.
23. Daniel Wank, "Institutionalizing Modern 'Religion' in China's Buddhism," in *Making Religion, Making the State*, ed. Yoshiko Ashiwa and David Wank (Stanford, Calif.: Stanford University Press, 2009), 126–150.

24. Gareth Fischer, "The Spiritual Land Rush: Merit and Morality in New Chinese Buddhist Temple Construction," *Journal of Asian Studies* 67, no.1 (2008): 143–170.
25. Nanlai Cao, "Christian Entrepreneurs and the Post-Mao State: An Ethnographic Account of Church-State Relations in China's Economic Transition," *Sociology of Religion* 68, no. 1 (2007): 45–66.
26. C. K. Yang, *Religion in Chinese Society* (Berkeley: University of California Press, 1961).

7

DISENCHANTMENT DEFERRED

Sudipta Kaviraj

The sparseness of the title of Charles Taylor's work is itself an incitement to further thinking. The work purports to be a description, analysis, and reflection on "a secular age"—but it is reticent about the question of space. It offers a story of a great transformation—but where does this narrative happen? There are two ways of taking this unspoken indeterminate site of the secular age. A dominant strand of social theory, aligned to powerful narratives of modernization, would view in it a double story: a story of a historic transformation that really occurred in some "Western societies"— though recent scholarship has cast doubts on this casually conceived space named "the West."[1] But conventionally, modern social science would also "see" in it another story with a strangely indeterminate narrative status because it is a story that has not happened but, its viewers are convinced, will happen in the future.[2] It is a supplemental story of something that has not happened, which always accompanies the European story as an expectation, that makes this view so interesting. This combination—of what has already happened and what has not but we are convinced will—makes this a historical *process*—in part finished, in part not—which exerts such a powerful influence in the theoretical imagination of modern social science. Read in this way, the title *A Secular Age* is both a narration and an announcement—it is the name of an age in an unfinished process of unfolding—something that has begun in the West since the seventeenth century and is still going on in different parts of the world today.

Yet, clearly, Taylor does not intend it that way: his reference is explicitly both spatially and temporally limited: he is telling the story of a fundamental transformation of society that happened in Latin Christendom—limited to that space and that precise span of historical time. There is a palpable resistance in Taylor's work to the effortless slide into historical generalization so common in social theory. By stressing the fact that this is a story of the Western space, it forcefully raises a question as an entailment: What happened elsewhere? Even this question—"What happened elsewhere?"—could be read in two contradictory ways: it could mean, as it did in Weber's *Religion of India*, why did the story of the West not happen in India or China?[3] Slowly, social scientists have now come to acknowledge how strange that way of framing the question is: Why should the history of Europe happen elsewhere?[4] Did those spaces not have a sufficiently singular history of themselves? The notable difference found in Taylor's book is that it drops that supplemental part of gratuitous expectation about history that had not yet happened. By making that gesture, it raises the question more forcefully. Those who believed in the older way of reading the idea need not have grappled with the complexities of non-European history because of their comfortable assumption of a routine replication of Europe's historical narrative. Those who have decisively given up that hope must now take up the task of providing an outline of those narratives of historical difference.

A Secular Age starts with a condensed and stylized history of the premodern period—when the default position of social belief was that there was a creator who established the order of the human world and it was a human being's fate to live by the rules of that order.[5] In the following sections, Taylor traces the merging trajectories of singular lines of transformation—of the economy through the rise of modern capitalism; of the state in the form of absolutism, nationalism, and democracy; of social life through the emergence and expansion of associational forms of market and civil society. Forms of modern economy, state, civil society, and culture emerge, support, and endorse one another—leading eventually to "the great transformation" toward modern secularity. The final part narrates the evolution of this modern world into its present state and its peculiar equilibrium of beliefs. Taylor does not repeat the conventional story. The most startling part of Taylor's narrative of Western secularization is its crucial revision of the received argument on one fundamental point. That narrative of secularization delineated a process of intellectual and institutional transformation that began in scientific revolutions and spread gradually to other adjacent spheres of belief—pulling down untenable forms of intellectual adhesions and commitments until these "subtractions" left only "an immanent framework" radically shorn of beliefs in God and the supernatural transcendent realm. Taylor's account is so unconventional and destabilizing of the conventional story precisely because of his claim that the establishment of the science-driven immanent frame does not inevitably lead people to a disenchanted universe of mandatory unbelief. Rather, modern human beings in the West generally accept the immanent frame: but they may still remain undecided between a belief in God and disbelief. In other words, assent to a scientific view of the world does not necessarily force people into disbelief in God for the sake of pure logical consistency. There is no inconsistency in an acceptance of a scientific view of the world and a belief in the existence and effectivity of transcendence. This has serious and complex implications for the study of the trajectories of non-Western cultures. The first story left two options for thinking about those cultures: either they remained immovably tradition bound, or they followed the same logic of change—with a time lag. Taylor's revised version of the European story does not have this implication and allows us to think about what really happened in these cultures without a constant reference to what happened in the West. It becomes possible to posit a seriously multilinear narrative of secularity.

To respond to *A Secular Age* with a parallel story, it is essential to follow a particular narrative frame: to ask first whether the state of premodernity in other cultures were sufficiently similar to the patterns found in the West, so we need not seek a different narrative of the premodern. Second, we must ask, in the Indian context, the question of the origins of Indian modernity—a question that has become enormously more complicated by recent research but, precisely for that reason, also more fascinating. When does "the modern" begin in Indian history? And why is that time the beginning of the modern?[6] Third, in the Indian context, the question of colonialism is unavoidably crucial: How are patterns of religious belief affected by the impact of deeply different ideas from the West? What were those ideas? How were they received? Were they modified, and in what direction? How did the debate between the modernists and their critics unfold? What were the significant forms of religiosity in the colonial modern period? And finally, what has happened to the questions of disenchantment and secularity in our contemporary times—after independence? What is the state of religious life in India today? To write about the secular age outside Latin Christendom is necessarily to ask a differently inflected version of the same question. Taylor's work is based on the conviction that the people in West do live in a secular age, and the book is a description of its historical path and present state. In the Indian case, we must rather ask, "Do we live in a secular age?" Given the primary features of beliefs in India today, should we call this age "secular"? In this essay I shall try to offer some necessarily sketchy answers to these vast historical questions.

In recent academic debates regarding Indian secularism, Rajeev Bhargava has suggested that to think lucidly about this complex of issues, we need to be clear about what the terms "secularism" and "secularization" mean; and in the Indian discussions in particular he has proposed a distinction between political and ethical secularism.[7] Ethical secularism denotes the predominantly modern intellectual condition in which belief in God as source of ethical order is fatally undermined by ideas of modern science. Political secularism refers to a condition in which the society's political authority itself tolerates diverse religious groups and encourages reciprocal toleration. The primary difference between these two states of affairs is that in the first, there can be, and usually is, a deep decline in religious belief: but in the second—political secularism—there is no attendant expectation of this kind. Indeed, what is called political secularism usually emerges and flourishes in societies marked by widespread deep religious belief, but an additional condition is that the society should be marked by religious diversity and conflict.[8] In societies that are entirely homogeneous in religious practice,⁹ the requirement for political secularism does not arise.

Theoretically, these two states of affairs could be viewed as two separate solutions to the problem of religious diversity. In one case, diversity of persuasions will result in religious conflict—both in the form of contestation of beliefs and in two forms of conflict—between political regimes and between political authorities and their own subjects if they are divided by religious faith. In another case, a plurality of faiths may not lead to conflict of that kind. In cases of political secularism, deep religious beliefs can exist in a society—without giving rise to conflict. In case of ethical secularism, conflict declines, because religious belief, which caused that conflict, becomes weaker. In this essay, I shall view these two as alternative "solutions" to the problem of religious conflict and shall try to analyze the long-term trends in Indian history through these two models of conflict and of adjustment.[10]

SOME OBSERVATIONS ON PREMODERN RELIGIOUS BELIEFS: ANCIENT IMMANENT FRAMES

Were there serious theoretical positions in premodern times that saw the world as radically immanent? And if they did, what was the extent of their influence on society in general? As in ancient Greece, ancient Indian intellectual life was characterized by a variety of philosophical and religious schools. A preliminary division of ancient Indian philosophical schools was between the *nāstikas*,[11] those who do not accept the existence of God and its implications for ethical life, and the *āstikas*,[12] those who accept the existence of God but formulate and shape this belief and its ethical implications at times in very different ways. Among the *nāstika* philosophical schools, one of the most prominent was the Cārvākas, who gained notoriety for their radical materialist ontology and skepticism about belief in God and an afterlife ordained by him. Working with a radically spare epistemology that accepted only direct sensory perception (*pratyakṣa*) as the only firm ground for belief (*pramāṇa*), the Cārvākas denied that the existence of God could be established by serious philosophical argument. Among the most famous of their ideas was their scornful rejection of an afterlife, or transmigration of souls. In a compressed expression of both their metaphysical and ethical theories, the Cārvākas exhorted human beings:

Yāvat jīvet sukham jīvet ṛnam kṛtvā ghṛtam pivet
Bhasmībhūtasya dehasya punarāgamanam kutah[13]

"As long as you live, you ought to live in pleasure. Borrow money to drink ghee. How can a body that has been consumed by fire [literally, "turned to ashes"] return [to take the consequences of its acts]?" Even in this highly condensed utterance, which is more like a slogan than a philosophical statement, the Cārvākas state their case with great sharpness and force.[14] This particular *sloka* does not directly refer to the existence of God and does not announce their characteristic belief in atheism, except by indirect allusion. The statement takes unerring aim at the karmic belief in the transmigration of the soul, in metempsychosis, which is a crucial part of *āstika* doctrines.[15] It is a fundamental constituent of those belief systems that in a just, immutable order ordained by God, animals and human beings assume bodily forms and enter a cycle of acts through a specific birth. At death that body is destroyed, but the soul assumes another form, determined by the nature of the acts done during its previous lifetime. A particular birth is linked to the karmic order, in which the *kartā* (the actor) assumes responsibility for its acts and is punished or rewarded in the next birth. The Cārvāka statement refutes this karmic theory of reincarnation by pouring scorn on the idea that a physical body "turned to ashes" can "return" (*punarāgamanam*) to suffer the responsibility of its acts after death. In principle, after this refutation, it is possible for the ensuing argument to take varying routes regarding ethical life. It is perfectly possible to argue that precisely because there is no afterlife, a person should try to lead a life of ethically irreproachable acts, because a judgment on his or her life will be based on an accounting at the end of it.[16] The Cārvākas, however, decided to follow a more cynically materialistic route about ethical reckoning. Their derivation of ethical principles simply draws the logically correct but morally dismal implication that since the body is not likely to return to suffer for its acts, people should simply enjoy a hedonistic existence without restraint. "Borrow money and have ghee" (ṛṇam kṛtvā ghṛtam pivet) became a proverb for nihilistic materialist attacks on the very possibility of ethics; though, it is at least sensible to conclude that if there were likely consequences a person had to face within the span of this life—for example, condemnation by fellow human beings—a materialist's advice would be to take those consequences seriously. Probably because of their extreme hedonism and rejection of ordinary tenets of ethical existence, the Cārvāka philosophy drew the heaviest fire from the *āstika* schools. Over the long term, although the Cārvāka view always remained a highly defined distinctive position on philosophy and moral conduct, its popular influence was restricted.[17] However, if the Cārvāka doctrine did not have such morally nihilistic implications and spread widely, it is conceivable that its effects could have been similar to a process of "disenchantment." It certainly posited a picture of an entirely immanent world and denied all transcendental authority, but its tenets made it a strand primarily confined to philosophical extremists, and it is not surprising that their doctrines have drawn admiration from modern Marxist commentators on Indian philosophy.[18] The continuing presence of Cārvāka doctrines in philosophical debates is evidenced by the discussion in the fairly late text *Sarvadarśanasaṃgraha* (Collection of All Philosophic Schools) by Mādhavācarya, a south Indian philosopher of the fourteenth century who begins his survey of philosophical schools with the Cārvākas.[19]

A far more serious dispute emerged in Indian religious and philosophical life with the emergence of Buddhism. Buddhism appeared, along with similar philosophical and religious doctrines like Jainism, to challenge conventional Vedic religion. Eventually, however, Buddhism constituted the major challenging doctrine to Vedic orthodoxy, which resulted in the sharpest philosophical debates with Vedic Hinduism and, eventually, the complete disappearance of Buddhism from the Indian subcontinent. Jaina theories of philosophy and a religious ethical life, though never a similar challenge to the Vedic theoretical and social order, survived and continued parallel to orthodox Brahminic faith, never attracting the same order of philosophical and social hostility.

The Buddhist challenge was fundamental, because it questioned traditional Vedic religion on at least three basic levels. It challenged Vedic and Brahminical doctrines of philosophy at the level of abstract ideas and arguments. But it also mounted an intense attack on the scriptural authority of the Brahmins and their claim to ritual social dominance. Finally, it undermined the conventional structure of the *varna* (ancient form of caste) society, though recent research has thrown some doubt on the extent of this challenge. It is probable that Buddhist religion challenged the authority and the ritual preeminence of the Brahmins as a social stratum rather than the entire conception of the caste order, as modern nationalist interpretations had sometimes suggested. But there is no doubt that Buddhism represented a challenge to Vedic Hinduism on philosophical, ritualist, and social-structural grounds. At least the early doctrines of Hinayana Buddhism, drawn from the Buddha's original teachings, did not require as much emphasis on transcendent horizons of human existence and metaphysical beliefs. It is doubtful whether Hinayana Buddhism even had a pronounced conception of God. Buddhism merely exhorted people to lead an ethical life by following a small number of powerful moral principles and performing an observant self-critical role toward their own attempts at ethical action—an uninterrupted series of these constituted an earthly "good life." As it did not require a powerful supramundane dimension for its fundamental beliefs, this early form of Buddhism could have had an extended and expanded life in Indian society, one that could also have possibly generated a powerful impulse toward something like disenchantment—a form of belief in which adherents accept a wholly immanent existence and pursue an ethical life without a pronounced conception of God, relying primarily on their own capacity for moral self-reflection. This possibility, however, was decisively obviated by the actual course of religious history. My point is that the first occasion of possible disenchantment could have emerged out of philosophical and religious views that were skeptical of the existence of God and accepted a wholly immanent universe. Both the materialist philosophical doctrines and early Buddhist religion contained powerful elements of such ideas. If these trends became dominant, Indian intellectual life might have moved toward an eventual decline of high religion toward an ancient form of secularity.

DOCTRINAL CONFLICT AND SKEPTICISM

A second possible line of development could also have emerged from the sheer fact of religious diversity. After the challenge of Buddhist heterodoxy, although Vedic religion recovered to control the social structure and retain the caste order, Indian society saw an extraordinary efflorescence of religious creeds. First, the challenge of Buddhism gave rise to new forms of Hindu faith that rejected a number of major Vedic beliefs and absorbed, often without explicit acknowledgment, important elements of the Buddhist heterodoxy. Probably the first new religion to experiment with new forms in this manner was Kashmiri Saivism,[20] after the eighth century. It deviated from Vedic orthodoxy in maintaining that all human beings could find a path to God, that *mokśa* or liberation could be found through the intercession of a preceptor (guru) and an initiation into an exemplary ethical life rather than strict observance of rituals. Saiva thinkers modified and showed skepticism about the rules of the caste order and karmic theology. As recent scholarship has shown, Saivism itself went through an extraordinary period of elaboration into new strands that offered different theologies, observance practices, rituals, and tantric specialisms.[21] Such features were to some extent absorbed from Buddhism or developed in response to its doctrinal suggestions.[22] Jayanta Bhatta's *Āgamadambara*[23] portrays a social state of this kind, wherein a large number of religious groups produce an energetic and vibrant life of ecclesiastical disputation. It is possible to argue that one potential result of such lively intellectual debate could have been a mutual destruction of their structures of justification, which might have left ordinary people initially bewildered and eventually drawn toward an abandonment of all religious doctrines, because no doctrine could offer certainty, and plurality simply produced either intellectual confusion or interminable social conflict. Something like this happened much later in early modern Europe. Religious diversity and acrimonious debates undermined the deep bases of religious belief itself. But this second possible line of development did not occur in India.

Actually, religious life in ancient and medieval India followed a third trajectory, which stamped Indian religious life with its specific character. From the fifth century C.E., diversity of religious beliefs and observances proliferated in India without restraint, probably because the predominant response of political power to this diversity of faiths was one of evolving institutional tolerance. Political tolerance could assume two distinct forms, as recent work on the basis of inscription material has pointed out. In an initial stage, after the rise of Buddhism, it was common for royal families to declare their adherence to a particular religious path; but they also made it known that they did not oppose their subjects' affiliation to other faiths; and it was clear that followers of faiths different from that of the ruler were not punished or persecuted. The social state described by the *Āgamaḍambara* confirms this model. The king in this story belongs to a particular form of worship, but it is made clear that the queen follows a different sect, making for diversity and the origin of tolerance within the royal household. Taking advantage of this culture of relative tolerance, the princess is attracted to the Nīlāmbaras, an extreme liberal sect whose members went around in couples covered by the same "black blankets."[24] The social world of *Āgamaḍambara* attests to the pervasiveness of religious difference in ancient Kashmir. The play shows a religious space shared between Vedicists, Buddhists, Jainas, Śaivas, Vaiṣṇavas, and atheists, and extreme new sects like the Nīlāmabaras engaged in a vibrantly contentious exchange of opinions and arguments. Royal power floats above them, providing protection to all sects without much discrimination, despite the fact that royal personages—the king and his queen—like all ordinary individuals, have to choose their own personal paths to God. What is truly remarkable is the existence of a fairly open public sphere of discussion and debate in which intellectual contestants had to follow collectively acknowledged rules of disputation, making it possible to decide without ambiguity which side was victorious in a particular exchange.

This "nova effect" was streamlined in the next few centuries, and the primary geometry of religious space in India settled down into a triangular configuration with Saivism, Vaisnavism, and Saktaism as the three dominant poles. In his study of the historical rise of Saiva and Vaisnavite doctrines during the Axial Age,[25] Jan Gonda described a process through which the original chaotic pantheon of Vedic deities are given a simpler and more structured shape. The thesis about the Axial Age is that religious life is reconceived in a fundamentally new fashion; and some of these Axial shifts can be discerned clearly in the historic movement from Vedic religion to new doctrines like *Pratyabhijñā*.[26] The ordinary Vedic conception of a good religious life placed the test of religiosity in the strict performance of elaborate rituals, leaving a householder's everyday life unburdened by the anguish of ethical reflection. By maintaining that attaining *mokśa* (that is, an identification with Siva) is possible in this life,[27] Saiva religion made the whole burden of exemplary activity internal to everyday life. This makes an ethically demanding reflexive orientation toward everyday life the central feature of a religious existence.

The soteriological impulse in the post-Vedic age was directly opposite to the Vedic scene. Vedic religion is primarily ritualistic and worships a great diversity of deities placed horizontally in a vast pantheon. The two founding texts of Saiva and Vaisnava doctrines—the Śvetāsvatara Upaniṣad for the Saivas and the Bhagavatgītā for the Vaisnavas—both show an impulse toward devotionalism and unity. The vast field of deities is restructured by elevating one—Siva or Visnu—as the equivalent to the Upanisadic *puruṣa*, invested with the magnificent characteristics of the *puruṣa-sūkta* but divested of its pronounced casteist associations,[28] because both Saiva and Vaisnava doctrines would seek to modify the hard versions of the *varna* system.[29] Eventually this simplification process would lead to one supreme deity being worshipped as Siva or Visnu. Gonda discerns two processes—the selection of some central features of Vedic religion, like the strand that identifies a *puruṣa* who is the creator and preserver of all existence, and the gradual identification of one of the lesser deities from a range of figures. The features of the great *purusa* are then merged into the figure of this singular deity to turn him into the *devādideva*— the God before and above all other gods. Two traditions accomplished this transformation successfully, later evolving into the Saiva and the

Vaisnava doctrines, because the two figures who emerged into prominence from the crowd of equally inconsequential small deities to acquire the characteristics of the great *purusa* were Siva and Visnu—reconciling power and loving-kindness.[30] Interestingly, although these religious forms emerged through processes of parallel evolution from a vast and inchoate field of pre-Axial Vedic worship, they were not always viewed as uniformly abominable heterodoxies that betrayed Vedic religion. Buddhism's challenge was at times viewed in that manner and considered *veda-viruddha* or *vedadrohī*. By contrast, the Saiva and Vaisnava doctrines differentiated themselves from the original Vedic religious form without causing offense as a fearsome heresy or a social betrayal. In early medieval India, religious difference evolved to assume a peculiar form that allowed diversity to flourish without leading to excessive conflict. Alexis Sanderson shows how forms of mantra and other new ritual practices were originally devised by the Saiva Siddhanta theorists for adepts and initiates in their specific religious form—generally called texts on *paddhatis* (methods of proper worship)—an intricate and elaborate structure of aural and bodily disciplines.[31] Subsequently, some of these techniques of elaborate worship were imitated or in some cases simply copied by Jaina and Vaisnava sects.

Such transfers—to use an appraisively neutral description—worked in two ways. First, these borrowings were driven by competition between contending sects, so that if something was considered attractive, it was emulated by others who did not want to fall behind in popularity. Despite the potentially conflictual side to these transfers, they also prepared the ground for a kind of tolerance in the long run, because although the sects worshipped different deities, they often worshipped them in remarkably similar ways. Competitive emulation created conditions for intelligibility, familiarity, and tolerance. Unlike the difference between Vedicists and Buddhists—with one group believing in caste and the other rejecting it—differences between Saivas, Saktas, and Vaisnavas evolved into a distinctly different pattern of competitive diversity without mortal conflict. Saivas and Saktas believed in soteriologies that were closely related: Sakti was often viewed as the creative cosmic power of Siva conceived as a separate figure of adoration, for instance, as in the great treatise of Kashmir Saivism, Abhinavagupta's *Īśvara-Pratyabhijñā-Vimarśinī*'s initial *mangalācarana*. To take a random and temporally distant example, the manner in which a Gaudiya Vaisnava text like the *Caitanyacaritāmṛta* from the fifteenth century opens its textual movement is astonishingly similar.[32] By this time, of course, this distinction between *isvara* and his *sakti* had had time to evolve in subtlety and intricacy, and the *Caitanyacaritāmṛta* could draw on this long tradition of formal elaboration. It says, very similarly, Krsna who is God in his full self (*kṛṣṇastu bhagavān svayam*), was initially self-subsistent, but his curiosity about his own powers required that he must have a complementary double. To see himself, he alienated himself into the feminine form of Rādhā. In much of the theology of Siva-Durgā—both in the Saiva and the Sakta traditions—this relationship is viewed in an identical manner.[33] Of course, in this vast and vibrant marketplace of devotion, religious sects had to defend their boundaries and claim relative superiority. Often this would be done by showing a competing deity as a worshipper or a supplicant to the supreme being. But there are instances of striking ingenuity in incorporation of different religious figures. Centuries after Buddhism had ceased to be a real threat to Hindu worship, the Eastern poet Jayadeva composed an invocation to the ten *avatāras* of Visnu. For Jayadeva, Krsna is God himself, and it would be illogical to view him as an *avatāra*. This vacates a place of an *avatāra*, and Jayadeva, in one of the most popular *daśāvatāra stotras* of all times, inserts the Buddha into the vacancy as the ninth descent of Visnu:

Nindasi yagna-vidherahaha śruti-jātam
sadaya-hṛdaya darśita paśu-ghātam
Keśavadhṛta Buddha-śarīra jaya jagadīśa hare[34]

Heinrich von Stietencron has persuasively argued that the modern historical language influenced by Orientalist concepts habituated observers to the idea that India was marked by a single religion called Hinduism comprising different sects.[35] To a less prejudging vision, these would appear as separate religious forms or communities of worship, coexisting in a large space. The interesting feature is the sociology of difference found in the culture of this vast subcontinent. Difference does not necessarily mean contestation, let alone violent conflict. It appears that these religious forms across the entire subcontinent devised a remarkable form of negotiation of religious difference. Boundaries of religious groups were in a sense zealously maintained. The Saiva tradition was riven down the middle between followers of Saiva Siddhanta schools and the more radical practitioners of renunciation like the *kapalikas*, despite their common devotion to Siva. In a parallel fashion, the Vaisnava religious tradition had internal divisions between the south Indian paths and the distinct Gaudiya form originating from Caitanya—with highly elaborated distinctive theologies, in spite of occasional mutual borrowings. Similarly, the Sakta religious strand gave rise to distinctive tendencies of the worship of Sakti in varying forms and eventually spawned an utterly radical nondomestic version in Vāmācāra—the "Left" practice that focused on deviant sexual disciplines and utterly disregarded rules of conventional domesticity. All three traditions developed radical groups in their fringes—Saiva *kapalikas*, Vaisnava *sahajiyas*, and Sakta Vamacaris or Kaulas—that frightened and troubled ordinary Hindu householders and were always kept warily at a distance. The significant point about religious controversy potentially giving rise to processes of intellectual disenchantment is that all major lines of religious devotion evolved internal differentiations but maintained a balance between distinctness and forbearance, practicing a form of benign indifference to others' practices and beliefs, except in the case of the fringe groups, whose extreme beliefs probably also kept their numbers small. Adopting these extreme religious positions could be done only at the cost of social renunciation or ostracism—because polite Hindu society claimed the fringe groups had rejected it, while the groups claimed they had rejected dull and staid domesticity. What is crucial in this short historical picture of religious evolution in India is the fact that religious diversity, accompanied by often spirited doctrinal disputation, did not lead to the consequence that initially some intellectual elites and eventually a major part of society lost faith in all religious forms. In some contexts, vibrant disputation between contending religious groups succeeds not in undermining the opposing view, but religion itself. In ancient and medieval

India, diversity in religious philosophy and practice evidently did not lead to this consequence.

FORMS OF RELIGIOUS DIVERSITY IN MEDIEVAL INDIA

The entry of Islam from the twelfth century did not alter the main contours of this picture in any fundamental way. Differences between Islam and the Hindu sectarian beliefs ran deep and were often sharply expressed.[36] The fundamental difference between a transcendent and an immanent conception of God was popularly expressed in the opposition between Islam's radical opposition to idolatry and the compulsive imagic vision of the Hindu sects. At one level, the conflict between Islam and Hindu religious ideas was quite similar to the previous contention between Vedic religion and Buddhism—translated in some cases into direct political conflict. But the underlying similarities of sociological features despite the doctrinal differences between the two religions are also quite striking.

Islam was in some ways as decentralized as Hindu religious society: its religious elite was not more united doctrinally or institutionally than the Brahmin stratum of Hinduism.[37] Politically, Islamic religious teaching marginalized the role of the state in a way quite similar to the Hindu caste order.[38] The fundamental similarity was that for both religious communities there was a "social constitution" ordained by religious authority, in the last instance by the power of God, taken as immutable. The task of political authority was not to modify but to protect it, because the state was not its creator in the first place. Political power had the responsibility of restoring that order if it was challenged or fell into disruption. Large groups of Hindus must have converted to Islam to produce the indigenous Muslim community, which remained bitterly divided for a long time sociologically between aristocratic "outsiders" and indigenous commoners, apart from the doctrinal divide between Sunnis and Shias. Broadly, the two communities stayed next to each other, practicing a form of benign indifference and reciprocal noninterference instead of all-out warfare through the agencies of the state.[39] Islamic states very quickly adopted positions of relative neutrality between differing religious communities and their claims, remarkably similar to the attitude of ancient Indian political rulers. Historical chronicles of military campaigns regularly show that armies were composed of soldiers taken from both religious communities, turning these conflicts mainly into contestations for power rather than religious warfare. Despite occasional rebukes and incitement from more radical clerical groups, Muslim rulers showed scant enthusiasm for using the power of the state toward large-scale conversion—often driving more aggressively devout intellectuals like Ziauddin Barani, the great chronicler of the Delhi sultanate, to despair.[40]

POLITICAL ARGUMENTS FOR ACCOMMODATION

As I have argued elsewhere,[41] two different responses emerged in medieval Indian Islam toward the principal question of relations with the Hindus. The response of *political* rulers was to claim the practical impossibility of conversion and more energetic application of strict Islamic law, as long as the Muslims, as Emperor Iltutmish remarked, were like "salt in food."[42] Energetic strategies for scrupulous application of Islamic law could be feasible only when Muslims were more numerous among the subjects, which could happen only if the efforts of religious leaders, the critics themselves, met with greater success. Rulers cleverly blamed the conservative religious elite for the imperfect state of affairs and shifted the responsibility to them. At times, advocates of accommodation would use scriptural authority in favor of their position by citing the verses in the Qur'an that described violence or pressure as inapplicable in the process of religious conversion.[43]

SUFI ARGUMENTS FOR ACCOMMODATION

A more radical argument for accommodation came from *religious* thinkers of popular Sufi orders, who achieved unprecedented influence in Indian religious life—eventually attracting devotion from numerous

Hindu followers as well.⁴⁴ Sufi traditions preached accommodation and started giving value to Hindu paths of devotion. But Sufi thinking was also diverse, with important and serious distinctions within it. From advice for toleration, Sufi orders often went over to a direct acceptance of the value of Hindu worship, especially the traditions of Krsnab-hakti.⁴⁵ Amir Khusrau, one of the earliest intellectuals to advocate a principled logic of accommodation of Hindu and Persianate religious and cultural forms said,⁴⁶

> O you who sneer at the idolatry of the Hindu /
> Learn also from him how worship is done.

The main Sufi orders retained their distinctly Islamic nature; but in cases like Kabir, accommodationist thinking gave rise to religious devotion which defied a denominational description. A major source of theological opposition between Islam and Hinduism turned on the question of the two images of God: transcendent and immanent. The Islamic argument that God was transcendent, a creator of the universe, who is simultaneously bigger than and beyond it, supported the injunction that no form should be used to represent him. In worship, human beings must recognize that he is unencompassable by human imagination. Opposed to this are the common Hindu notions that God is infinite, but the human mind is finite; and therefore, the human mind cannot realistically think it can have any understanding of God except through some finite representation. Also, God in creating the universe has left an intimation of his existence in everything. This is a massively difficult opposition to reconcile, or mediate with Islamic faith. But verses by Sufis surmounted this difficulty with effortless grace. Zaheen Shah Taji's ghazal melds these two ideas:

> Tha shart jis ki yad mein har shai ko bhulna
> Har shai ki yad se wahi yad a raha hai kya

"I forgot (turned away from) all things, because that was the condition for knowing Him. But now I find that the remembrance of every thing reminds me of Him."⁴⁷

Clearly, this incorporates beautifully the notion of a God immanent in everything into an Islamic reflection on the meaning of worshipfulness.[48] Sufi writers wrote the first narrative poems and made a crucial contribution to the formation of the Hindi language.[49] A medieval Bengali author wrote a long poem, *Nabībaṃśa* (The Family of the Prophet), in which the genealogy of the Prophet is extended beyond Adam into more unconventional pre-Adamic time. God, it maintains, created the world may times—at least nine times before Adam; and every time it was rescued and recreated by a new incarnation of God—the first nine of the ten *avataras* of the Hindu *daśāvatāra* myth. To the possible objection that adding Hindu myths to the conventional Muslim ones constitutes mixing illegitimate elements into the purity of the Islamic corpus, these narrators often answer that the purpose of the mythic stories was to proclaim the majesty of God. It does not diminish his majesty to suggest that he created the world many times, not once. It adds to our contemplation of his creative powers by adding to the sense of his majesty.[50]

At times, Sufi thinking went further. Kabir's famous poems often claimed, in God's own pretended words: "I am not in the temples, not in the mosque, not in the Kabaa, nor in Kailasa, where you are seeking me, my servant, I am near you/inside you/ in your grasp . . . You can find me in a moment's search"—by looking inside your heart.[51] Parallel to these developments in high religious thought, there emerged popular and folk traditions in some of the regions where the line of Islamic expansion in India came to a rest—Kashmir, Bengal, and the Deccan—where the cults of local Pirs and Babas fused the two religions and their iconographies and languages of worship.[52] Songs of the Bauls of Bengal, particularly by figures like Lālan Phakir and Hāsan Rājā, express a similar sensibility, completely merging the two languages of devotion.[53] Interestingly, the honorific designation "Baba" came to be applied equally to both Muslim and Hindu saints. Again, this evidence does not show that religious difference led to a mutual and eventually comprehensive destruction of all structures of justification, tending toward a Weberian form of disenchantment. Rather, it seems that the development of diverse adjacent religious sects produced generally the opposite result: they learned to coexist in a range of attitude from muted hostility to mutual respect. But there is one instance of a peculiar and unusual development in a somewhat later period—in the extraordinary culture of Akbar's royal court.

AN EXTRAORDINARY MOMENT IN HISTORY: MEDIEVAL DISENCHANTMENT? BADAYUNI'S PORTRAYAL OF AKBAR'S COURT

Badayuni's celebrated account of Akbar's court advances the interesting suggestion that intense rationalism began to destroy the grounds of religious belief itself. Badayuni, of course, was an intellectual of deeply conventional religiosity, unattracted to the unconventionalities of Indic Sufi traditions, and he shows the anxiety that Hinduism's absorptive capacity will dissolve the theological distinctiveness of Islam.[54] He wonders, for instance, about whether he acquires religious guilt by translating one of the *sargas* of the Mahabharata's sacrilegious tale at Akbar's insistence. He finds reassurance in the thought that God could not be blind to the workings of political power in the mundane world, and surely he would understand that Badayuni's labor in translating the loathsome and corrupt narrative, though he had to give it proper scholarly attention, was not because of his own intent, but of the compulsion of his station. So the relevant intention was not his scribal intentionality in attentive and serious translation but the emperor's far more serious and culpable intentionality in getting those ideas translated and rendered accessible and worthy of attention to a community of Muslims.[55]

The historical record of Akbar's court is quite well known and does not require any recounting. I want to note a strand of Badayuni's narrative that is usually ignored or rejected as an evidence of his spite against Abul Fazl and the emperor. Akbar's announcement of the Din-i-Ilahi is a famously interpretatively contentious subject.[56] Abul Fazl's account of Akbar's rule[57] and the brief record of the emperor's direct views on religious matters[58] are used for an understanding of the astonishing culture of debate in the imperial court, but that account had been dulled by a tiresomely repetitive anachronistic adulation.[59] By contrast, Badayuni's chronicle is mistrusted by secularist historians as marred by the bigotry of a conservative scholar.[60] But the special character of what happened in Akbar's times, particularly in the lighted circle of his presence, comes into relief more sharply precisely if we read Badayuni's generally disapproving and reproachful narration of the innovations in religious imagination. Both Badayuni and Abul Fazl provide an account of an initial period when Akbar ruled according to conventions of ordinary Muslim empires, followed by a stage of increasingly profound and searching religious questioning. Both chroniclers agree that initially he was primarily interested in variations of Islamic faith, but the Muslim clerics were so abusive to one another,[61] he found their squabbles offensive and decided to widen the circle of his quest, again, at first to neighboring faiths like Persian fire worship.[62] Eventually he invited Christians, and finally Jainas and Hindus into the most intense religious disputation. During his gradual change of opinion, he became drawn toward sun-worship — ritually important for the Parsees but philosophically justified by Hindu ideas — supplemented by distinctly secular arguments like the one that it was the source of all energy and all life. [63]He decided later to mutter the Gayatri mantra at sunrise. Surprisingly detailed accounts of the religious disputations have survived and show how fierce the debates between the different faiths were.[64] Ultimately, to Badayuni's deep disapproval, he decided to propagate what the chronicler regarded as a heretical sect that rejected the fundamental tenets of Islam. Din-i-Ilahi can be interpreted in different ways: it is often viewed as a contending religion that would have challenged and competed with Islam and conventional Hinduism, supported by the power of the state.[65] From most readings it appears more plausible to regard it as a comportment of refinement, rationality, and tolerance in a field of great religious diversity, a stance of selective admiration for elements of divergent religious paths. Akbar's own close associates sometimes did not see it this way. The emperor's preeminent general, Man Singh, Badayuni reports, refused to accept it, and allegedly told the emperor that he did not have to prove his loyalty the Mughal cause, which he had proven beyond any possible doubt in many military crises. If the emperor demanded, he would convert to Islam; but he could not follow a third line, because he acknowledged only two faiths — Hinduism and Islam.[66]

Badayuni seems to have been most disturbed by the spreading atmosphere of rationalist freethinking in the court. Leading figures in court circles showed their intellectual daring by making fun of the Prophet and engaged in a competition in holding irreligious opinions. Badayuni showed great perspicacity in noting what could be the stirrings of a profound shift in intellectual life—driving rationality to a point that comprehensively undermined the entire religious conception of life. Seen from a different angle, Badayuni's account shows the possibility of the crossing of a threshold from a religious to a completely immanent, exclusively humanist position. This was a more profound threat to religiosity than the very different threat to domesticity from deviant practices in Hindu sects—the *kapalikas*, the kaulas, and the *sahajiyas* paths. Deviant sects threatened the ideals of ordinary domesticity; unbelief threatened the entire conception of religion. However, this is a rare example of a tendency of intellectual religious disputes to cross over into a secular humanism. Jahangir, the next emperor, continued many of Akbar's political practices of accommodation, following the Mughal theory of rule, but did not follow the daring rationalist tendencies of his father's courtly associates.[67]

Probably a philosophically more accurate picture of the experimentation in Akbar's circle is presented in the *Dabistan-i-Mazahib*,[68] a text on religious diversity composed in the mid-seventeenth century. Its approach to the debates is fundamentally different from Badayuni's, but it records, from a different appraisive point of view, similar intellectual trends. At the end of its detailed account of the disputes between religious schools—which include Shias, Sunnis, Jews, Christians, and Hindus—the *Dabistan* presents the ideas of a "learned philosopher" who eventually makes a case for following Akbar's lead in religious matters. Religious groups and their prophets must be judged by two criteria, he suggests: first, whether their teachings conform to the tests of human reason; and secondly, whether in their lives the prophets or *avatāras* can be said to have lived entirely unblemished moral lives. He concludes that none of the moral ideals presented by Hinduism (Krsna, Rama), Christianity (Jesus), or Judaism (Moses) could pass the test of a pure life: it is possible to find faults with what they preached and practiced. All existing religious doctrines contained significant elements that could not be accepted by rationalist reasoning. From our angle of interest, the crucial point comes here: instead of taking an atheistic-skeptical turn and declaring all religious teachings are unreliable, it makes a different philosophical turn, suggesting that attractive elements should be extracted from all religious faiths and turned into a composite religious ideal of the kind Akbar recommended in his Din-i-Ilahi.[69] Remarkably, Akbar's solution to religious diversity moved away from a purely practical argument like the one advanced by Iltutmish. Rather, it grounded religious toleration in principles, instead of mere political prudence. Unlike the Sufis, however, who recommended forbearance toward all faiths, whose adherents should be allowed to practice their religions, this suggested something more—an eclectic combination of religious ideas and practices that cut across religious boundaries. It is one thing to suggest that Hindus and Muslims should live adjacently and practice their religions, quite another to say that they should absorb ideas and acts of worship from other faiths in an active religious life, and abandon elements which fail the test of reason.

The practice of the Sufis represented a different response to religious diversity—an attempt to refuse the temptation of rejecting the other faith and to accommodate the contending religion as another and equally estimable way to God. Just as the first move could lead to disenchantment of a kind, the second was the best guarantee of the comfortable survival and continuance of intense religious life. By preventing religious creeds from producing violence, accommodation removed the main cause of peoples' disillusionment with religious belief. Ultimately, despite the immense impact of modern intellectual currents, religion was never seriously undermined in India, because premodern Indians on neither side viewed it as a threat to social peace and a potent cause of destructive violence.

MODERNITY AND RELIGIOUS CHANGE: THE NINETEENTH CENTURY

In Indian history, the period equivalent to the historical phase that comprises the largest part of Taylor's analysis was the nineteenth century.

Weber's work simply advanced a powerfully plausible hypothesis about the process of disenchantment, proposing a contrast between the medieval and the modern responses to religion in a very long-term historical-sociological theory. Since that theory takes up a very large span of time as its unit of analysis, it is correct in producing the contrastive pictures of a religious premodernity and an increasingly disenchanted and irreligious modernity. It is also right in indicating that the fundamental intellectual shift that eventually results in this revolutionary transformation to the immanent frame is driven by the scientific revolution of the seventeenth century. The trouble with this historical sociology is that it is not historical enough. By highlighting the contrast, Weber's theory absolutizes the difference, and by not looking at the small changes that lead to the big change, it enhances the finality of the change and obscures the contingency of every step. Simply by telling the story with greater detail, *A Secular Age* provides us with a truer picture that restores the contingencies, the cross pressures, the near misses through which the big change occurred. Telling the story this way makes it possible to modify the epistemic character of the big change and its historical implications. Interestingly, some intellectual figures who suggest crucial intellectual innovations in this process are not atheistic deniers of God's existence but intellectuals of deep Christian faith, whose ideas nonetheless result in intellectual secularization in the long term. By telling a story in which contingencies are restored and the narrative teleology is correspondingly softened up, Taylor's account makes it possible to use the western European story in comparative historical analyses in a very different fashion. It shows how similar the Western story was for much of the time to the story of other cultures, and when it comes to the process of disenchantment, it is able to show several things about the use of the western European experience in the discourse of social theory.

1. It shows how a process that occurs in specific countries in western Europe is presented as a general trend covering the West (i.e., all of Europe and America).
2. It turns this exceptional turn in western European history into a precedent to be followed by the rest of the world.

This illicitly converts what was a regional development in world history into the first occurrence of an iron law. Taylor's account thus helps us form the opposite hypothesis—that what happened in the West was perhaps the exception, not the rule that every other society was to follow. By viewing Taylor's work in this fashion, we can strive to produce a global historical sociology that works in a way opposite to Weber's. Instead of regarding the exceptionalism of the Western story as a precedental narrative, the first instance which inaugurates a long chain of similar events that have not yet happened, it can help us turn it into a exception in the true sense—that is, a story different from others and unlikely to be followed identically elsewhere. So the "uniqueness" of the West remains a fact in both cases, but the historical implications are seen in the opposite manner. Looking at the resources of modern social theory this way, we can hypothesize that in the long history of religious life there are stages when interreligious conflict threatens to undermine the whole basis of religious life itself, when the observing popular audience might lose faith not in one but in all religions. But this is a *possibility*, not a necessity; given the complex architecture of historical conditions, these occasions might also pass without that possibility being taken in the direction of popular disenchantment. In the history of other cultures, therefore, it is more promising to look for stages and events of striking importance in their own narratives rather than turn the history of other cultures into an endless waiting for the recurrence of the history of Europe.[70]

The rise of Europe's colonial powers makes it possible to advance a dissemination argument of a quite different kind. To understand this argument, we should attend carefully to some features of the first, Weberian thesis. The general version of the Weberian argument does not use power as a crucial explanatory category. It views rationalization as a general feature of human thought, and therefore a kind of disenchantment produced by rationalization as a property inherent in all religious cultures.[71] It is in the nature of human thought to be "rationalizing" in Weber's sense, and we can therefore expect rationalization processes to occur in all religious traditions, quite independent of the intellectual influence or political domination of one over another. Our analysis till this point shows there is no clear warrant in the actual historical record for such a strong expectation of "rationalization" in human history.

But the *colonial* argument is different, and it draws its strength from a different source. The rise of modern structures in European societies—especially Holland, England, and France—represented by the intensive disciplinary political powers of the modern nation-state and coupled with the equally intensive productive powers of early capitalist economies, created unprecedented capacities of political and economic expansion for these societies, leading to the colonization of vast territories of the world. An argument favored by some Marxist and other radical historians suggested that although these societies might have had entirely independent trajectories of evolution before, colonial power ended such independent historical paths and brought them under the dominance of the societal logics that governed European modernity. Once within the grasp of European colonialism, all societies became a general theater for the unfolding of the specific logics of modern structures. This reading of history then suggests that after the nineteenth century, the history of modern Europe becomes the history of the world with a pattern of delays.

AMBIGUITIES OF COLONIAL POLICY TOWARD NATIVE RELIGION

A review of Indian history after its contact with European colonization shows both interesting similarities in detail and divergences in the overall pattern of evolution. The first thing that strikes us is the exaggeration and simplicity of the picture of colonialism in this theory of colonial modernity. It is true that European modernity affected societies in distant continents only through colonialism, but colonialism was a vast and internally complex enterprise; and it was by no means predetermined that European states, after the establishment of their imperial domains, would intend to replicate in their colonies all aspects of modern European life. European powers remained anxious about the cultural complexities of these societies and sought to exercise a form of political rule that studiedly avoided interference in cultural matters. In particular, European powers feared that religious faith had especially combustible potential; at least in the first period of colonization, British authorities often followed a deliberate policy of conspicuous noninterference in religious affairs. Colonial policy was thus often quite opposed to energetic efforts at Europeanization of these societies. Guided by the overriding ideas of orientalism, colonial power often encouraged a retraditionalization of these cultures rather than their forcible modernization.[72] Intellectual opinion among the literate elites remained divided about the real historical effect of European colonization. While thinkers like Gandhi saw it as a massive project of Westernization of Indian society, other equally influential interpreters of history, like Nehru, thought just the opposite—that colonialism was the primary obstacle to the *real* modernization of Indian society. Thus it is simply not historically accurate to think of the colonial period of Indian history as a massive attempt by British authorities to impose Western institutions on an unwilling Indian populace. The actual story of cultural response to colonialism was far more complex and interesting—combining strands of serious imposition of institutional forms, successful resistance by both Indian elites and subaltern populations, emulation by modernist groups—often thwarted by nervous colonial authorities. Two examples can show the complexity of colonial cultural initiatives.

The famous case of the abolition of sati—burning of widows with their deceased husbands among upper-caste Hindus in Bengal—in fact illustrates the complexity of colonial cultural change.[73] It is true that without the existence of a Western colonial state, such reform would have been impossible. Yet the reform was not in the first place proposed by colonial authorities but by modernist Bengali elites.[74] The government agreed to pass the legislation with some residual anxiety about its potential effects.[75] Laws effecting reform of Hindu society—like widow remarriage, the age of consent, and so on—were all similar initiatives, initiated by Hindu elites and sanctioned by an initially indifferent or reluctant colonial administration. The second case was the conversion of Indian subjects to Christianity. Initially, enthusiastic missionaries started preparations for large-scale conversion of natives to the "true religion." Not surprisingly, they faced strong intellectual opposition from the modernist Hindu elite, who showed eagerness to adopt rationalistic thought but not the Christian religion. Hindu reformers like Ram Mohan Roy indeed mocked Christians for their belief in ideas like "the Immaculate Conception" despite claims to a strict rationality.[76] His successors, among them Bankimchandra Chatterjee, maintained that a reformed version of Hinduism, purged mercilessly of supernatural and irrational ideas, was a better vehicle for a rationalist ethical life than Christian doctrine.[77] But more surprisingly, colonial political officials themselves obstructed zealous missionary efforts at large-scale conversion and refused to supplement their doctrinal preaching by the material force of the state.[78] After the rebellion of 1857, when India was turned into a Crown Colony, the imperial government hurried to assure its subjects of noninterference in matters of religious belief. The colonial state and its institutions were not simple instruments of transference of European secularity to its colonial domains.

RELIGION IN BENGALI MODERNITY

In the rest of this chapter, I shall try to provide an account of complex religious changes that happened in Bengal, the first part of the subcontinent to experience the impact of colonialism and Western intellectual culture. There is no attendant claim that this is *representative* of what occurred in other parts of India, only that this is an interesting enough trajectory to understand the evolving history of secularity.

Not colonial state power, but Western education began to produce the most significant cultural alterations in Bengali society. After the establishment of the Hindu College in 1817, the Bengali elite were affected by Western-style syllabi delivered in the English language. Initiation of Western education immediately produced a deep ferment of ideas, and three types of responses to Western education could be discerned in its very early phase. One early trend, following a charismatic Eurasian lecturer, Derozio, argued passionately in favor of acceptance of Western-style rationalism and its corollaries—rejection of conventional religious faiths (in their case, primarily the Hindu faith), eating forbidden food (beef), and adopting European social habits.[79]

Ranged against them on the other side—entirely hostile to absorption of rationalist Western ideas—were large segments of Hindu conservative opinion who believed that the collapse of their ancestral religion would mean a cultural erasure of their identity as a people. But a significant section responded with greater discrimination and intellectual finesse, selectively incorporating elements of the new Western intellectual tradition and reforming the conventional Hindu religious faith. Ram Mohan Roy, one of the major figures of this era, represented this third, more eclectic, and intellectually innovative trend. Two of these tendencies of new thinking certainly introduced highly significant changes in Hindu religious ideas. Of the three, the first, radical rationalism, evinced propensities toward what could eventually turn into general disenchantment. Subjecting traditional Hindu beliefs—about the nature of God, the order of society, the pattern of religious observances—to a pitiless critique, many of these radicals became entirely unmoored from religious ideas. Some were so utterly alienated from Hindu ideas that they embraced Christianity. An interesting example of this trend was the life of the great poet Michael Madhusudan Dutt, the iconoclastic author of the *Meghnādbadhkāvya*, which completely upturned the narrative values of the *Rāmāyana* by turning Rāvana into the hero of his epic.[80]

THE HISTORIC SIGNIFICANCE OF BRAHMO REFORMS

Brahmos, Ram Mohan's intellectual successors, followed a different but equally transformative line of thinking regarding the Hindu faith. Rejecting a great deal of its past textual tradition, they ignored the two conventional Hindu theologies in Bengal[81] and shaped an entirely new, modernist version of Hinduism—eventually questioning the social strictures of the caste system.[82] Their reformation of Hindu worship was striking in every sense: instead of individual prayer, they introduced a form of collective, communal worship inside buildings that were farthest removed in their interior character from conventional Hindu temples. These had no idols, no riotously chaotic ceremonials, no priestly intermediaries. In its observances, Brahmo religion owed more to the congregational forms of Protestantism than to conventional Hindu piety. In other ways, too, Brahmo innovations in religious life transformed intellectual habits in Bengal. Their journal, the revolutionary *Tattvabodhinā Patrikā*, began with an introductory notice that was an exemplary presentation of ideas of what Taylor has called "providential deism," much indebted to the ideas of the Scottish Enlightenment.[83] The Brahmos' acceptance of rationalism did not stop at a reformation of ideas internal to religious life but spilled over into an enthusiastic reception of modern science.[84] J. C. Bose, the Cambridge scientist, became a pioneer in scientific experimentation and philosophical thinking.[85] Curiously, Bose also illustrated a highly significant feature of this great intellectual transformation. As in early modern Europe, many modern Bengali intellectuals embraced an immanent frame and accepted entirely the scientific picture of the universe, but did not find that incompatible with an intense belief in the distant God. Providential deism in fact made this philosophically easy to accomplish. The majesty of God's creation, the infinity of his powers, was revealed in the infiniteness of the natural universe and its structure of harmonious complexity. For them that was a much clearer evidence of his omnipotence than the capricious use of supernatural capacity—as the Hindu traditionalists believed.[86] God became increasingly powerful and increasingly distant from the world in this worldview, with the impossibly intricate laws of nature the legible trace of his presence. This left open the path to enthusiastic scientific enquiry and acceptance of scientific thinking as something that was not merely compatible with theism, but in fact in a sense a part of the search for God, of knowing God's mind by knowing what he made.

Interestingly, although the actual adherents of Brahmo religion remained confined to a small highly sophisticated elite, the influence of this modernist mode of religious faith gradually dominated Bengali intellectual life.[87] Two remarkable examples, Bankim Chandra Chatterjee, the novelist and writer, and Bhudev Mukhopadhyay, the first major social theorist of modern Bengal, were sharply critical of the Brahmos but entirely accepted deist ideas. Bankim remarked against authors who wanted God to constantly interfere in human affairs—in their favor—that God did not run the universe the way a coachman drove his coach on Calcutta streets.[88] Bhudev claimed that the Hindu was the greatest believer in casual rules of the universe, as the doctrine of transmigration of souls and rebirth simply showed that nothing, including birth in a particular family, happened by chance, without a proper operation of causality.[89] Birth was always just deserts for acts done in a previous birth, which were cognitively inaccessible to humans but known to their creator.[90] Despite their quarrels about other matters, the conception of God—an infinitely distant and infinitely powerful being—was strikingly similar between these contending strands of modern Hindu thinking. This was one powerful trajectory of intellectual change affecting Bengali society. Eventually, the successors to this tradition of radicalizing Brahmo thinking evolved into political rationalisms of varying kinds; it is hardly surprising that from the 1940s a large section of Brahmo intellectuals were attracted to Marxism and contributed significantly to a highly sophisticated Marxist tradition in Bengal. In this segment alone, the logic begun in Ram Mohan Roy went all the way to a militant revolutionary form of the immanent frame and radical disenchantment. Communist intellectuals in the 1940s and 1950s would scrupulously avoid any connection with carnivalesque forms of popular religious ceremony like the Durga Pūjā, and they practiced a robust, passionately extreme form of fundamentalist secularism. It was only in them that the logic of intellectual evolution described in Weber came to be fully realized. Not surprisingly, they could be regarded by less radical intellectuals as exceptionally "Westernized."[91]

However, this line of evolution was exceptional and was represented by a small group of radical intellectuals. Educated Bengalis generally did not accept such comprehensive rejection of religious life. They remained comfortable with one of two different resolutions to the challenge of the immanent frame. The first, illustrated by Rabindranath Tagore, was an acceptance of a scientific picture of the world (though he had grave misgivings about the effects of modern technology) that was reconciled with a deep faith in a deist God whose presence is worshipped primarily through artistic epiphany.[92] The second consisted in a skillful deployment of practical inconsistency that separated two spheres of their lives—a sphere of rationalist action in the office, in material life, and in research, and a sphere containing the domestic, the emotional, and the religious—viewing them as two disconnected circles of appropriate forms of conduct. Individuals who acted impeccably according to rules of the immanent frame in one could simply drop them as they crossed the boundary into the sacred and could happily practice the most traditional forms of devotion in the domestic *pūjā* ceremony.[93] A statistically larger number of educated Bengalis functioned in the second way of comfortable inconsistency rather than the first. The Brahmo intervention in Bengali culture is highly significant for a comparative analysis, as it constitutes a historical point similar to early modern Europe, where, in Taylor's story, a small but highly energetic elite (1) conceived of an entirely new way of being in the world and (2) were able to refashion the social imaginary of the whole society. This process of imposing the new imagination was a complex process of persuasion by dazzling intellectual performances, silent coercion by new institutional forms, and the insistent disciplinary shaping of subjectivities. Akeel Bilgrami's essay, though focused on Gandhi, brings an essential element into the picture by demonstrating that this refashioning of social imaginaries did not occur without deep contestation by two groups of dissenters. Some opposed this change from the standpoint of a traditional Christian social imaginary; but others—like the Diggers and the Babouvians—desired a different constellation of modernity itself.[94]

In early colonial Bengal, the course of intellectual history was fundamentally different from comparable stages in modern Europe. The Brahmo form of modernized religion—accepting science, a distant hidden God who wrote his thoughts in the laws of nature, viewing society as a space of association and mutual benefit, valorizing commerce, separation of a private sphere—were the ideas of a small elite. Eventually, the Brahmos were victims of the self-segregating tendency of social elites. Eliteness is a strangely contradictory quality of being leaders of ordinary people and being separate from them at the same time. Elites must remain sufficiently connected to their followers to be able to fashion them but sufficiently distinguished to maintain their superiority and distinction and the claim to lead. But the radical intellectual trajectory that moved from Brahmo deism into the secular atheism of the leftists became vanguardist and was so advanced that it did not notice when it lost contact with the masses behind them.⁹⁵

DEBATES WITHIN MODERN RELIGION

Not surprisingly, the Brahmo intellectual movement, became more internally diverse as it gathered momentum, giving rise to intense controversies about the direction it should take.⁹⁶ Arguments of strictly modernist belief tended in some cases to slide irresistibly toward atheist, or at least agnostic, conclusions. In the case of most Brahmos it stopped short of atheism. Constant invocation of the Sanskrit adage "sa jīvati mano yasya mananena hi jīvati" ("only that person could be said to live, whose mind lives by [critical] reflection"; that is, live your life reflexively) by preachers like Sibnath Sastri fatally undermined ordinary Hindu ritualism. But gradually some intellectuals felt an absence of three elements essential to religious life. The first absence was of enthusiasm. Later Brahmo figures like Keshub Chandra Sen thought that their faith was rationalistically desiccated, without any room for passionate attachment to either God or the religious community. Secondly, in a related way, the emphasis on trusting one's own reason led to an isolationist atomism in Brahmos that went with their embrace of a Western-style social individualism. Instead of transforming the rest of the society by their example, they turned others against them. Finally, the evolution of forms in the main Brahmo Samaj disavowed all connection to the great repertoire of religious forms in indigenous Indian culture and cut themselves off from the deep resources of community-making in their own history. Brahmo Samaj demanded a disdainful alienation from indigenous culture, and it was not without reason that Brahmos were seen as an artificially and slavishly Westernized subculture of Bengali society, politically subordinated, servile to colonial power, and consequently rewarded by their masters with easily manipulable prosperity.⁹⁷ Each element of the high Brahmo self-image could be turned into its degraded double in the distorting mirrors of colonial culture—rationalism as imitation of the British,⁹⁸ self-reliance as malicious selfishness, affluence as just deserts for commercial enterprise viewed as economic prizes for political servility.⁹⁹

The later history of the Brahmo movement was marked by intense conflict on these themes. Sen initially came to dominate the Brahmo intellectual scene with Debendranath Tagore and Sibnath Sastri, to subsequently make a theatrical break with the mainstream. His followers incorporated into Brahmo religion an essential element of passionate devotion, a sense of the festive, and even practiced traditional forms of singing like *kīrtan*; and some wondered if Sen was an *avatāra*. His search for the convivial in his own religious traditions took him to a revival of musical and worship forms of Bengali Vaisnavism—an expressive grammar easily intelligible to ordinary lower-class Bengalis. Former friends in the main Brahmo movement watched with sullen disapproval as, in their judgment, he got swept away by torrents of devotional enthusiasm from the narrow path of rationalist solemnity of Brahmo worship. This showed that even among the new devotees of Western knowledge and rationalistic reform there was both a sense of anxiety and a sense of loss—particularly on the related problems of leaving behind their own cultural traditions and alienating themselves from the masses into typical elite isolation. It is remarkable how even a movement as self-consciously rationalistic as Brahmo Samaj slowly fell back into more conventional Hindu practices—in matters of observance of caste, forms of worship, and core religious beliefs. Unlike the religious elites of modern Europe, crucially, they could not reshape the rest of the society in the image of their own ideals. Yet it would be deeply misleading to suggest that newer forms of Hinduism did not absorb anything from Brahmo thinking and, indirectly, from Western contact. The elements Taylor describes in the modern social imaginaries were taken up, absorbed, and at times modified selectively to suit their local historical purposes. Overall, however, these selective changes altered Bengali society seriously—but not into an image of the secular societies of modern Europe.

REASSERTION OF TRADITIONAL RELIGIOSITY

Keshub Chandra Sen, in his wide-ranging religious quest, developed an intimate exchange of ideas with Ramakrishna Paramhansa—a fascinating figure in the complex story of modern Bengali religiosity. Illiterate in modern terms, he came from a village to work as a priest in a temple founded by a rich Calcutta zamindar family, and for a long time, he acted single-handedly as a powerful foil to the rationalist impulses of Brahmo religious reform. He professed to do his religion in every way that educated Brahmos execrated. Ramakrishna flaunted his lack of formal education, constantly baited highly educated people on their claim to superior ethical knowledge. Usually through a Socratic dialogue he revealed their own shallow ethical understanding to themselves, often forcing them to a surprising surrender.[100] He openly claimed to talk to Kali, his deity, went into trances, showed a childlike curiosity about everything, including modern science, and eventually completely disarmed some of the most formidable intellects of Calcutta. His preeminent disciple, Vivekananda, again shaped an extremely interesting form of religiosity—only partly drawing on Ramakrishna's folkish religion, supplementing it with generous borrowings from the high Hindu traditions of Advaita and the Upanisads.[101]

Other Hindu intellectuals made distinctive attempts to resist secular disenchantment. Bhudev Mukhopadhyay provided a powerful, highly consistent, two-sided argument: the first part was an insightful and searching attack on aspects of Western modernity, and the second offered a reasoned defense of Hindu customs and rituals (*ācāra*).[102] Bhudev inaugurated a powerful and subtle style of argument that would later become widely popular among Indian critics of the West. Western education imparts to modernist elites a readiness to believe the worst about others: particularly their fellow Bengalis who did not have modern education.[103] He selected an extreme and provocative example to illustrate his criticism. Modernist elites deride Hindu rituals of worship of forefathers: they think that believers think that if they do not sacrifice to their ancestors, evil spirits will wring their necks at night. In fact, the underlying logic of the ritual, explained Bhudev, was subtle and gracious. Ancestor worship was a ceremony of intergenerational gratitude. Human beings, in Bhudev's philosophical anthropology, are the most vulnerable of animals. Tigers take a year to learn to hunt and become full adults of their species. Humans are born and remain helpless for an inordinately long time. If we consider how we came into the world, in a state of utter vulnerability, and how we were received, as if the whole world was waiting for our arrival, we would feel a spontaneous sense of gratitude. If we are thoughtful, we will recognize that we are always in debt to our forefathers, who came before us and prepared the world for our habitation by creating a civilized universe we can inherit and continue. Debts have to be repaid, but this is a debt that is impossible to repay, because by the time we are adults and are able to pay our debt, those we are indebted to have passed away. The only way we can repay the debt of our birth—*pitṛ-ṛṇa*—is by doing the same thing for later generations, leaving them a world undegraded compared with one in which we were born. Western educated modernists do not appreciate this because they are unrestrained egotists and think they are historical atoms without obligation to anyone before or after. But they also do not understand the logic of Hindu ritual and condemn people who are really more subtle and thoughtful as less intelligent than themselves. Modernist elites are both arrogant and stupid: they are unable to learn. Western education and social privilege fortifies their ignorance.[104]

This is a single example, from many spirited intellectual defenses of religious tradition—a part of a massive pushback from critics of Western modernity. The culture of nineteenth-century Bengal resounds with this murmur of dissent against surrender to rationalist secularity. The remarkable features of the narrative of Bengali religious reform were that at the initial stage, the introduction of Western ideas produced something like what Taylor calls a "nova effect"—an extraordinary eruption of new forms of religious thinking, moving in different, often contradictory, directions. Some of these certainly went in the direction of a specific use of the immanent frame that produced exclusive humanism, exemplified primarily by the secular Brahmos and the Marxists. Other strands of experimentation did not abandon their commitment to religion but changed its character. At times, the new religious forms were more intense than traditional ones and demanded much deeper commitment to their ethical principles. This certainly changed the character of religious life in Bengal, but equally certainly it did not undermine religion in general. Finally, Ramakrishna represented something more fundamental—a forceful counterattack from traditional religion, which refused to be shamed by rationalistic attacks but devised powerful counterarguments. Transformations in the nineteenth century show a culture of deep religious questioning and energetic experimentation, but certainly not a decline of religious life. Had religious reform not occurred through the Brahmo intervention and associated quests for a new kind of religious thought, conventional ritualistic Hindu religion might have suffered a terminal decline. The ingenuity of thinkers like Ram Mohan Roy, Bankimchandra Chattopadhyay, Debendranath Tagore, Vivekananda, and Rabindranath Tagore ensured that versions of Hinduism that could reconcile rationalistic beliefs about the immanent frame and belief in transcendence became available to increasingly educated generations of Bengali Hindus—exactly what Taylor argued against the teleological visions of Weberian sociology. Rationalistic forms of thought should be thought of at two levels: at one level they are a *repertoire*, a tool kit for reasoning; at another level they are a specific set of distinctive theoretical *doctrines*. Use of rationalistic techniques as a repertoire can produce doctrines of diverse kinds, often quite different from ideas characteristic of the European Enlightenment. Nineteenth-century Bengal saw an enthusiastic absorption of this repertoire, which was then utilized to fashion doctrines quite different from the "subtraction stories" of European disenchantment. Indeed, large segments of the modern Bengali intelligentsia mourned the possible loss of the enchanted from their lives and devised ingenious ways of retaining its charming colors around the white circle of rational beliefs.[105] Only a small segment of radicals allowed their faith in reason to lead them to an entirely disenchanted Godless world.

STRANDS AGAINST INDIVIDUALISM

In selective absorption of the various elements of modernity, some segments of Bengali society responded enthusiastically to the opportunities of capitalist commerce. There was more general enthusiasm for the development of a public sphere and the growth of a new kind of nationalist political solidarity. Bengali intellectuals, including the most militant modernists, often condemned European modernity as egotistic, materialist, unrestrained, and prone to collective violence. Bhudev Mukhopdhayay produced the first systematic and forceful critique of European modernity, with a powerful message that Indians should not learn anything from them except modern science and political economy.[106] Bankimchandra rejected what he saw as excessive individualism in utilitarian doctrines, and eventually also in positivism, though he was initially drawn to both.[107] After an initial phase of anti-individualistic criticism, Bengali political thinking turned decisively toward socialist radicalism. Bengali Marxists, while adopting a radical secular atheism, continued the critique of individualism of the earlier generations.

There could be, in this sense, an interesting latent connection underlying different parts of modern Bengali culture. At one level, communist secularists were entirely opposed to and separated from the ordinary Bengali worshipper of Vaisnava and Sakta deities. Ordinary people were immersed in a religious world of constant domestic worship of scores of small divinities—from deities of snakebites, smallpox, children's welfare, domestic prosperity, education, and music to the great autumn festival of Durga, the goddess of deliverance from evil.[108] Marxist intellectuals treated such superstition with appropriate disdain and professed a crusading belief in science. But on another level, there were deep underlying similarities that both sides denied. Both these trends of thought were deeply hostile to the ideal of a society of the associational order of mutual benefit, or unrestrained bourgeois individualism, of an atomistic interpretation of modern liberty. Radicals denounced it as a structure of capitalist values; the popular masses viewed it as the unnatural selfishness of Western-educated elites. The radicals opposed this order in the name of an imagined collective of the future; the ordinary religious devotee in the name of a great collective tradition of the past. Both rejected an unconditional embrace of the package of moral values of Western modernity. The great religious debates of the nineteenth century had a double and somewhat contradictory effect viewed from a Weberian perspective. On the one side, they caused an acceptance of an immanent order across most sections of society; but at the same time Bengal's nineteenth-century discourses contained and rolled back "the expanding universe of unbelief."[109]

As a result, the great question at the heart of Taylor's narrative, "How is it that five centuries ago it was common to believe in God, and it is equally common now not to believe in him?," remains inapplicable to the Bengali and, I presume, also the Indian case. For the simple reason that the second clause is factually inappropriate: in the Indian cultural world, it is simply not common not to believe in God.

RELIGION TODAY

Since the time of Rabindranath Tagore an immense shift toward a qualified disenchantment can be observed in Bengali literature. In Tagore's poetry and song cycles there was an intense presence of a feeling of high artistic devotion.[110] Tagore's poetry is inconceivable without a deep sense of a divine presence in the universe, and art arose in epiphanic wonder at its harmony. From the 1950s Bengali poetry showed a sudden death of God. Poetic creation flourished, but it was left spiritually desolate by this disappearance: its primary themes were mundane suffering and social injustice.[111] In nineteenth-century fiction, religion was present on every page. Figures like *kāpālikas* constantly appeared in Bankim's novels, *baāuls* and *bairagīs* in Tagore's stories and plays; but by the time of Saratchandra Chattopadhyay, a celebrated writer of social novels, these characters had literally died out—totally incongruous in a literature that swung between the melancholy of degradation and the exhilaration of imminent revolution.

THE FESTIVE AND THE CONVIVIAL: THE RETURN OF THE COLLECTIVE IN BENGALI CULTURE

It could be objected that this reading of what Bengalis think is prejudiced toward high intellectualism, that my picture assumes, which it does, that a people necessarily think the way their intellectuals do, a typical intellectualist error. But I believe a decisive rejection of the package of European modernity could be found in social practices as well in intellectual doctrines. Social practice is an infinite field; I shall illustrate my case by the single but significant instance of the autumnal festival of Durga Pūjā. Interestingly, the mass audience that adoringly read the novels of Saratchandra and the communist poets lived in a world full of vibrant everyday religiosity, particularly exemplified by the festivals of Durga Pūjā. It causes little surprise that the poor youth who supply the cadres for the Communist Party rallies also collect subscriptions for the neighborhood's seasonal *pūjās*.

Critics of modern individualism saw it as impoverishing the character and content of *collective* life. Rabindranath Tagore wrote an interesting essay on the necessity of festivals—*Utsav*—for a vivid life of society. A society requires periodic reminders of interdependence and solidarity among its members, and festivals (*utsav* in Bengali) provide that utterly necessary representation of a community to itself.[112] Tagore wrote an elaborate reflection on the nature of the festive. The life of work, of the everyday, is driven by interest: it does not allow people to come together; interest drives them apart. The festival is the inversion of this everyday condition: it is the upside-down time in which people are united by love, not separated by self-interest. The time most appropriate for the festive is the night, because the day is the time for work and the night is for togetherness.[113] "The night is the special time of the festive."[114] The Durga Pūjā functions exactly like that in modern Bengali culture and has undergone a fascinating historical evolution since the coming of colonial wealth in Calcutta, the imperial metropolis.

The Durga Pūjā was a long-standing medieval festival, originally performed in village temples.[115] With the establishment of Calcutta as the imperial capital and the irresistible rise of the class of colonial landlords, the festival was brought to the city and transformed into a predominantly urban spectacle. Conventional village worship was not spectacular in the modern sense: the idols were highly conventionalized images, crafted from conventional materials, worshipped in the precincts of old temples. The migration of the goddess to the colonial city transformed the nature of the celebration. In Calcutta the Durga Pūjā was transmuted into a real spectacle of wealth, pomp, and power. Initially these were called *bāro-yāri pūjās*,[116] during which primarily the family of a wealthy landlord and his associates in Calcutta's elite society enjoyed a social gathering. But these ceremonials did have a more public side as well. The pageantry of the occasions and the competitive spending between rival zamindar families on music, decorations, and feasts were a spectacle meant for others—to measure their organizers' wealth and munificence. Unlike traditional village society, wealth in Calcutta came out of the secrecy of careful hoarding and became a source of conspicuous display. On one day, usually, the ceremonies organized a *kāngalī bhojan*—a feast for the destitute. For one day poor neighbors of wealthy magnates got a brief glimpse of their wealth and received a sumptuous meal, a fleeting break from their usually indigent life.[117] But somewhat like the transformation of royal spectacles of power in Europe that changed from a show of the personal wealth of the monarch to a pageant for the country, the *pjā* ceremonial in time subtly but decisively changed its significance. By the middle of the twentieth century, after the formal abolition of zamindari, there was also a change in the city of Calcutta. From a village studded with mansions of the wealthy, it turned into a sprawling city dominated by its modern middle class comprising the entire range from affluent managerial professionals to impecunious clerks who nevertheless shared a proud culture of the *bhadralok*. They stamped their character on the city and its festivals decisively; the Durga Pūjā shifted from a show of ostentatious private wealth to a collective self-adoration of the *pāḍā* (the neighborhood). Earlier *pūjās* were financed by single families, others were guests, spectators, and bystanders. Later, the *pūjās* became genuinely collective affairs funded not by personal opulence of the zamindars but by subscriptions from all middle-class householders. All households therefore had a collective sense of ownership over the festival. It was a *public* spectacle in a peculiar sense: first, public in the sense that the idol was not inside a family house but in a public space, turned toward the outside for a spectatorial view of its artistic qualities; it was also public in the sense of being the *common* festival of the *pāḍā*. All rivalries between families and frequent feuds among factions were supposed to be left aside as the spectacle assumed the characteristics of the carnival in Mikhail Bakhtin's sense.[118] It represented an exceptional time when what happened in the ordinary time of the whole year was set aside, and special things happened: a high time when all that was valuable about the community was put on exhibition. It was an occasion on which the *pāḍā* worshipped itself—in a strongly Durkheimian sense—an extraordinary time of exceptional solidarity against the selfish, individualistic pulls of quotidian existence. The *pūjā* was also a reminder of what a society should be when it transiently imitated its ideal self.

Observers suggest that since the 1980s the Durga Pūjā seems to have entered into a new stage. Democratic politics after independence was given a particularly sharp participatory edge by leftist parties who specially mobilized the urban poor and demanded that they share these common festivals with the middle classes of urban neighborhoods. Under political pressure, eventually, the middle classes reluctantly allowed them into these festival committees, turning these into more crowded, less prim, more inclusive, but also more fractious *pāḍā* organizations, which, under altered circumstances, have to show similar strategies of producing temporary solidarity and class truce. Ordinary everyday conflicts between the middle classes and the poor over land, water, electricity, sanitation, crowding, noise, and political affiliations have to be muted if the annual spectacle of *pāḍā* solidarity is to be presented to the world, representing the ideal image of the harmonious collective.

In the last decades the Durga Pūjā has also acquired some artistic characteristics highly relevant to our investigation of the present as history. Recently, the Pūjā festivals have become stages for exhibitions of a local, intrinsically Bengali, art of making the *pandals* (large marquees) into extraordinarily fanciful shapes. Local artisans who earlier made the common standardized *pandals* for marriages and festivals—a bamboo structure covered by red and white cotton sheets to announce its festive character—have in the last decades morphed into architect-artists of the most amazing imitations of the exotic—ancient temples, modern buildings, the White House—answering the most extravagant and quixotic impulses of the local imagination. They can materialize into a transient reality any conceivable architectural shape. They also create through the combination of these bamboo fabrications and ingenious lighting, which, incidentally, the technicians learned from the technical stagecraft of the vibrant Bengali theatre, a truly unreal city of dreams.

After nightfall, when a kindly darkness covers the filth and chaos of Calcutta's grimy streets and these illuminated shapes dominate the field of vision, the fetid disorder of this metropolis of poverty turns into a dreamland, a transient illuminated paradise, for five days. Bengalis, who have suffered from steep economic decline since independence and bristle at the derision of both outsiders and insiders at the decline of their once preeminent culture, can engage in a collective celebration of themselves—because the *pandals* and the great creativity on display are transient but true. What the local worship does to the *pāḍā*, the festival as a whole does to the self-image of the entire city. For five days, all classes in the city get a taste of an unreal, temporary, unreliable paradise—a land of visual poetry—undeniably real for that week, destined to vanish at its end.

The forms of religiosity of the crowds are historically interesting and paradoxical. Few among the thousands tramping through the marquees exhibit the conventional comportment of the Hindu devotee: there is hardly any space to bend and bow, to do even the most perfunctory *pranām* to the idol. It is a vast river of people out to have fun—through dress, food, visual spectacle. This is undoubtedly different from conventional forms of worship, what the Bengali term *pūjā*—both noun and verb—meant even in the mid-1950s. The verb has faded, only the noun has remained, but with a meaning and material existence that is vastly expanded with the immensely powerful use of the whole range of modern technologies. The Hindu *pūjā* is not resistant to technology; it is amazingly adaptive. Every single technological innovation is ingeniously modified to serve a new use for this constantly self-renewing religion. The forces of modernity—the technology of lights, sounds, and materials; the power of democratic change; the decline of a supplicating abjection to the terrifying forms of the divine; a new comportment of self-affirmation reflected in the fact that young people see the idols as artistic objects rather than images charged by a divine force— are all at work in the modern festival. All these are secular or at least secularizing forces, yet their effect is not a decline of religion but its transformation into something that is a powerful modern vision. "Religion" is as undeniably visible in the streets of Calcutta in the twenty-first century as in the 1950s; yet in another sense the culture of the city is distinctly less religious by traditional definition. What is the sense of "the religious" in this description? Is one form of "the religious" less historically true than another? Is there anything more to historical truth than the indelible existence of a social fact? Why must a historical fact in an Indian city conform to another historical fact plucked from the distant history of modern Europe or seem somehow historically diminished and less real?

RELIGIOUS AND SECULAR TRANSCENDENCE

Taylor's rich reflections about the value that religion brings to human life end with an analysis of contemporary trends in the West for seeking a sense of fullness. Modern Indian life suggests undetected connections between traditional and modern religion—a religion without conventional religiosity. It appears that traditional religion—both the singular, intense, individual prayer and the riotous, popular festival—had a similar purpose—to seek transcendence. It was driven by a dissatisfaction with the everyday, with what human effort had achieved. At times, these produced strange forms of solidarity—for instance, during long pilgrimages when people walked hundreds of miles in the company of strangers suddenly brought together into a strange intimacy of fellow seekers or in carnivalesque gatherings in front of temples or on the hajj. These were all carefully arranged, widely understood, and deeply felt escapes from the monotonous degradation of everyday life. The meaning of "transcendence" has remained the same in the more secular carnivals of modern India. Secular people, it appears, need and desire transcendence as intensely as the devout. They seek it in art, in music, and in festivals that create an uncanny combination of the various registers of transcendence—in a promiscuous alliance of all forms of creativity, an indescribable secularized religious spectacle. It is impossible to deny that the Pūjā is secularized in some ways and equally impossible to deny that it remains a religious festival.

Is this a deferral or a denial of secularity? Is it merely that the trajectory of the European modern is simply lying in wait sometime in the future for Indian history? Is there "a secular age" outside the Western world? It is hard to tell, but it would be good for the sake of intellectual hygiene to train ourselves not to speak about the facts of one history always through the language of another.

NOTES

1. Casanova suggests that something similar to this "theoreticized" story happened in certain Protestant societies but definitely not in parts of Europe dominated by Catholic faith; Rajeev Bhargava, ed., *Secularism and Its Critics* (Oxford: Oxford University Press, 2005).
2. This will interestingly deprive the idea of the future of its defining quality of indeterminateness.
3. Max Weber, Hans Heinrich Gerth, and Don Martindale, *Religion of India* (New York: Free Press, 1962). For criticisms of Weber's analysis of India, see Romila Thapar, *Durkheim and Weber on Theories Relating to Pre-colonial India*, Sociological Theories: Race and Colonialism (Paris: UNESCO, 1980).
4. A similar debate regarding the medieval period in Indian history took place in the 1980s: see Harbans Mukhia, "Was There Feudalism in Indian History?," *Journal of Peasant Studies* 8, no. 3 (1981): 273–310.
5. Charles Taylor, *A Secular Age* (Cambridge: Belknap, 2007), 25–89.
6. In Indian historical research, a vibrant debate has erupted on the question "Is there a modernity before colonial modernity?" And if so, how do we see the relation between these two constellations of the modern? Sheldon Pollock, Sanjay Subrahmaniam, V. Narayana Rao, and David Shulman have contributed primarily to this new development.
7. Bhargava, *Secularism*.
8. Because diversity does not necessarily lead to conflict. An elementary move required for this discussion is a conception of a long continuum, on one side of which is conflict, and at the other end is Sufi tolerance, which does not merely accommodate others but values diversity as an enhancement of its own self. But in the middle there are many possible states of affairs—a less than Sufi tolerance that treats the others' practices with indifference, because they are basically similar; a mild disapproval of the others that treats them with strategies of distance; repugnance for others that still tolerates their ways; deep hostility that does not explode into conflict. On close inspection, we shall find examples of all such states in India's long religious history.
9. This sounds innocuous and possible, but on closer inspection, societies that appear homogeneous at first sight might turn out to contain internal diversity with the potential for causing considerable irritation. This is not merely true of the notorious case of Hinduism, which many scholars believe was misconceived

as a singular religion by primarily modern Western observers; it is also true of the great internal divide in Islam between Shia and Sunni versions of faith. For Hinduism, see H. Stietencron, "Hinduism," in *Hinduism Reconsidered*, ed. Gunter-Dietz Sondteimer and Hermann Kulke (Delhi: Manohar, 2001); and David Lorenzen, "Who Invented Hinduism?," *Comparative Studies in Society and History*, 41, no. 4 (1999): 630–659.

10. There is a lot of overlap between this essay and the analysis in my paper "Modernity, State, and Toleration in Indian History: Exploring Accommodations and Partitions," in *Boundaries of Toleration*, ed. Alfred Stepan and Charles Taylor (New York: Columbia University Press, 2014).

11. From the Sanskrit *nāsti*—does not exist.

12. From the corresponding antonym *asti*—does exist.

13. This is the proverbial version of Cārvāka doctrine. The *Sarvadarśanasaṃgraha* of Mādhavacārya has a less frivolous, more poignant version: instead of "ṛṇam kṛtvā ghṛtam pivet," it says "nāsti mṛtyor-agocaraḥ"—that is, no one escapes death. *Sarvadarśanasaṃgraha*, chap. 1. For modern studies of Cārvāka doctrines, see Debiprasad Chattopadhyay, *Lokāyata* (Delhi: People's Publishing House, 1973); and more recently, Ramkrishna Bhattacharya, "Carvaka Fragments: A New Collection," *Journal of Indian Philosophy* 30, no.6 (2002): 597–640.

14. Interestingly, even in dramatic and narrative presentations of Cārvāka materialists there is a noticeable characteristic of philosophical sharpness of argument. Even though they are quite often shown to be bested in a philosophic dispute, the intellectual sympathies of a modern reader might go toward them; at least their frequent narrative "defeat" by Buddhist or Vedicist antagonists might not appear so conclusive. For an example, see the dispute between the Carvaka and the Saiva philosophic protagonist in the famous philosophical play, *Āgamaḍambara*, written by the Kashimiri Saiva philosopher Jayanta Bhatta. In the play the materialist is shown to be defeated and speechless, and describes him as "*maunam bhūmim ālikhati*" (silently drawing lines on the ground); *Āgamaḍambara, Much Ado About Religion*, trans. and ed. Csaba Dezso (New York: New York University Press, 2005), 151–169, here 169. Yet it could be doubted that the actual theoretical exchange was so utterly decisive.

15. Consider the direct contrast with the famous lines in the Bhagavatgita:
    Vāsaṃsi jīrṇani yathā vihāya parāni gṛhṇāti naro 'parani
    Tathā śarīrani vihāya jantu parāni gṛhṇāti navāni dehī
    [Just as a person leaves worn out clothes and wears new ones, the soul (dehī = the possessor of the body) leaves one body to take up a new one].

    Gita 2.22.

But the text provides the supporting idea without which this one cannot stand:

Nainaṃ bhindanti śastrāṇi nainaṃ dahati pāvakah
Ajo nityaṃ śāśvatoyaṃ purāno na hanyate hanyamāne śarīre

Gita 2.23

[Weapons cannot tear it, fire cannot burn it, it is birthless, changeless, deathless, ancient; it is not destroyed with the destructible body].

16. Some ancient philosophies like Buddhism would have inclined to this view, just like modern secular ethics.
17. It is remarkable that references to Cārvāka doctrines can be found in a seventeenth-century Islamic digest like the *Dabistan-e-Mazahib*; *The Dabistan or School of Manners*, vol. 2, trans. David Shea and Anthony Troyer (Paris and London: Allen, 1843), 197ff (hereafter *The Dabistan*).
18. For a well-known and influential account from a conventional Marxist point of view, see Debiprasad Chattopadhyay, *Lokayata: A Study in Ancient Indian Materialism* (Delhi: People's Publishing House, 1973).
19. *Sarvadarśanasaṃgraha*, chap. 1.
20. For a wide-ranging scholarly analysis, see Alexis Sanderson, "The Saiva Age," in *Genesis and Development of Tantrism*, ed. Shingo Einoo (Tokyo: University of Tokyo, 2009).
21. Sanderson, "The Saiva Age."
22. The distinguished Sanskritist, V. Raghavan, made a similar suggestion about the specific evolution of *rasa* theory in aesthetics in *The Number of Rasas* (Madras: Adyar Library and Research Centre, 1967).
23. Jayanta Bhatta, *Much Ado About Religion*, Clay Sanskrit Series, (New York: New York University Press), 2005.
24. The name Nilambara comes from this—literally "black cloth."
25. Gonda does not use the arguments about the Axial Age transformations, but his analysis follows very similar lines. Jan Gonda, *Visnuism and Sivaism: A Comparison* (London: SOAS and Athlone, 1970).
26. The *pratyabhijñā* philosophy evolved in ancient Kashmir from an originator, Somadatta, but was developed powerfully in the works of later philosophers like Utpaladeva. By general consensus, its greatest heights were reached in the commentarial expansions by Abhinavagupta in his *Īśvara-Pratyabhijñā-Vimarśinī* in the tenth century.
27. This change in the meaning of *moksha* is announced in the first *mangalācarana sloka* of the *Īśvara-Pratyabhijñā-Vimarśinī*.
28. Because the *sukta* from the *Kṛṣṇayajurveda* also stated that the four castes emerged from the *puruṣa*'s head, hands, thighs, and feet.
29. Some of these revisions are recorded in the very different understanding of caste difference in the *Śukranīti*:

Na jātyā brāhmaṇaścātra kṣatriyo vaiśya eva na
Na śūdro na ca vai mleccho bheditā guṇa-karmabhih
[Here Brahmins are not decided by birth, nor *ksatriyas*, or *vaisya*; not *sudras*, not even *mlecchas*; they are distinguished by their qualities and actions.]

Śukranīti, chap. 30, sloka 9

30. Gonda, *Sivaism and Visnuism*, 32–33.
31. Sanderson, "The Saiva Age."
32. Caitanyacaritāmṛta,

    Rādhā-kṛṣṇa-praṇaya-vikṛtir-hladinīṣaktir-asmād
    Ekānātmanavapi bhuvi pura dehabhedam gatau tau
    Caitanyākhyam prakata-madhuna tad-dvayam caikamāptam
    Rādhā-bhāva-dyuti-suvalitam naumi kṛṣṇa-svarūpam

33. For a historical analysis of this theology, see Rachel McDermott, *Revelry, Rivalry and Longing for the Goddess of Bengal: The Fortunes of Hindu Festivals* (New York: Columbia University Press, 2011).
34. Canto 1, 1.9 in Jayadeva, *Gitagovinda*, trans. Lee Siegel (New York: New York University Press, 2009), 10.

    You condemned the sacrifice of living beings sanctioned by Vedic texts,
    your compassionate heart saddened by slaughter of animals. Let Hari,
    the lord of the universe, triumph.
    (My translation).

35. Heinrich von Stietencron, "Hinduism."
36. One central methodological point in this discussion is not to transfer into premodern times the modern picture of Hinduism and Islam as two large homogeneous "religious communities." Communities revolve around much smaller sects and worship groups among both Hindus and Muslims. A confirmation of this idea is the manner in which premodern treatises discuss religious or philosophic communities. *The Dabistan*, for instance, uses the terms "Hindu" and "Muslim" clearly not to denote real religious communities but as second-order descriptive categories: the actual communities it describes in detail are smaller, more numerous and diverse.
37. At times, doctrinal disputation between different sects within Islam—particularly between Shias and Sunnis—could be fierce. For an account of such acrimonious and bitter debate, see *The Dabistan*, vol. 3, 50–63.
38. For a fuller version of this argument, see my paper in *The Boundaries of Toleration*.
39. I had once suggested that they created a form of back-to-back neighborliness, not a frontal public sphere of open interaction, except in the spheres of administration, art, and music.
40. Barani deplores the lukewarmness of Islamic rulers in their pursuit of their religious duty and approves of the rather tyrannical Alauddin Khalji for

ensuring that Hindus are made to live in poverty and political fear. "Sultan Alauddin requested his councilors to suggest some rule or regulation, whereby the Hindus might be ground down, and their property or wealth, which is the source of rebellion and disaffection, might no longer remain with them . . . and so much should not be left to the Hindus as to admit of their riding horses, wearing fine clothes, and indulging in sumptuous and luxurious habits." "The Reign of Alauddin Khilji," in Ziauddin Barani, *Tarikh I Firuzshahi*, trans. A. R. Fuller and A. Khallaque (Calcutta: Pilgrim, 1967), 76. And as a result of these policies, "it was not possible in fact for a Hindu to hold up his head, and in their houses not a sign was left of gold and silver, and articles of luxury, which are the main incentives of disaffection and rebellion. In consequence of their impoverished state, the wives of the landed proprietors and chief men even used to go to the houses of Musalmans and do work there, and receive wages for it" (79).

41. My paper in *Boundaries of Toleration*.
42. S. Nurul Hasan, *Religion, State and Society in Medieval India*, ed. Satish Chandra (Delhi: Oxford University Press, 2006).
43. This is also an argument made directly by Akbar in Abul Fazl's discussion of his views. He stated that a truly religious conversion must be free from fear of coercion or the enticement of favor, and additionally, conversion should be open to both sides. Abul Fazl, *Ain-i-Akbari*, vol. 3, chapter on "Happy Sayings of His Majesty," p. 424ff.
44. For an excellent account of Indian Sufi orders, see Carl W. Ernst and Bruce Lawrence, *Sufi Martyrs of Love* (New York: Palgrave Macmillan, 2002).
45. Although this question cannot be treated in detail here, the similarity between Sufi musical lyrics with *kṛṣṇabhakti padas* is quite astonishing. And in contrast to the highly conventionalized autobiography of bhakti, it could be surmised that there were serious transactions between Vaisnava and Sufiana thought about the love of God. Lines attributed to Amir Khusrau like these: "main nizam se naina lagayi re / ghar nari gawanri chahe so kahe" are very similar to lines of *thumris* to Krsna.
46. Amir Khusrau, quoted in K. A. Nizami, *Studies in Islamic History and Culture*, vol. 2 (Delhi: Idarah-i Adabiyat-i Delli, 2009), 57.
47. The lines clearly play on the opposition between *bhulna* and *yād*—forgetting (*bhulna*) and remembering (*yād ānā*). It is also notable that it uses the philosophic term *shart*, literally meaning a logical condition.
48. Nizami, *On Islamic History and Culture*, vol. 2, 57.
49. Cf. the work of Aditya Behl on the *Candayan*.
50. Syed Sultan, *Nabībaṃśa* or *Rasul-carit* (Dhaka: Bangla Akademi, 1978). See also, Rahul Peter Das, ed., *Essays in Middle Bengali Literature* (Calcutta: Firma KLM, 1999). For a similar argument from a north Indian Sufi author, see Muzaffar

Alam, "Strategy and Imagination in a Mughal Sufi Story of Creation," *Indian Economic and Social History Review* 49, no. 2 (2012): 151–195.

51. The last phrase of the line, "main to tere pas mein," combines the three meanings into one untranslatable idea.
52. Richard Eaton, *Rise of Islam and the Bengal Frontier* (Berkeley: University of California Press, 1993); and Tony Stewart, *Fabulous Females and Peerless Pirs: Tales of Mad Adventures in Old Bengal* (New York: Oxford University Press, 2004).
53. For a remarkable analysis of the folk traditions as part of mainstream Hinduism, see K. M. Sen, *Hinduism* (Baltimore: Penguin, 1962).
54. K. A. Nizami comments on the long history of this anxiety in Indian Islam in "Islam in Modern India," in *On Islamic History and Culture*, vol. 2 (Delhi: Idarah-i Adabiyat-i Delli, 1995), 56–58.
55. Badayuni, *Muntakhab ut Tawarikh* (Calcutta: Baptist Mission Press, 1884).
56. For a generally informative account, Makhanlal Raychaudhuri, *Din-i-Ilahi: or the Religion of Akbar* (Calcutta: University of Calcutta, 1941).
57. In his *Ain-i-Akbari* and *Akbarnama*.
58. The penultimate chapter of the *Ain* collects some of Akbar's thoughts on assorted themes. *Ain-i-Akbari*, vol 3, book 5.
59. This line of thought tends to portray Akbar as a modern secularist—ahead of his time.
60. For instance, the assessment of Badayuni in the works of the leading Aligarh historians like Iqtedar Alam Khan.
61. For a graphic exchange of insults between Shias and Sunnis, see *The Dabistan*, 3:50–65.
62. Two religious figures from other religions became influential in his own evolution, the Parsee saint from Navsari and Rudolfo Acquaviva, the Jesuit priest from Goa.
63. Raychauduri, drawing upon Abul Fazl. *The Dabistan* attributes these ideas about the sun to Raja Birbal (3:93).
64. *The Dabistan*, 3:50ff.
65. Colonial historians like Vincent Smith supported this view, partly because of their definition of "religion" and partly to fortify their arguments about Oriental despotism. For a spirited critique of Smith, see Raychaudhuri.
66. *Muntakhab ut Tawarikh*.
67. On a more brutally mundane level, he got Abul Fazl assassinated by one of his Hindu allies.
68. *The Dabistan*, 3: chap. 10.
69. *The Dabistan*, 3: chap. 10, pp. 70–86.
70. For a critique of this kind of historical expectation, see Dipesh Chakrabarti, *Provincializing Europe* (Princeton: Princeton University Press, 2000).

71. Max Weber, *Sociology of Religion* (Boston: Beacon, 1993).
72. This has been forcefully argued by some historians like Nicholas Dirks.
73. Interestingly, there are references and occasional discussions about the practice of sati in Mughal discourse. Both Abul Fazl's *Ain-i-Akbari* and the *Dabistan-e-Mazahib* mention this custom and different responses to it.
74. Ram Mohan Ray played a vital role in this two-sided persuasion, which involved his native elite groups denouncing the custom and the British authorities legislating against it.
75. For a detailed historical analysis of the history of the sati legislation, see Lata Mani, *Contentious Traditions: The Debate on Sati in Colonial India* (Berkeley: University of California Press, 1998).
76. Again, *The Dabistan* shows that such criticisms were not unknown in the religious debates in Mughal India.
77. Bankimchandra Chattopadhyay, *Krishnacharitra, Bankim Rachanabali*, vol. 1 (Calcutta: Sahitya Samsad, 1974), 196.
78. Incidentally, this stance of religious neutrality was supported by theorists like John Stuart Mill.
79. Sibnath Sastri narrates the story of a teacher in the college who walked the streets of Calcutta asking strangers he met, "Garu khābi, garu khābi?" ("Would you eat beef?"). Sibnath Sastri, *Ramtanu Lahiri O Tatkalin Banga Samaj*.
80. Michael Madhusudan Dutt, *Meghnadbadhkavya*, trans. Clinton Seeley (New York: Oxford University Press, 2005).
81. The Shaktas and Vaishnavas.
82. Brahmos were distinctly more daring in intellectual than in social life. They challenged Hindu religious doctrines and ethical ideals with great intensity but took some time to deviate from caste practices in social intercourse. See Debendranath Thakur, *Atmajivani* (Calcutta: Visvabharati Granthalay, 1962).
83. The opening notice of the first number of the *Tattvabodhini Patrika*. See also Brian Hatcher, *Bourgeois Hinduism or the Faith of the Modern Vedantists* (New York: Oxford University Press, 2008).
84. David Kopf, *Brahmo Samaj and the Shaping of the Modern Indian Mind* (Princeton: Princeton University Press, 1979).
85. For more on J. C. Bose, see Kopf, *Brahmo Samaj*, chap. 5; for a more interesting and searching analysis, see Ashis Nandy, *Alternative Sciences: creativity and authenticity in two Indian scientists*, (Delhi: Oxford University Press, 2001).
86. In fact, this is not true of Hindu traditionalists generally. Certainly beliefs in popular Hinduism gave credence to this idea, but serious exploration of Hindu theology shows immensely powerful and intricate reflection on God's nature and the ways in which finite human cognitive capacities could approach the question of "knowing" him. For instance, the *Īśvara Pratyabhignyā Vimarśinī* by the tenth-century Kashmiri philosopher Abhinavagupta is one example of an

exercise of this kind—the text dealing with the question "What could be meaning of an enterprise of knowing God?" But the ignorance of the moderns about the ancients, produced by colonial education protected the Western-educated elite from this knowledge and seemed to confirm their beliefs about common Hindu beliefs. So Hindus may not have believed in these ideas, but there is no doubt that modernist intellectuals believed that Hindus did.

87. Kopf, *Brahmo Samaj*.
88. Chattopadhyay, *Krishnacharitra*, 1:434.
89. This, strictly speaking, is true of the Vedic view of karma.
90. Bhudev Mukhopadhyay, *Samajik Prabandha*, ed. Jahnavi Kumar Chakrabarti (Calcutta: Paschim Banga Rajya Pustak Parshad,1984), 36.
91. T. N. Madan and Ashis Nandy, for instance, make this charge against Nehru, whose actual thinking on religion, as his biographer Gopal notes briefly, is more nuanced. In some of his later writings, Nehru would describe himself as agnostic, while communists would have presented themselves as ebullient atheists.
92. One of his famous songs runs:
    Ākāś bharā surya tārā, viśva bharā prāṇ,
    Tāhāri mājh khāne āmi peyechi mor sthān,
    Vismaye tāi jāge āmār gān
    [The sky is filled with suns and stars, the earth is filled with life. My music rises out of my wonder that I found a place in its midst].
    Note that the operative emotion is not even one of gratitude but the cognitivistic sense of wonderment. Rabindranath Thakur, *Gitabitan* (Calcutta: Visvabharati, 1970), 430.
93. It would be entirely common and unremarkable for a family of a high-level engineer to have a domestic celebration of the Saraswati *pūjā*, worship of the goddess of learning—whose support was crucial in getting ahead in the world of education.
94. Akeel Bilgrami, chap. 9 in this volume.
95. Taylor's emphasis on the elites' capacity to transform the culture of ordinary people is another critical point. Often the story of non-Western cultures simply seeks singular examples of modernist thought to announce the inauguration of a modern age.
96. Kopf, *Brahmo Samaj*.
97. In Bankim's searing condemnation, "prisoners boasted of the length of their chain" (Chattopadhyay, Bankim Rachanabali, vol. 1). But Rabindranath Tagore's novel *Gora* also explored this sensitive question—intellectual emancipation construed as a mask for political obsequiousness.
98. Again, Bankim, "Ingrajstotra," in Chattopadhyay, Bankim Rachanabali, 1:9–10.
99. Tagore's novel *Gora* indicates that Rabindranath thought these criticisms contained some truth.

100. The book containing his discourses, *Kathamrta*, begins with an encounter with the compiler who diffidently said his wife was ignorant in religious matters. Ramakrsna Kathamrta, Complete Edition (Calcutta: Ananda Publishers, 1990).
101. Tapan Raychaudhuri, *Europe Reconsidered* (Delhi: Oxford University Press, 1989).
102. Bhudev Mukhopadhyay, *Samajik Prabandha* and *Acar Prabandha* in *Prabandha Samagra* (Calcutta: Charchapad, 2014).
103. Mukhopadhyay, *Samajik Prabandha*.
104. Mukhopadhyay, *Samajik Prabandha*.
105. This was especially through literature—particularly mytho-historic fiction (Abanindranath Tagore: *Rajkahini*, *Nalak*, and *Buro-Angla*) and fantastic poetry (Sukumar Ray: *Aboltabol*)—a device that could retain enchantment in a modern world. The painter Abanindranath Tagore's renowned lectures on art made a powerful case for entrusting to art the task of maintaining enchantment in human life. Abanindranath Tagore, *Bageshwari Shilpa Prabandavali* (Calcutta: Ananda, 1999).
106. Mukhopadhyay, *Samajik Prabandha*.
107. Bankimchandra Chattopadhyay, "Udar-darsan" (Philosophy of the belly) and "Bidal" (The cat), in *Krishnacharitra*, vol. 1.
108. For a genealogy of the festival, see McDermott, *Revelry, Rivalry and Longing for the Goddess of Bengal*.
109. Charles Taylor, *A Secular Age* (Cambridge: Belknap, 2007), 352–376.
110. The first cycle of his three cycles of songs, *Gitabitan*, is *Pūjā* (Worship).
111. Both the leftist and apolitical strands of modern Bengali poetry are godless in their own ways. The immensely influential surrealist poetry of Jibananda Das shows no sense of transcendence.
112. Rabindranath Thakur, "Utsav," in *Dharma* (Calcutta: Visvabharati, 2002).
113. "To taste the flavor of togetherness, to feel a sense of serenity in the midst of the distractions of everyday, human beings invite all people to a festival. On that day, his conduct becomes the opposite of his everyday behavior." *Dharma*, 11. But Tagore also has an apprehension that modernity is fundamentally inimical to this sense of collective life: "Even on this day we turn coming together into mere crowding, the enterprise into an exhibition" (14).
114. "Din o ratri," *Dharma*, 20. "Darkness reveals more to us than it obscures. Without it, we would not have received the messages from distant parts of the universe; light would have confined us in a prison"(20).
115. See McDermott, *Revelry, Rivalry and Longing for the Goddess of Bengal*. For a more traditional exploration of theology of Durga and Kali in Bengal, see the deeply learned and insightful study by Sasibhusan Dasgupta, *Bharater Sakti-sadhana O Sakta Sahitya* (Calcutta: Sahitya Samsad, 1960).
116. Literally, ceremonies organized by a dozen friends: *baro* = twelve and *yar* = friends.

117. There is a particularly rich tradition of literary—mostly satirical—commentary on the *baro-yari pujas* in early modern Bengali literature. One of the earliest and most distinguished is the one by Kaliprasanna Sinha, a zamindar himself, and a writer of a celebrated work, *Hutom Pencar Naksa* (Sketches of the owl) with the telling subtitle: *Apanar Mukh Apani Dekho* (See your own face)—a mirror held up to the feckless zamindari class.
118. Mikhail Bakhtin, *Rabelais and His World*, trans. Helen Iswolsky (Cambridge: MIT Press, 1968).

8

AN ANCIENT INDIAN SECULAR AGE?

Rajeev Bhargava

Charles Taylor's *A Secular Age* is a book about the social imaginary of the North Atlantic and, to some extent, European modernity.[1] But much of its argument, and I believe the reason for its success, lies in its characterization of what the secular age leaves behind, what no longer exists, perhaps what it has lost. It is a feature of Taylor's work that he enables us to experience the transition from one kind of life-world to another. Among these lost worlds, he discusses "early religions" that still exist in some parts of the world. This essay must be viewed as part of a larger project that hopes to explore the transition in India from what appears to be its world of "early religions" to a world with a marked resemblance to one inhabited by post-Axial religions.

A fragment of a larger project, this entire chapter is written as an answer to a very narrow question. If Charles Taylor is correct about his understanding of what is meant by "secular" (which, by the way, is closer to the modern Indian understanding of secular than to the more mainstream Western understanding of the term), and if further, he is correct in his characterization of the secular age, is it at all conceivable that a secular age existed in ancient India—not India the modern nation-state but India the territorial-cum-civilizational unit? Is it plausible to suggest this? Such a question I would have found preposterous only a few years ago, but our current conjuncture appear to be full of momentous possibilities for rethinking the history of thought, and thus this intellectual adventure appears worth undertaking. To take just one example, suppose that the answer, assuming that all the distinctiveness and specificities of each secular age are revealed only by more detailed conceptual and historical studies, is *yes*, what profound implications might this have for a theory of modernity? It is taken for granted by virtually every Western theory that a close link exists between the secular and the modern. But if an ancient secular age exists, then the link between secularity and modernity is severed. I am not in a position to answer these questions in this essay, but equally I must register and index the unfolding of a space where one can ask a question such as: "What would theories of secularities look like if secularity and modernity are uncoupled?"

Three more sets of preliminary remarks are in order. First, I am neither a historian of ancient India nor a philologist. Given these inadequacies, I do not make any substantive claims of my own, at least not directly. However, I cannot deny that this essay has implications for the substantive claims made more explicitly by other scholars. I suspect much of what I say might wittingly or unwittingly have implications for the claims made by theorists, particularly theorists of modernity.

Second, I make uninhibited use of an entire vocabulary that comes from two traditions believed to constitute the Western world: the Judeo-Christian, originating in Palestine, and the Greco-Roman, originating in the area around Mediterranean. I offer two justifications why I risk using this vocabulary to describe a state of affairs in ancient India. These justifications are required because of the very real and obvious danger of reading into ancient India features of the two aforementioned worlds that are markedly different from it. The first reason is methodological. Despite the warning usually provided by good historians of thought and hermeneuticians, I feel somewhat less ill at ease about my approach because I believe that the connection between word meaning and context is not as strong as some people like to believe. Words travel faster than their meanings. Oftentimes, the original meaning of a word gets lost on the way, but another meaning from roughly the same family, residing in a different, perhaps a new home, is drawn ineluctably to the signifier. A suitable but imperfect translation occurs.

Shifts, displacements, even subversions occur, but hidden similarities are revealed too, and new similarities are born. Perhaps a time has come to not overread or overplay differences across time and space.

My second justification concerns, more importantly, the vocabulary that I deploy, which is also used extensively by historians of the ancient world, including ancient India. I am almost tempted to pin the blame for my own inevitable errors onto the historians and philologists on whom I rely. It is their language that is found in my essay. Furthermore, the two traditions that provide the resources for the vocabulary of the paper are much closer to ancient India than many modernists realize. Egypt, Palestine, Mesopotamia, Persia, India, and China constituted an intercommunicating global universe and had more in common in the period that interests me than what the modern West shares with the two traditions from which it is believed to have originated.

Third, the project to which this paper belongs must not be conflated with the more normative intellectual undertaking with which I am also associated. In some of my previous and current work I have delved into the ancient Indian past to explore the conceptual resources for a normative political response to religious diversity and conflict. I have frequently used the term "political secularism" for the cluster of this particular normative vocabulary used by modern Indians, the precursors of which can be found in diverse political figures separated by thousands of years, such as Asoka, Akbar, and Nehru.[2] In short, I have been attempting to outline the rudimentary history of conceptual, value-laden elements from which political secularism has been fashioned and refashioned in India. It needs to be clarified that the project of the present paper is only remotely connected, if at all, to this other more normative project of political secularism and its history.

***

The India of early religions was not monolithic. There were varieties of religious experience in ancient India. Multiple Indian secularities were also available. The sheer diversity of ethical perspectives is breathtaking. Perhaps this was the case in other similar places too. Whatever the case, a question that arises is: "Why, when the option between 'belief' and 'unbelief' was available in ancient India, is it inappropriate to speak of an ancient secular age?"³ After all, the title of Taylor's book itself admits the possibility of other secular ages. The book is not called "*The* Secular Age." It is tempting at this stage to simply assume a constitutive link between secularity and modernity. The book is entitled "A Secular Age" because there are other contemporary secular ages, perhaps a Chinese, a Latin American, a North African, an Indian— multiple modern secular ages similar to multiple modernities. I think this would be a mistake and I believe Taylor does not assume this. His point is more subtle.

However, Taylor's question needs modification before it can be explored any further. The phrase "an option between belief and unbelief" is a profoundly Christian and perhaps even a post-Enlightenment formulation. It possesses an Enlightenment flavor because of a predisposition to intellectualize ordinary beliefs and practices, characteristic of the elites of the time. The term "belief" is itself a pointer in this direction. From connoting "to hold dear," "to love" (a link still found in the German *beleiben* by virtue of its link with *leiben* [love]), "to give allegiance or be loyal to what is highly valued," it began to mean a state of mind that may be true or false.⁴ More importantly, the identification of religious perspective as a system, primarily of belief, presupposes an exceptionally prominent place of doctrine typical of Christianity. Other religious perspectives such as Islam and Judaism have bestowed much greater significance to law than to doctrinal belief. Still others, like Indian soteriologies, talk of the ends of life and the pivotal nature of certain practices but hardly ever speak of systematic intellectual doctrine.⁵ So, in the Indian context, it would be more appropriate to ask whether an option exists between at least two lifeworlds or experiences, one that presupposes the existence of gods and goddesses and the other that does not.

EARLY RELIGION: RIG VEDIC INDIA

Early religion, Taylor tells us was embedded in three different senses. First, human agency was embedded in society. Second, society was embedded in the cosmos and finally, the cosmos incorporated the divine.⁶ It is hard to disagree with Taylor. Each of these is true of Rig Vedic religion (1500–1000 B.C.E.). First, for an individual to view himself or act outside the social matrix was inconceivable. For the Rig Vedics (henceforth referred to merely as Vedics), an individual was the social role he inherited. The Brahman or the Kshatriya was nothing but a Brahman or a Kshatriya. To use these terms somewhat anachronistically, their social identity was their personal identity. A second sense in which agency was socially embedded had to do with the primary religious act, ritual sacrifice. No sacrifice could be performed by any agent all by himself. The sacrifice was offered by the Kshatriya, the primary householder, but it had to be executed by the Brahman, who alone had the know-how and thereby the authority to do so. Ritual sacrifice was then jointly performed by the two social agents, each complementing the other: one caused the ritual to be performed, the *yajaman*, and therefore was the primary recipient of the benefits accruing from it, and the other actually performed it, for which he received a gift/fee (*dakshina*). And why did the *yajaman* perform it? For the sake of society? As its protector and benefactor? Not really. The routine wishes of a Vedic householder, to be fulfilled by the performance of the sacrifice, were "sons, rain, cattle, superiority within his clan and tribe, living for the proverbial 100 years, and then finding his way to heaven."⁷ In short, what Vedic men hoped to achieve through sacrifice were very much goods of this-worldly human flourishing.⁸ There is little supramundane about their ambition. This is underlined by the fact that life in heaven was a further continuation of a pleasant life on earth.⁹ The idea of the *sanyasi* is still not conceived.¹⁰ Nor is the normative idea born that one should strive to escape life in this world.¹¹ Indeed, in the Rig Veda, Richard Gombrich tells us, "man is born and dies only once."¹² There is no rebirth. *Amratva* (immortality) in some passages of the Rig Veda appears to be nothing but the continuation of a long life on earth.¹³ Would it be wrong then to say that ritual sacrifice was the nodal point through which transactions occurred between socially constituted men? Was this, too, a moral order (like the modern moral order) constructed for mutual benefit, for the reciprocal exchange of goods and services? This would not be entirely correct, for there were also others who benefited secondarily or indirectly from the *yajna*—for the sacrifice also sustained the entire social and cosmic order (*Rta*).¹⁴ Since everyone benefited, albeit differentially, one could say that it was performed on behalf of and for the sake of all, for the entire society. Perhaps this alone made the act sacred and lent it the religiosity it would not otherwise possess.

Even this Durkheimian account does not get it right, however. The impression it creates that men associated with one another for the sake of mutual benefit and largely for ordinary human flourishing, though not incorrect, misses out on two crucial points. First, there were two more clearly specified participants in the ritual act whom we have failed thus far to mention: ancestors and gods. Second, the Vedic world of here and now was nevertheless thoroughly enchanted. In short, a sociology of ritual sacrifice will simply not do. We need rather a cosmo-sociology. Relations between men were thoroughly implicated with and mediated by relations of men to their ancestors and gods.¹⁵ These latter were the other participants in rituals, for gods and ancestors were invited to the sacrifice too. Except for Agni and Soma, all remained invisible. Yet a formal meal was offered to all these worthy dignitaries. A ceremonial offering of food (including animals) was made to fire so that Agni could carry it to other gods who ate it as smoke and aroma (*medha*). The leftovers were the more immediate and reciprocal gift of gods to the *yajaman*. The food offerings made to the Brahman, in addition to his *dakshina*, were meant to go to the ancestors. Somehow the food consumed by Brahmans was transmitted to them. Hence the importance of ritual feasts. A failure to do so would starve the ancestors and wreck the sacrifice. Thus, ritual sacrifice connected men not only to other men but also to gods and ancestors who lived either in heaven or somewhere between heaven and earth. As Taylor rightly puts it, society is embedded in the cosmos and the cosmos incorporates the divine (gods).¹⁶

Thus reciprocity and mutual benefit were certainly key to ritual sacrifice, but the system of mutual exchange crucially involved gods and ancestors. Gifts, mainly food, were offered to the gods to procure mundane goods and for ultramundane, quite instrumental-seeming reasons—to get something in return. The Vedic mantra was: "Give me, I give you." Of course, even in the Rig Vedic period, this must not be understood as a simple and true exchange or return of favors. The logic of reciprocity implied the principle of different and deferred returns. Equivalences were never sought by humans. Reciprocity entailed long-term relationships in which giving and receiving were never really over. If the sacrifice was performed exclusively for self-interest and without a sense of genuine gratitude, it was bound to fail.[17] Thus, it does not appear entirely correct to say that "these were not then offerings to the almighty out of gratitude." Nor were they given out of "celebratory exuberance."[18] They were, as Jamison and Witzel admit, "mandated by the reciprocal system."[19] But the thoroughly enchanted world of porous Vedic selves has enough elements to keep the secularist and the humanist interested: There is no other world. No rebirth. One is born once and one dies only once. The only ends to be sought are this-worldly. There is no higher goal of human flourishing.

Much in this early religion, then, comes close to what Taylor calls exclusive humanism. Three features mark his characterization of it. First, there is no other world but this, the only one we have. Second, following straight from the first, no human flourishing exists except in this world, nothing beyond and higher than flourishing here and now. Finally, it is achieved by human agency without help from or grace of God or gods. Exclusive humanism is self-sufficing. Early Vedic religion appears to meet the first two requirements but not the third. For Taylor, enchantment and exclusive humanism simply do not go together. Exclusive humanism is possible only for buffered selves. But Vedic selves are porous through and through.

Or are they? Matters are much too complicated in the Vedic world. In some passages, gods are manipulated and not just propitiated by humans, implying a power struggle between the two.[20] In others, sacrifice acquires coercive power to which gods submit. At least some of the power of gods is usurped by ritual sacrifice performed by humans. The sacrifice yields the desired result regardless of the wishes of gods. As Gombrich says, "In the early Vedic period, when gods were powerful supermen it was up to them to grant or withhold the benefits for which the sacrificer asked. Later it did not depend upon divine caprice. Sacrifice must work unless badly performed."[21] The correct performance of ritual, independent of gods, achieves everything desired in this world. This is socially embedded agency that works on its own, without help or hindrance from any other power. This indeed is self-sufficing, exclusive humanism as far as I can see in a relatively disenchanted world, for gods and spirits are inconsequential even if they exist. (Their existence is compatible with disenchantment as long as their role is negligible.) The causal efficacy resides in the power of skilled men, in this case Brahmans, who by putting into words a significant and non-self-evident truth acquire spiritual force.[22] In fact, in some other passages, as pointed out by Gonda, the formulation of cosmic truth turns Brahmans into gods.[23] If godhood is simply a state to be achieved by humans themselves, then any reference to gods expresses superhumanism, which is undoubtedly a form of exclusive humanism. Indeed a continuing ambiguity exists in the early Hindu tradition on the referent of "god." The Sanskrit word for it, *deva*, is used sometimes for gods and sometimes for men, including kings and Brahmans.[24]

This existence of something akin to exclusive humanism is not unique or entirely surprising, for Taylor acknowledges the presence of exclusive humanism in Greece, represented by Epicureanism, a tradition that admitted gods but found them "irrelevant to humans."[25] And what was possible in Greece is conceivable in India, too. In fact, two of the major Indian "religions" in first millennium before the Common Era, though very distant from Epicureanism, do not admit gods in their ontology. The original "asocial Buddhism" (a term used by Greg Bailey and Ian Mabbett) certainly took the same view on the relevance of gods.[26] [M]ichael Carrithers makes the same point, "Neither Socrates nor Buddha was much interested in God, gods or the supernatural, but both were passionately concerned with the ends and the conduct of human life."[27] The Jaina teachings, of greater antiquity than the teachings of the Buddha[28] but which certainly came to fruition at the same time as the Buddha, also show little interest in "God, gods or the supernatural." They do, of course, believe in the cycle of rebirth and the impact of a person's karma on the possibility of escaping it, but liberation is to be achieved exclusively by human agency, in this case by complete cessation of all action, by a state of complete motionlessness of both mind and body.[29] This actionlessness is the only answer to the problem of rebirth, because on the Jaina view all karma results in demerit and therefore in rebirth. Karma sticks to the soul like dirt in objects.[30] One is born with the demerit of the karma of previous births. The only way out of this predicament is self-mortification, massive physical austerities to get rid of bad karma of past actions and births and henceforth to cease acting.[31] The only way to break the cycle is by attaining a condition of motionlessness and thoughtlessness and move gradually and eventually to death.[32] Very different from, perhaps even the opposite of, Epicureanism, but exclusively humanist all the same and like other non-Vedic soteriologies, extremely focused on individual karma and responsibility in the extreme.

Something in these accounts throws up the temptation, then, to introduce here the idea of an ancient secular age (parts of the late Vedic or early Upanisadic period that overlap with disappearing Rig Vedic, emergent Buddhist, and continuing Jaina perspectives) But this is a mistake. For Taylor warns that exclusive humanism must not be conflated with the secular age.[33] For Taylor, a secular age is characterized by three features, only one of which is the presence of (1) exclusive humanism. The other two are (2) the availability of a seriously meaningful option between belief and unbelief (in the Indian case, let us say, between lifeworlds presupposing the existence of God or gods and goddesses, an enchanted world, a conception of human flourishing beyond here and now, and the denial of lifeworlds that presuppose the existence of God or gods and goddesses or their relevance, a conception of human flourishing with no reference to anything beyond here and now and a belief in the self-sufficiency of human agency). Finally, (3) the availability of this option not just to a few people (elites' theory) but to a large mass of people. The options must be widely available if not to all, to a vast majority of people in society. It is hard to tell how this condition can be met in any nonmodern or ancient society. Yet scholars have used reason and imagination to propose a view on how ordinary people may have lived their religious lives. For instance, Louis Renou claims that in Jainism the lay community always played an important part in the administration of its religion and in the cult. For him the richness of extracanonical literature and its variety of genres testify to the fact that what is known as Jainism is sustained not only by monks and nuns but by male and female lay followers.[34] However, this points to the social role of laypersons in the overall life of their religion. There is no phenomenology available of this period. Indeed, historians of the ancient world have wrestled with this troubling issue for eternity. The textual accounts invariably provide the perspective of those who knew how to compose and write, typically the elite cultural producers. For the period before printing and mass literacy, the reconstruction of the phenomenology of the life of ordinary people is extraordinarily difficult. And so, Taylor's third condition rules out virtually any assessment of the secularity of the ancient world. How in earlier eras could a specific set of conditions of belief, a wholly new context or background that shapes any experience of belief or unbelief, be available, more or less identically, to large sections of people in large societies? Although very little hard evidence exists to test whether or not such conditions were widely available in ancient India, it seems preposterous to suggest that a particular social imaginary associated with the modern West could also be present in ancient India. However, this also makes a secular age, by definition, available exclusively to technologically advanced societies with a large infrastructure of diffusion and dissemination.[35] I therefore propose a modification of Taylor's criteria that an age may be characterized as secular if (1) in addition to some form of exclusive humanism, other philosophical and religious perspectives exist. (2) This diversity is accompanied by a condition that allows for viewing these different outlooks as meaningful options and a third, different criterion, namely, (3) there is freedom of movement across them. A person could move from one to another or simultaneously partake of many, indeed, in principle participate in all of them.

Did such an age exist in ancient India? It is quite clear, since at least the early Rig Vedic period continuing well into our own times, that large sections of Indian people have practiced some form of ritual sacrifice and committed themselves to the existence of multiple gods and goddesses. From the later Rig Vedic period there has, from time to time, also been a discourse of some form of inclusive monotheism, for example, prayer to *Ishwara*. However, in the entire first millennium before the Common Era, possibly earlier and quite certainly later, the Indic world also witnessed three varieties of exclusive humanisms in roughly the sense outlined above. First, regardless of the existence and propitiation of gods, the correct performance of the ritual act by a specially qualified group of people can result in both the achievement of all the goods crucial to human flourishing and to maintaining the entire cosmic order. Second, at least on one interpretation, for the Jain view, the ultimate end of human life, the complete cessation of thought and action can be achieved by self-sufficing, austere, and disciplined human action. Finally, a third view prevalent among the Buddhists that the ultimate goal of human flourishing can well be achieved by following the middle path, that is, acting in a way that is neither self-indulgent nor excessively austere and that gives at least equal weight to a self-related ethic as it does to other-related morality. Each of these outlooks satisfies the conditions of exclusive humanism.

It is hard to tell whether exclusive humanism was restricted to a small group of Brahmans and Shramanas. But both the teachings of Buddha and Jaina were available to non-Brahmans and non-*kshatriyas* especially to *vis* (ordinary people). Indeed, there was free movement of Brahmans and kshatriyas from one outlook to another. Recall that exclusive humanists do not have to deny the existence of gods. They presuppose the self-sufficiency of their own acts and find gods irrelevant to achieving their main goals. Some Vedic Brahmans were quite certainly exclusive humanists in this sense, but like the Epicureans, who must have been small in numbers, these Brahmanic exclusive humanists must have been a tiny minority. However, the same cannot be said of the Jainas and the Buddhists. In my view, they too are exclusive humanists and their number might have increased quite rapidly in the first millennium B.C.E. The more important point, however, is not how large the group of exclusive humanists was in ancient India (a similar problem might well arise for the modern West today; relative to others, exclusive humanists may well be a tiny group), but as mentioned, is that exclusive humanism was a significant presence and coexisted with those for whom gods were unquestionably present and relevant and furthermore, that there was free movement from one outlook to another. It is these two conditions that compel me to entertain the possibility of an ancient secular age in India. The possibility of multiple options does not entail anything like what Taylor calls the "nova effect" in ancient India or that any form of exclusive humanism was widely pervasive and dominant. But there is also no reason to believe, from whatever thin evidence that is available, that the availability of the option of moving from some outlooks to others was not part of the background condition of a very large number of people who communicated with one another. I hope to have made my point clear despite the difficulties of prevalence of exclusive humanism in the ancient period. I am trying to make a case that different forms of exclusive humanisms (Vedic Brahmanical, Buddhists, Jainas, and philosophical traditions of Carvaka) existed in India. All but one of them rejected ritual sacrifice as central to their worldview. And the one for which ritual sacrifice was pivotal does not appear to think of gods as relevant. These perspectives existed with lifeworlds that presupposed the existence of gods and goddesses, so that a meaningful option existed between these. I must now confess to muddling my way through two slightly different criteria that define a secular age. The first is Taylor's own, set out in *A Secular Age*. The other criterion appears to drop the acceptance of exclusive humanism by the masses in order to concentrate more fully on mobility conditions embedded in criteria 1 and 2.[36] It seems to me that Indic peoples invested far more in an exclusive humanist worldview than even the Greeks. This appears to be true of the period of my focus, that is, the first millennium B.C.E. I would not venture to make this claim for later periods.[37]

Since I have supplied a new element in Taylor's criteria, modified it, must elaborate it. So I turn now to what I hope would be a richer discussion of mobility conditions. What in India were the broader contexts within which religions/secularities were chosen, entered into, exited from? How could people cohabit amidst such diversity? What did it mean to have an option or choice between rival world views? What did it mean to choose a religion? and to exit one?

I begin this discussion by Richard Gombrich's characterization of religion in India.[38] According to him, "religion" might refer to (1) *marga*, a path, providing an answer to the question "What must I do to be saved." In short, religion might be a soteriology, a meaning endowing perspective, specifying ultimate goals, that gives individual life its point and direction, especially when confronted with the certainty of death. Equally, it refers to (2) those embedded beliefs and practices that structure the social life and normative expectations of individuals, particularly in relations with one another. Rituals, rites of passage, rules of hygiene, and traditional norms can also be subsumed under this conception of religion. Richard Gombrich calls it "communal religion."

This distinction is important, because it enables us to see how it is possible in India and more generally in Asia for many individuals to belong to two or more religions, for they can be attached at once to one of the many soteriologies (religion 1) and to a quite different set of communal practices (religion 2). They could continue to follow the set of practices they participated in before the new attachment. Hinduism has over time spawned many soteriologies but with minor regional variations has tended to keep a stable set of communal practices. These communal religious elements have sometimes been so entrenched that even conversion to other religions, those which claim to perform both soteriological and communal functions, has not unsettled them. Thus, many converts to Islam and Christianity long continued with "communal" aspects of Hinduism, despite a change in their soteriology. Many Buddhists believe in gods but claim that this has nothing to do with and therefore is not inconsistent with their religion (soteriology). Gods, for them, have much to do with their this-worldly concerns and have no bearing on their pursuit of Nibbana (nirvana). This also allows a ruler to respect all "faiths." Since one might without contradiction follow the soteriological beliefs of one religion and the communal practices of another, one must respect both and so must the ruler, who himself may follow one or many "religions." It is clear that one should not view Hinduism and Buddhism as two mutually exclusive religions. To do so would be to utterly distort both.

What are the conditions of the possibility of moving easily from one religion (soteriology) to another (soteriology)? Three immediately come to mind. First, the religion in question must not impose heavy costs or forbid movement across religions. It should contain conceptual resources of ideological freedom rather than unfreedom. This is primarily a cognitive but also an emotional matter. Second, closely related to 1, it must not possess an internal institutional structure with enormous social power. This is matter of social organization, of loose or tight internal social relations, of openness and flexibility within.

Third, it must not provide direct legitimation to or become too closely aligned with political power. Neither political rule nor political violence must be sanctioned by religion. This is an issue of the relationship between religion and political power, a matter of toleration or political secularity. I shall call these the theological, the social, and the political conditions of free movement across religions.

THE THEOLOGICAL CONDITION

The theological condition (the term is my own) can be discerned in the writings of several scholars, and in particular in the writings of Jan Assmann.[39] Several quite distinct ways of meeting this condition exist. First, the implicit or explicit theology of a religion must allow for translation of gods.[40] In virtually all cultures of classical antiquity, each god performed a function based on his or her cosmic competence. Thus, there are gods of love, war, knowledge, craftsmanship. Likewise, each god embodied an entity of potentially cosmic significance. Hence, gods of fire, rain, earth, time, sun, moon, and sea, or primal gods who create, destroy, preserve, and so on. The god of love in one culture could then also acquire the name of the god of love from another culture. This way differences continue to be viewed as irreducible and yet translatable.[41] One might even call this feature of translatability, a theology of recognition—the gods of each culture are recognized within the background of a common semantic universe. Eventually, this theological mode of coping with diversity can be enlarged to include soteriologies that do not depend on gods. One can deploy the more general term "ethic of self-realization," which includes both god-dependent and god-free ethics pertaining to humans and even nonhuman selves. Each of these ethics can be treated as a way of being or relating to the ultimate, in whichever way the latter is defined or understood. Certainly, this inclusive monotheism or perhaps globalism of ethics permits easy movement across religions. If the different names refer to the same god or the same god has different cultural backgrounds, then why create too much fuss about leaving one and embracing another? Indeed, why not embrace both?

A second strategy widely practiced in ancient Egypt involves the collocation of two or three gods, leading to hyphenated cosmic deities such as Amun-Re.[42] The two, Re and Amun, Assmann tells us, do not merge. They retain their individuality, quite like in the mode of translation. But here each becomes a crucial aspect of the other. Thus, Re becomes the cosmic aspect of Amun, and Amun becomes the local and cultic aspect of Re. Each aspect complements the other, without subsumption or domination. This strategy was also available and practiced in India.

Finally, a strategy even more common in all ancient cultures involves ontological subordination of one god to another god.[43] Thus, one god becomes the supreme deity of which all other are gods are manifestations, as Ram and Krishna become avatars of Vishnu. Or we might have a pantheon of equal gods with very diverse primal functions and others who are but manifestations or relations of the supreme deity.

Each of these strategies meets the theological condition of free movement across different cultures and religions. Freedom of conversion would not be the appropriate term here. Conversion implies one's permanent departure from the worship of one god to the exclusive worship of another. But this goes against the very point of these strategies of translation, hyphenation, and hierarchical assimilation. For here there can be a free movement back and forth and indeed the simultaneous commitment to all. This is true both when unity is explicitly claimed (inclusive monotheism) or when it is merely implied (as in polytheism).

The contrast to the above-mentioned strategies is provided by perspectives that block translation. Translation becomes impossible if you show the irreducible nonequivalence of the terms sought to be translated, if two terms simply cannot refer to the same entity. So, here we confront two irreducibly different entities. If the worlds centered on the two entities are incompatibly different, then one can either live in one or in the other, but not in both. Such blockages can occur in the natural course of things, without being intended. But on its own, what follows from this is structured irrevocable plurality: a very different multitheistic universe without conversation, a world peopled by groups that are internally intimate, but fundamentally and irreconcilably estranged from one another. But the blockage in question is grounded in a set of reasons that provide the motive for why it must proceed. The reason is that there is this one god who is the "real thing," the true god, and all other gods are false. Therefore, any act of translation is fundamentally impossible, even though it can be imagined under some kind of hallucinatory delusion. Since it can be imagined, and we can, in the false belief of the possibility of translation, be tempted by the idea that all gods are the same, the act of translation must be expressly forbidden. Hence, the command: there is only one true or real GOD and thou shalt not worship other (false or unreal) gods. This is not inclusive but *exclusive* monotheism, grounded in what Assmann calls the "Mosaic distinction," the distinction between true and false in religion.[44] There are no compromises when this distinction becomes part of lived experience. Quite possibly, the distinction between those who follow true religion and believers in false religion (us and them) can slide easily under some circumstances into a radical difference between friend and enemy. (The enemy outside [infidel] and the enemy within [heretic]).

This idea can be easily misunderstood to be anti-Semitic, the product of a terrible essentialization.[45] I do not think this is fair. The fact is that such a distinction exists, has developed from somewhere, in some context, and has been politically deployed by church and state both. It was activated during the Crusades. It was deployed during the Crusades and in the Reformation—as Taylor shows graphically[46]—and deployed extensively in the wars of religion, in the ethnic cleansings in Europe that resulted in the expulsion of Jews and Muslims from several regions,[47] and is in play even in contemporary nonviolent evangelical movements. It is imperative that we understand and explain it, that we trace its genealogy, if only to better surmount some of its difficulties. At any rate, since it is part of the explicit theology of some religions, the Mosaic distinction must be viewed as a conceptual resource that can be drawn upon when believers of these religions are motivated to do so. It is not permanently central to any of the monotheistic religions. Indeed, no living religion can be radically monotheistic in this way. It can even travel to other cultures and play a transformative albeit negative role as is illustrated by the development of what following Assmann can be called "Mosaic Hinduism." But this does not detract from the fact that whether or not it can be deployed depends on many factors, social, historical, cultural, and political.

The Mosaic distinction, perhaps an unfortunate term for a very real and important distinction, does not meet the theological condition of free movement across religions. In fact, it actively destroys it. If you believe and live by this distinction, then you will hold on to your true religion with all your strength and fight against all other religions with all your might. The choice to move out or to live comfortably with others is ruled out under these conditions. The Mosaic distinction was unavailable to anyone in ancient India. This partly, but only partly, explains why different soteriologies could comfortably coexist. There were, however, some elements that drew Vedic Brahmanism into orthopraxy.

THE SOCIAL CONDITION

This brings me to the second condition, the social condition. Cantwell Smith has a very interesting discussion of how modern religions were formed. A glimpse of the portrait he draws might go somewhat like this. If you view the formation of religion as a process, you might find that in the beginning there is a teacher, often a dissenter from an existing outlook, who begins to attract a set of followers. These loyalists are attracted by his teachings and his example and begin to see themselves first as wandering followers of a certain set of teachings and then as a community. But this may or may not happen. When such a community becomes large, it acquires an institutional structure. Such an institutionalized, rule-bound community might be called a church. This too is not inevitable and therefore may or may not happen. This happens more or less side by side with the formulation of an intellectual doctrine. So we now have a well-demarcated community distinguished from others by its founder and his teachings, reflected in a scripture, and possessing an organizational structure and an explicit theology. At the completion of this process, one might say that we have the birth of a religion proper. Now clearly much depends on how much the Buddhist *sangha* resembles a church and when Buddhist teachings become "Buddhism," a religion.

Now, one of my tentative proposals here is that the formation of a church places enormous restrictions on freedom of movement across *margas* or faiths and that such "churches" did not exist in ancient India. The *sangha* appears to have come closest to a church, but is not the same thing. It is, as Gombrich points out, "a body of men who meet regularly and in their face-to-face relations have some of the qualities of the family."[48] Furthermore, the function of the *sangha* is to help its members lead a disciplined life to achieve goals prescribed by Buddha. Members are not gatekeepers scrupulously watching whether rules of entry or exit are observed but rather follow one another's example to lead disciplined lives within the order. Moreover, as Cantwell Smith points out, Buddhism is a missionary religion, but "Buddhist missionaries, in all their compassionate zeal as they moved across all of Asia, did not expect that those who listened and responded to their message should abandon what other religious involvements they had. The result has been that from Ceylon to Japan those who Westerners call "Buddhists" are in almost every case simultaneously participants in at least one other religious "complex" It follows that some of the key steps after the formation of *margis* may not have been taken in the ancient period. Even Buddhist *sanghas* were different from churches and did not place social restrictions on the free movement of *margis*.

THE POLITICAL CONDITION

A third condition, the political condition, is the absence of political restrictions on religious and philosophical dissent, on formation of opposing alternatives to mainstream faiths and philosophies, or on movement from one philosophical/religious outlook to another.[49] This condition seems to be frequently present in ancient India. A glorious illustration is to be found in the edicts of Asoka, the builder of a large empire in third century B.C.E.

Two Asokan edicts are particularly relevant for our purpose. The seventh edict begins with "The beloved of the gods wishes that all Pasandas[50] must dwell everywhere, in every part of his kingdom."[51] This seems like a simple, quite inconsequential statement, but in fact it articulates a normatively defensible response to religious coexistence and freedom.[52] To begin with, many outlooks in that period were deeply opposed to one another. Vedic Brahmanism, centered around animal sacrifice in order to propitiate the gods and get their assistance to secure this-worldly goods, was still pervasive. This was deeply offensive to the Jainas, who rejected a this-worldly soteriology and believed in the principle of *ahimsa*. The teachings of the Buddha disagreed deeply both with the indulgences of Vedic Brahmanism and with the radical ascetism of the Jainas. Buddha introduced an other-related ethics that was as concerned with self-fulfillment as with right conduct toward others, especially the poor, the needy, and the vulnerable. This morality encompassed all living beings—not only humans but animals too. It required enormous political courage and imagination to build an inclusive polity where different religious groups could coexist and publicly debate their differences. After all, a number of morally dubious responses were also conceivable—extermination, expulsion, or back-to-back neighborliness rather than face-to-face discussion.

In edict twelve, we find a discussion of the basis of such coexistence. For Asoka, *dhamma* constitutes the all-important common ground, the essentials, of all *pasandas*, and the fundamental content of *dhamma*, its core principle *vacaguti*, is variously interpreted as restraint on speech or control on tongue. We do not have much evidence of the verbal battles and the agonistic energies that were expressed in these vitriolic tongue-lashings. But the edicts imply that verbal wars in that period were intense and brutal. They simply had to be reined in. But what kind of speech must be curbed? Edict twelve says that speech disparaging other *pasandas* without reason must be restrained. Speech critical of others may be freely enunciated only if we have good reasons to do so. However, even when we have good reasons to be critical, we may do so only on appropriate occasions, and even when the occasion is appropriate, we must never be immoderate. Critique should never belittle or humiliate others. Thus, there is a multilayered, ever deepening restraint on one's verbal speech against others. Let us call it *other-related self-restraint*. However, the edicts do not stop at this. They go on to say that one must not extol one's own *pasanda* without good reason. Undue praise of one's own *pasanda* is as morally objectionable as unmerited criticism of the faith of others. Moreover, the edicts add that even when there is good reason to praise one's own *pasanda*, it too should be done only on appropriate occasions, and even on those occasions, never immoderately. Undue or excessive self-glorification is also a way to make others feel small. For Asoka, blaming other *pasandas* out of devotion to one's own *pasandas* and unreflective, uncritical, effulgent self-praise can only damage one's *pasanda*. Offending and thereby estranging others undermines one's capacity for mutual interaction and possible influence. Thus, there must be equally multitextured, ever deepening restraint for oneself. Let this be *self-related self-restraint*.

Elsewhere, in the seventh edict, Asoka emphasizes the need not only for self-restraint, *samyama*, but also *bhaavshuddhi*, again a self-oriented act. *Bhaavshuddhi* is frequently interpreted as self-purification, purity of mind. However, this term is ambiguous between self-purification within an ethic of individual self-realization or one that at least includes cleansing one's self of ill will toward others. My own view is that in the context of the relevant edicts, the moral feeling of goodwill toward others or at least an absence of ill will toward others must be a constitutive feature of what is meant by *bhaavshuddhi*. Self-restraint and self-purification are not just matters of etiquette or prudence. They have moral significance.

Given all this, and to advance mutual understanding and mutual appreciation, it is better, the edict says, to have *samovaya*, concourse: an assembly of *pasandas* in which they can hear one another out, communicate with one another. They may then become *bahushruta*, one who listens to all, the perfect listener, and open-minded. This way they will not only have *atmapasandavraddhi*, the growth in self-understanding of one's own *pasanda*, but also the growth of the essentials of all. The edicts here imply that the ethical self-understanding of *pasandas* is not static but constantly evolving, and such growth is crucially dependent on mutual communication and dialogue with one another. Immoderately blaming others without good reason disrupts this process and, apart from damaging *dhamma*, diminishes mutual growth.

The edicts add that no matter how generous you are with gifts and how sincere your devotion to rituals, if you lack *samyama*, *bhaavshuddhi*, and the quality of *bahushruta*, then all the liberality in the world is in vain. Conversely, one who is unable to offer gifts but possesses the aforementioned virtues lives a *dhammic* life. Thus, one whose speech disrespects no one, who has no ill will toward others, and who does no violence to living beings is truly dhammic. Dhamma is realized not by sacrifice but by right speech and conduct.

Both these edicts point not to persecution but to civility across religions; but the more general point I wish to convey through this discussion is that no single philosophy legitimated a political rule, and therefore the distance between state power and religion/philosophy was always maintained. I believe this point is of a piece with Sheldon Pollock's view that nothing compels us to believe that "legitimation, or its higher form, ideology . . . have anything like the salience in noncapitalist nonmodernity that scholars have attributed to them."[53] In conjunction with other conditions, a continuing tradition of refusal to use any religious outlook for political legitimation helped both religious diversity and accommodation as well as freedom of movement from one religion to another.

I suspect that one might speak of a postpagan, secular age in the modern West because the availability of these conditions has re-emerged in "the West" in recent times. In the Western world, modernity marked the formation of its first "secular age." This has happened because first, the ties between religions and states have weakened. Even exclusive humanism in western Europe and the North Atlantic does not directly legitimate political rule. Second, the church has lost the vast social power it once possessed. The emergence of exclusive humanism and the prestige of its initial and continuing association with modern science helped undermine the church. Finally, although no doctrinal changes have occurred to dissolve what Assmann calls the "Mosaic distinction," its significance has been considerably weakened.

Let me return to a discussion of India. It is obviously not my contention that there is an identity or continuity between the ancients and the moderns because a secular age figured in both worlds. But some possible, tentative conclusions, needing more investigation, might be drawn from the essay. First, there might have been many a complex of movements leading to diverse secular ages spread across several centuries and across many regions. We must both explore these different secularities and unearth the different movements that engendered and shaped them. Second, each of these was distinct and different from others, but there is no prima facie ground to lump them under the rubric "primitive" and view others as "developed." Even a more sophisticated cognitive and moral evaluation cannot assume a naïve progressivism. That judgment will vary from feature to feature and will be context dependent. Third, despite all the differences, there are ways in which these might be similar, and these similarities might turn out to be as illuminating as all the differences. Here I draw inspiration from a remark of Bernard Williams in *Shame and Necessity*. Williams refers not to similarities due more or less to biologically based need, nor to unconscious similarities, but to unacknowledged similarities concerning concepts we continue to use in interpreting our own and other people's feelings and actions and to which, for cultural and historical reasons—and in the case of postcolonial societies such as India, political reasons—we have become blind. Most Indians believe that when they participate in traditions they call "secular," they could not but take part in modern Western patterns of thought and practice. It would be intellectually exciting to find that in some respects such participation might take us to traditions of an entirely different set of ancestors who had some vague relation to us but who we had dismissed as too exotic and remote. Perhaps this might give us reasons to treat the peoples of ancient India as our cultural ancestors in quite the same way that Europeans so uninhibitedly view Greeks as theirs. This, after all, has implications even for how we view Hinduism.

My own sense of where we currently are in India is hazy and somewhat chaotic—a huge and important difference from Taylor's own masterly grasp of modern social imaginary. But it is obvious that a better sense of the *transition* to contemporary social imaginary—and not merely an idea of what it is—depends upon what this is a transition *from*. My hunch is that what modern "Western" worlds appear to have left behind—the ancient, the medieval, the early modern—is still around in India, not in the same form or to the same extent, but still recognizable. Despite massive changes and against the wisdom literature of history and social science, continuities between the old and the new appear to abound in India. [E]ric R. Dodds, one of the great scholars of ancient Greece lamented the difficulty of retrieving the beliefs and feelings of persons long dead, most of whom had left no evidence or record of what they thought and felt. However, he also noticed the remarkable continuity between accounts of ancient Greek rituals and anthropological descriptions of current Greek rituals. The continuities in India might be more abundant. To take just one example, the core marriage ritual of going around the fire has been unchanged for three millennia. Both Witzel and Pollock note the recitation of Vedic hymns in parts of India are virtual tape recordings of past recitals. Sometimes one wonders whether our inability to grasp many ancient phenomena in India is due less to their prolonged absence and more to their continuing presence. They still lie so close to us that we barely notice them!

An intellectual experiment might help demonstrate this point. The following paragraph is written in the present tense. But were I to change it to the past tense, it would ring as true for a period three thousand years earlier!

> Indians are unusually this-worldly. Their religious life inclines them to turn toward, not away from the world, to be at home rather than in exile. It also secretes proclivities to accept rather than change the world. They take the business of living in this world very seriously, as also their duties as a householder to produce and reproduce life, practices without which societies die. To procure these worldly goods, their own action—karma—is crucial but equally or more significant is help from various gods. Gods could either directly facilitate the outcome or block the obstructive machinations of evil spirits and malicious humans. They must be beckoned by ritual and prayer to the aid of their devotees and appeased on public festivals to secure collective benefits. The world of Indians is largely non-transcendent, propelled by the pursuit of this-worldly goods and is wonderfully enchanted.
>
> A large number believe in rebirth and hope that they would be reborn as humans. The key to long life and rebirth as a human is the performance of correct daily and seasonal rituals. Quite possibly, another world beyond this one, the abode of ancestors and gods, exists, but a belief in radical transcendence does not follow. For most Hindus, *moksha* is of little consequence, a legitimate goal of full-time salvation

seekers such as *sadhus* and *sanyasis*, rare anyway in today's *kalyuga*. Heaven is a more achievable goal but really it would be best to continue living on earth. Hindus, it seems, really can't have enough of life here and now.

NOTES

1. Charles Taylor, *A Secular Age* (Cambridge: Harvard University Press, 2007).
2. Amartya Sen, *The Argumentative Indian* (New York: Picador, 2006).
3. Taylor, *A Secular Age*.
4. Wilfred Cantwell Smith, *Modern Culture from a Comparative Perspective* (Albany: State University of New York Press, 1997).
5. Ibid.
6. Taylor, *A Secular Age*, 152.
7. S. W. Jamison and M. Witzel, *Vedic Hinduism* (1992), 38. www.people.fas.harvard.edu/~witzel/vedica.pdf
8. B. Nakamura claims that in doing so the "Brahmins became strongly this-worldly." Hajime Nakamura, *A Comparative History of Ideas* (Delhi: Motilal Banarsidass, 1992), 38.
9. Richard Gombrich, *Theravada Buddhism: A Social History from Ancient Benares to Modern Colombo* (London: Routledge & Kegan Paul, 1988), 30. Also see Nakamura, *A Comparative History of Ideas*, 39.
10. Jamison and Witzel, *Vedic Hinduism*, 47.
11. Ibid., 76.
12. Gombrich, *Theravada Buddhism*, 30.
13. Brian Black, *The Character of the Self in Ancient India* (Albany: State University of New York Press, 2007), 11.
14. Jamison and Witzel, *Vedic Hinduism*, 67.
15. Ibid., 74.
16. Taylor, *A Secular Age*, 26.
17. For a good discussion of these issues, though in a different context, see Daniel C. Ullucci, *The Christian Rejection of Animal Sacrifice* (Oxford: Oxford University Press, 2012), 26.
18. Jamison and Witzel, *Vedic Hinduism*, 63.
19. Ibid., 65.
20. Ibid., 60.
21. Gombrich, *Theravada Buddhism*, 33.
22. Jamison and Witzel, *Vedic Hinduism*, 66.
23. Jan Gonda, *Selected Studies*, vol. 6 (Leiden: Brill, 1991).

24. For an interesting discussion see Madhav Deshpande, "Interpreting the Asokan Epithet Devanampiya," in *Asoka: In History and Historical Memory*, ed. Patrick Olivelle (Delhi: Motilal Banarsidass, 2009), 19–44.
25. Taylor, *A Secular Age*, 19–27.
26. Greg Bailey and Ian Mabbett, *The Sociology of Early Buddhism* (Cambridge: Cambridge University Press, 2006).
27. [M]ichael Carrithers, *The Buddha* (Oxford: Oxford University Press, 1983).
28. Louis Renou, *Religions of Ancient India*, Jordan Lectures 1951 (London: Anthlone, 1953), 120.
29. Ibid., 132.
30. As Renou (*Religions of Ancient India*) puts it "Karman is a real substance, a sort of *poison* that infects the soul and renders it liable to be invaded by the other substances, space and time" (132).
31. "The procedure is to destroy former karman and ward off the approach of new karman; this is accomplished by asceticism and the other methods of purification, both ritual and mental." Renou, *Religions of Ancient India*, 132.
32. Ibid., 124–127.
33. Taylor, *A Secular Age*, 19–20.
34. Renou, *Religions of Ancient India*, 122.
35. Since I believe a crucial link exists between the wide availability of options to a very large population and what Taylor calls the "immanent frame," I am arguing that while immanent frame is what characterizes a modern "secular age," other secular ages may be conceived differently, even without the presence of the immanent frame.
36. For drawing my attention to two sets of criteria, I must thank Charles Taylor, personal communication, January 6, 2013.
37. On the distinction between inclusive and exclusive monotheism, see Jan Assmann, *Of Gods and Gods* (Madison: University of Wisconsin Press, 2008), 13.
38. Gombrich, *Theravada Buddhism*, 25–26.
39. Assmann, *Of Gods and Gods*; and Assmann, *The Price of Monotheism* (Stanford, Calif.: Stanford University Press, 2010).
40. On the distinction between implicit and explicit theology, see Assmann, *Of Gods and Gods*, 13.
41. Ibid., 54–58.
42. Ibid., 58.
43. Ibid., 58–62.
44. Assmann, *The Price of Monotheisim*, 8–30.
45. Ibid.
46. Taylor, *A Secular Age*, 79–80, 445.
47. Benjamin Kaplan, *Divided by Faith* (Cambridge: Harvard University Press, 2009).

48. Gombrich, *Theravada Buddhism*, 90.
49. W. Cantwell Smith, *Modern Culture from a Comparative Perspective*, 29–30.
50. This is one of the most difficult terms to translate. Its standard meaning is "heretic," but clearly Asoka does not use it in this sense. The standard translation is "sect," which is unsatisfactory because of its Christian association. There is an imaginative suggestion, now rejected, that it might be linked to *prasha*, a term in avestha and similar to *prashna* in Sanskrit, meaning "question." An imaginative translation could then have been a group of questioners or enquirers. But there is no strong evidence to support this view. Radha Kumud Mookerjee links it to *parishad*, meaning "assembly." But that too is not accepted by everyone. Perhaps, the best translation would be "followers of a school of thought or teachings." This last is the meaning I intend here. I will continue to use the Prakrit word *pasanda* in the main text.
51. The identification of King Priya-darshi with Ashoka was confirmed by an inscription discovered in 1837.
52. For a detailed discussion see Rajeev Bhargava, "Beyond Toleration: Civility and Principled Coexistence in Ashokan Edicts," in *Boundaries of Toleration*, eds. Alfred Stepan and Charles Taylor (New York: Columbia University Press, 2014).
53. See Sheldon Pollock, *The Language of the Gods in the World of Men, Sanskrit, Culture and Power in Premodern India* (Berkeley: University of California Press, 2006), 517. Pollock's account is far more complex than suggested here, and it is beyond the scope of this paper to get any further into its details.

BIBLIOGRAPHY

Assmann, Jan, *Of God and Gods*. Madison: University of Wisconsin Press, 2008.
——. *The Price of Monotheism*. California: Stanford University Press, 2010.
Gombrich, Richard. *Theravada Buddhism: A Social History from Ancient Benares to Modern Colombo*. London: Routledge & Kegan Paul, 1988.
Heesterman, J. C. *The Broken World of Sacrifice: An Essay in Ancient Ritual*. Chicago: University of Chicago Press, 1993.
Hiltebeitel, Alf. *Dharma*. Honolulu: University of Hawaii Press, 2010.
Kaplan, Benjamin. *Divided by Faith*. Cambridge: Harvard University Press, 2009.
Nakamura, Hajime. *A Comparative History of Ideas*. Delhi: Motilal Banarsidass, 1992.
Olivelle, Patrick, ed. *Asoka: In History and Historical Memory*. Delhi: Motilal Banarsidass, 2009.
——. *Dharma: Studies in Its Semantic, Cultural and Religious History*. Delhi: Motilal Banarsidass, 2009.
Pandey, Govind Chandra. *Studies in the Origins of Buddhism*. Delhi: Motilal Banarsidass, 2006.

Pollock, Sheldon. *The Language of the Gods in the World of Men: Sanskrit, Culture and Power in Premodern India*. Oakland: University of California Press, 2006.

Renou, Louis. *Religions of Ancient India*. Jordan Lectures 1951. London: Anthlone, 1953.

———. "Vedic India." In *Classical India*. Vol. 3. Delhi: Indological, 1971.

Smith, Wilfred Cantwell. *Modern Culture from a Comparative Perspective*. Albany: State University of New York Press, 1997.

Taylor, Charles. *A Secular Age*. Cambridge: Harvard University Press, 2007.

Ullucci, Daniel C. *The Christian Rejection of Animal Sacrifice*. Oxford: Oxford University Press, 2012.

Williams, Bernard. *Shame and Necessity*. Berkeley: University of California Press, 1993.

Witzel, Michael. "Vedas and Upanisads." In *The Blackwell Companion to Hinduism*, ed. Gavin Flood. Oxford: Blackwell, 2005.

9

GANDHI'S RADICALISM
AN INTERPRETATION

Akeel Bilgrami

Gandhi never really came to any detailed grip with the concept of class, to say nothing of "class struggle," in the remarkable politics he espoused and generated. Yet I believe that there is a radical and "left-wing" Gandhi in a broad but genuine sense of that term. But if that is so, then there are interpretative tasks ahead. We need to reconcile this Gandhi with the ease with which he seems susceptible, and rightly susceptible, to an antimodernist reading.

I would like in this short essay to suggest that if we follow a method that is superbly exemplified in illuminating detail in Taylor's *A Secular Age*, we can construct a line of argument to show how Gandhi's seeming antimodernism may be read side by side with his radicalism.[1] The method is essentially genealogical and can be found in the sections of *A Secular Age* in which our secularity is seen not as a subtraction of religious elements from our past worldview but as a deliberate construction of the early modern period, a construction in which aspects of religion itself played a central role, especially the providential aspects of a newly emerging deism in that period. Since my subject is Gandhi, my own application of this method is bound to focus more than Taylor does on the fallout in *political economy* and *politics*, of the changes in religion and theology at that time.

The governing interpretative idea I propose to reconcile the seeming contradiction of his antimodernism with his radicalism is this: Gandhi's antimodernism reflects the deep *continuity* of his *radicalism* with a tradition of *early* modern dissenting tradition in Europe, especially in England, which Gandhi himself did not mention (or even perhaps know of) but with which his own alleged *anti*modern ideas shared a deep and detailed affinity. This genealogical grounding of his radicalism offers up a very specific historical dialectic, and I will argue that what seems antimodern in his thought would not seem so if we kept the dialectic firmly in our sights.

In general, that elements with affinities to the radical dissenting ideas voiced in the *early* modern period should appear to us as *anti*modern is due to a confluence of two closely related factors: first, our tendency to think of the path from early to late modernity as a teleological inevitability and, consequently, second, our tendency from the perspective of our lateness to stamp out the significance and the substantial presence of the *dissenting* voices in the earlier period, which lost out in the arena of social and political, and intellectual conflicts of those times. These two factors conspire to make it seem as if any assertion of some of the radical ideas to be found in early modern dissenting traditions at a date as late as, for instance, 1909, when Gandhi wrote *Hind Swaraj*[2] necessarily occupies a stubbornly reactionary position—something they would not seem to do if we viewed the teleology as uncompulsory, as Gandhi certainly did, and if we kept fully in our view of the past the power and pregnant possibilities that those dissenting ideas possessed, despite their having lost out.

If it were possible to use the expression "early modern" as an entirely innocuous description of a period of time in Europe, with no built-in implications of describing only those antecedents that would unfold into the developments of late modernity there, the radicalism of that period might give us a sense of the possibilities that Gandhi still held out for in the India of the early twentieth century, *which he took to be at the sort of cusp that Europe was at in the "early modern" period*. So, to repeat the crucial dialectical point, at the risk of causing tedium: that we should see this stance as antimodern, rather than as the radical ideas they were with a *serious potential for preempting* in India in the early part of the twentieth century the lamentable path in political economy and aspects of political governance that had developed over the modern period in Europe, is only because the directional certainties of an assumed teleology that have the effect of writing out of history the great significance that dissenting voices had at the earlier time, leaving the impression only of those antecedents that make our own conditions seem inevitable for our own time. How to correct this tendency in us by elaborating this dialectical reversal of it is the chief preoccupation of this short essay.

Why, in this explanatory dialectic, am I fastening on, of all things, the radicalism of seventeenth-century Europe, especially England, as the right frameworking antecedent to illuminate Gandhi's seeming antimodernism?

Hind Swaraj is a work of passionate and instinctive criticism. Yet it sets down themes that recur steadily in subsequent writings and, when studied together with them, yields something much more systematic that a reader might construct. My own construction[3] has been to stress that Gandhi's ideas that originated in that text and were haphazardly developed over time can be given some structure if we take one question as central for him and see his answer to it as having a range of implications that he himself interestingly draws, though not always quite as explicitly in the way I will elaborate later. At its most general, that question is: "When and how did we transform our concept of the world as not merely a place to live in but a place to master and control?"

Gandhi believed that in our answer to this question, we can aptly put the blame for the transformation about which the question inquires on certain developments in the West that have to do with modern science, a central theme of *Hind Swaraj*. It is for this reason that I think we must turn to the early modern period of the mid- and late seventeenth century in Europe, when the new science was first fully formulated and then consolidated in ways that went well beyond the narrow confines of science itself.

A sympathetically careful study of his writings allows us to see past some of Gandhi's occasionally crude rhetoric and find that his is not really a critique of science as some careless words he writes suggest, or even of modern science, but really a critique of a *metaphysical outlook* generated by certain developments around the rise of modern science, and *its implications* for society, politics, political economy, and culture. (He even scrupled to say that he was not against technology as such but against the *mentality* generated by technology when it was in the control of elites who had no other motive but to use it for their own gain.[4])

The reason why I stress "outlook" and "mentality" rather than science itself in characterizing the target of Gandhi's criticisms is because a range of metaphysical concepts and attitudes that were getting entrenched around the new science in the late seventeenth century and after were vehemently opposed—in terms closely anticipating Gandhi—by some (dissenting) *scientists*, who had no quarrel whatever with the new science that had reached its most systematic formulation in Newton's laws. What exactly, then, were these dissenting scientists protesting, if it was not the laws themselves? The answer to this question that I will try and present in summary has such a detailed echo in Gandhi's thought that it would be a failure of historical imagination on our part not to make something interpretatively significant of it in coming to an understanding of Gandhi's own criticisms of "modern science" and "Western science" as he sometimes (too) simply put it.

I have said that Gandhi's finding the fault line in modern science for a whole spectrum of social and political harms should be seen as his answer to his own most underlying omnibus question: "How and why did we transform our concept of the world as not merely a place to live in, but to master and control?" The question is an omnibus one, because in it the term "world" is a term of art whose meaning is highly layered, connoting nature, the human inhabitants of nature, and the relations between nature and its inhabitants, as well as the social relations between the inhabitants. *All of this* as an *integrated* whole, he claimed, was conceptually transformed by a certain metaphysical outlook that accompanied the new science, but for the sake of making his question and his own answer more tractable, it is worth breaking the integrated elements down into different transformations, despite the integrity that the term "world" would suggest.

One could begin with "nature" and ask more specifically about it, echoing the more general question: "How and when did we transform the concept of nature into the concept of natural resources?" We could then also ask how and when did we transform the concept of human beings (the inhabitants of nature) into the concept of citizens,[5] and the concept of people into the concept of "populations." And I think, as we proceed to answer these questions along the broad lines suggested by Gandhi's attribution of blame for these transformations to the changes wrought by science in the modern period, a final question emerges, which is roughly: "How did we transform the concept of *knowledges to live by* into the concept of *an expertise to rule by*?" It is a mark of Gandhi's extraordinary intellectual ambition that he thought *all* of these seemingly diverse questions were highly integrated, that these various transformations were really, at bottom, *the same transformation*, owing to a fault line to be found in the outlooks generated by modern science. (Hence the formulation of the question in omnibus terms of "the world" as a place to master and control.) Were he to have had Karl Marx's understanding of political economy and the notion of class, he would have noticed that Marx too had developed a parallel template for a range of transformations in his discussion of alienation, wherein he explored the making into resources and means, and therefore into objects, the entire realm of human subjectivity. I will say a little more about this in a moment, but for now, let me begin with the theme of nature.

Gandhi's understanding of nature derived heavily from his Bhakti ideals, in which nature is sacral, suffused with the divine, continuous with the atman that suffuses each of its inhabitants, a divinity available therefore to all at all times, should they perceive and find him through devotion.[6] Such a conception of nature was pervasive also in the popular religious understanding of much of early modern Europe; often described by intellectual historians as "Neoplatonism," it received explicit articulations in the writings of such radicals, for instance, as the Digger, Gerard Winstanley, and the Ranter, Jacob Bauthumley, to name just two in England.[7] It was this conception that was undermined in the late seventeenth century by a very markedly providentialist turn in which God was not to be viewed as immanent within nature but rather placed at a distance outside the universe, described often by the Latin expression *Deus absconditus*—a God put away for safeguarding. Newton's writings had much to do with this exile of God to a place outside the universe, though nothing in Newton's science demanded it.

That is to say, nothing in the Newtonian laws, nor basic concepts such as gravity, required that God be seen as being in a place external to his creation. The idea that nature and matter were inert and desacralized and that motion came about as a result of a push by God from an *external*, Archimedean point was no more demanded as an underlying explanation of motion by Newton's laws than the idea that motion was made possible by a divine *inner* source of dynamism in matter and nature. Both views were perfectly compatible with the laws and with the notion of gravity. Yet in the late seventeenth century the Royal Society's ideologues (figures such as, for instance, Samuel Clarke and Richard Bentley) insisted that the immanentist explanation of the broadly pantheistic, dissenting view (the brilliant and highly volatile Dissenter, John Toland, is said to have coined the term "pantheism," though not, of course, the doctrine) was dangerously wrong and that it was built into Newtonian science that God be seen as occupying a providential distance from and an external control of the universe. Newton himself acquiesced in this public presentation of his view—despite his well-documented Neoplatonism and alchemical obsessions in his private study—calling nature and matter "stupid" and "brute."[8]

This desacralization of nature was vociferously protested by dissenting scientists (then, of course, called "natural philosophers") such as Toland and Anthony Collins, who despite their embrace of the new science formulated by Newton, saw in this *metaphysical interpretation* of it, a whole range of consequences for politics and political economy that they denounced, invoking the ideas and practice of the earlier radical sectaries in their denunciation and anticipating in detail a number of Gandhi's criticisms of the destruction of agrarian village life. In particular, they claimed that a conception of a brute and inert nature was being mobilized by the orthodox figures in the Royal Society in open alliances they had formed with commercial and mercantile interests and an Anglican orthodoxy to make nature available for a much larger-scale and much more systematic plunder than ever before. They were responding to a deliberately constructed ideological framework pronounced in remarks such as this one by a contemporary scientist and early economist of this period, and a prominent figure in the Royal Society, William Petty, who said, in a publication of 1682: "What may be the meaning of the glorified bodies, in case of the place of the blessed shall be, without the convex of the orb of the fixed stars, *is that the whole system of the World was made for the use of our earth's men.*"⁹ From an anima mundi, there were built-in constraints to what one could take from nature, and such taking as was done was often accompanied by rituals of respect shown to nature and the divine presence within it, before cycles of planting and hunting. Now, without any such metaphysical constraint, they argued, things were openly being set up to take from nature with impunity, and they presciently saw that this would make the hitherto fitful practice of forced enclosures, a systematic and legally backed practice, depriving the poor of the collective cultivation of the commons and generating a future that pointed to what we today call "agribusiness," thereby destroying the local forms of egalitarianism the radical sects had envisioned and even, in the case of the Diggers, briefly put into practice.

It is quite apparent even at a cursory glance that the remark I cite from William Petty is an early statement of the implications of a metaphysical outlook that Gandhi deplored. It is evident, for instance, in the tremendously interesting correspondence between Gandhi and Tagore. Tagore echoes Petty when he says: "If the cultivation of science by Europe has any moral significance, it is in its rescue of man from outrage by nature, not its use of man as a machine but its use of the machine to harness the forces of nature in man's service."¹⁰ By contrast, Gandhi's view was that one could not find one's way to treat humanity as ends rather than means, unless one's fundamental metaphysical outlook toward nature was different from what is suggested by Petty and Tagore, unless, that is, we see nature itself as containing value properties, properties that go beyond the properties that natural science studies, properties that are not merely resources for exploitation, but rather properties which make normative demands on us and thus constrain us normatively. Gandhi, of course, presented these normative demands of nature as having a sacralized source. That was the Bhakti influence. To dismiss this as antimodern merely because of that fact would be shallow in the extreme. Marx had such a view of nature's relation to its human inhabitants too, though it is embedded in an entirely secular framework. It can be found in several passages in *The Economic and Philosophical Manuscripts of 1844*. Here is just one: "Only here does nature exist as the foundation of his own human existence. Only here has what is to him his *natural* existence become his *human* existence, and nature become man for him. Thus society is the unity of being of man with nature—the true resurrection of nature—the naturalism of man and the *humanism of nature* both brought to fulfillment."[11] How exactly to relate passages such as these that stress highly abstract metaphysical claims about the unalienated human existence that comes from our human agency being in sync in this way with the normative demands of nature[12] with Marx's far more specific claims about what makes for an unalienated form of labor is a delicate philosophical task, yet it is absolutely necessary to understand his overall conception of labor and alienation in modern capitalist society. The proximity with Gandhi on these issues is striking and well worth elaborating, but I cannot possibly do so here.

The dissent in early modern Europe, though it had as a central component such a protest as I have been expounding—a protest against the metaphysical support given by the orthodoxies congealing around the new science to emerging ideas of systematically destructive extractive capitalist economies—was by no means restricted to this component. It linked this component integrally to much broader issues in politics and culture.

One of the clearest goals of the ideologues of the Royal Society was to use the new science in the preservation of order and stability in society. Here again they were joined in an alliance with the latitudinarian Anglican as well as commercial interests for whom the revolutionary unrest of the pre-Restoration period was a palpable danger. Thus, for instance, the Boyle Lectures to be given regularly at the Royal Society had a fully articulated rationale to this effect, hardly disguising the keenness to present a Christianity and a commercial ethos that was an antidote to the "enthusiasm" (a widely used term of disparagement at that time) of popular religion and the dissenting philosophical and scientific voices that had affinities with it. It was enthusiasm after all that sought to turn "the world upside down." Toland and others were targeted, and many Dissenters sought haven in Rotterdam and other Dutch and European cities.

What about the scientific dissenting ideas was *political* anathema? How could opposition to something as arcane as the desacralization of nature and matter be a source of anxiety, not just about converting nature into a resource for zealous extraction for profit, but about governance? The inferences are not hard to draw, and they were forcefully drawn in the debates of the time. The exile of God from his immanence in nature and in all bodies was literally conceived as "putting him into *safekeeping*" as the Latin term *conditus* in the phrase *Deus absconditus* suggests (*abs* for its part connoting "putting him far *away*"). Why should a scientific establishment and its worldly allies want such a thing? And why should Dissenters so urgently oppose it?

If God's presence was no longer available in all bodies and all matter to the visionary temperaments of all who inhabited his earth, the values and virtues to live by that he enshrined were now the prerogative of learned and scriptural judgments, of university-trained divines. The Dissenters wanted that reversed, arguing that the *democratization of the polity* turned crucially on this not being an elite possession. It should be stressed that this form of dissent was not at all an instance of the quite different and far more general attack on popery in the Protestant Reformation, demanding an individual relation with God unmediated by the orthodoxies and institutions of the Roman Catholic Church. That in fact had yielded quite the opposite of what the Dissenters wanted, it yielded what political theorists have called a "possessive individualism" of the domesticated forms of Protestantism that emerged from the Reformation. The Dissenters were precisely opposing this Protestant establishment in England (and in the Netherlands) and its alliances with the economic and scientific establishment.[13] Such an individualism was a far cry from the democratized communities they sought, embedded in the collective cultivation of the commons that the radical sects of a few decades earlier had tried to draw from their ideas of a divine presence in all bodies and all persons. Winstanley, like Gandhi, had in fact explicitly described this Neoplatonism, with its close affinities with the Bhakti ideal that also saw God as available to the most humble of men and women (not restricted to "scholars bred up in human letters"[14]) as having a "great leveling purpose." This was indeed one of the chief sources of anxiety about the radical sects that led to them being charged with "enthusiasm."[15] The Dissenters saw the privilege of only a learned and trained accessibility to God as a quite local symptom of a much more general antidemocratic elite tendency that led to the law being handed over to feed lawyers and medicine being unavailable freely or cheaply, and in the end to a model of governance that revolved around the restored monarch and his court.[16]

Their fears were entirely borne out. Governance did indeed come to have this form in the post-Restoration period, and all radical dissent seemed to have been made irrelevant when even *liberal* ideals went on a little later to present essentially this form of governance as a "revolution" (the Glorious Revolution of 1688), aligning themselves firmly with ideals of civility in society and orderly governance by law that would stand behind the rule over a brute populace by a monarch, reflecting on earth a mundane version of the rule of an external providential God over a brute and material universe. Early liberalism in Europe, thereby, emerged as a legally and constitutionally codified successor to now-outmoded ideas of the divine right of kings.

Ideals of civility around the monarch and his court in the early Enlightenment have been well studied by a range of intellectual historians, including, of course, Norbert Elias.[17] They all attest to their relevance for the polity, but none, so far as I know, say what it most came to imply. They were intended to mark a form of codified decorum in behavior that defined the small and privileged class that ruled and was *defined against* the behaviors and lifestyles of the rude "populace" over which it ruled, a lifestyle characterized by cruelty and violence in their everyday lives. In the seventeenth century "cruelty" was considered the opposite of "civility." Thus to label a people "cruel" was to justify being cruel to them. So "cruel" was the opposite of "civil," but opposing cruelty with cruelty was not understood as cruelty, because it could come in the name of a defense of ideals of civility. Thus, it was that a stipulative semantics of this sort around "civility" created a screen by which the courts and the propertied classes hid from themselves the cruelties of *their own* perpetration. In the high Enlightenment, the notion of civility with this built-in screening function morphed into something much more abstractly specified in the quite different vocabulary of rights and constitutions. This transformation now had cruelty as something recognized, never as occurring in polities governed by the rights that their citizens possessed, but rather as occurring only in distant places that lacked such rights and constitutions. However, justly celebrated rights are—and they are deservedly so, for obvious reasons no one should deny—this new version of the self-deceptive screen hid from Western powers the cruelties that they perpetrated on distant lands, which lands alone—because they lacked notions of rights and constitutions—were recognized as given to cruelty. And, as is well known, a pedagogical framework was often set up as a justification for colonization, to bring civility and rights to the colonized lands (a perfectly familiar ploy, still masquerading under the label "liberal empire"). Gandhi was perfectly aware of this historical screening function of notions of civility and rights and thought that it only came to pass because of a loss of the genuine democratization that lies in the availability to the visionary temperaments of *all* people of the values to live by in a sacralized (Bhakti) conception of the ordinary perceptible world around one—and it explains to a considerable extent his studied indifference to the vocabulary and codifications of rights.

I think a deliberate "indifference" is the right description of his attitude. It is not as if he was hostile to the idea of rights: he seemed more to have been unimpressed by the intensity of enthusiasm for them among liberals around him and the well-known doctrines of the colonial masters from which these were drawn. And the considerations I have just mentioned were fortified in his mind by a sense of the provenance of these liberal ideas and how they spoke to a situation that he felt should not be allowed to arise in the first place in India. All these codifications were the unfolding achievement (if achievement is what it was) of a form of polity that emerged from the Westphalian peace. It was central to the Westphalian ideal that it needed to find a legitimacy for a new form of state that could no longer find its justifications as earlier monarchical forms often had, from a purely divine right. It sought a more mundane legitimacy in a new idea of the nation that required of its people a *feeling* for it *as a nation*, a nationa*lism*, as it is often called; and feelings for the nation, or nationalism (as opposed to any project of improving the conditions of its people), as a legitimizer of a particular form of state in the Westphalian ideal was generated in Europe by what is now a very familiar pattern that came to be called "majoritarianism." The preponderance of a nation's people came to feel for the nation most easily and most intensely by finding some "minority" or minorities and stigmatizing them as implicit outsiders. Once a nation-state was consolidated on these grounds of an abiding mix of prejudice and discrimination, an entire set of principles had then to be formulated to constrain the effects of such a nationalism, and so a variety of ideas of political secularism and multiculturalism codified in the form of rights and freedoms for *all* citizens of the nation had to be introduced. Gandhi had nothing intrinsically against these rights and these ideas (though quite possibly he doubted they would go deep enough to be efficacious against the deep roots of a majoritarian national ideal built up along these lines), he rather did not want for India, *in the first place,* the larger context of a noninclusive nationalism in which they were adopted as a subsequent constraint on its ill effects. He found the entire trajectory of the Westphalian ideal of the nation with its majoritarian-legitimizing nationalism deplorable; and he saw no reason for India to go down that path. The "modern" figure whom he most opposed, therefore, was Savarkar, not Nehru (who in fact often spoke in accord with Gandhi in finding distasteful the entire Westphalian ideal). Savarkar's admiration for this aspect of European modernity was explicit in his ideal of Hindutva,[18] and it is what Gandhi most recoiled from. His indifference to rights and other such codifications was only that he saw them as necessary within such a development as Savarkar desired. Independent of that development, human beings did not become better human beings by being made over into citizens of a nation-state and constrained by its codes and constitutions.[19]

I have tried in these few pages to show how a deep commitment to Bhakti ideals with their close affinities to the Neoplatonism of an earlier period of European history and intellectual history bring out the radicalism of Gandhi's political thought in the early part of the twentieth century. If it is right to suggest as I have that he thought, in 1908, that India stood at the sort of cusp that Europe stood at in the early modern period, then it is possible to read a whole range of his anxieties for India as being quite of a piece with the prescient anxieties that the scientific dissenters, invoking the earlier, radical sects, had expressed about developments in political economy and political governance that were being generated by worldly alliances between the ideologues of a new science and commercial and oligarchic and established religious interests that were setting up for a period of ruthless capitalist extraction and an incipient centralized form of government dominated by elites to facilitate it. To speak with a sense of resistance against a future for India that fell prey to these developments would only seem reactionary and antimodern, if there was something about these developments that was inevitable. But its inevitability only seems so if we write our histories as if there was no substantial dissent that had any significance in early modern Europe, a victor's history, as it were, a Whiggish complacence in our understanding of the past.

I will not deny that there are interesting questions to be raised about how deterministic we should reckon our understanding of the modern period to be. It is possible that, with the onset of a full-fledged capitalist society, there are deeply deterministic tendencies set up, what Marxist economists, following Oskar Lange, have sometimes called the "spontaneity" of capital.[20] But we, in the present paper, are talking of a period at the cusp, *before* the onset of a thoroughgoing capitalist formation, and it is not obvious at all that anything like the same idea of deterministic dispositions and tendencies can be mapped onto that earlier period because, as this version of the Marxist view makes clear, the tendencies are *immanent* tendencies, immanent, that is, to *capital*. It would take both the bite and the detail out of this understanding of determinism, which is focused on capitalism, to glibly extend it to contexts prior to the appearance of those details in the history of political economy. Nor is it obvious that a general doctrine that we have come to think of as "historical materialism" speaks to a strict and generalizable teleology of this kind. Marx's own writings are not fully committed on this subject, and it is interesting to note that the specific economic argument, tied to Oskar Lange's notion of capitalism's "spontaneous" tendencies that I mentioned, nowhere suggests that there is a generalizable form of determinism, of which this particular analysis of capitalism is only a particular instance.

I conclude, then, that it was part of the creativity in Gandhi that he should have relied on the resources of religious traditions in India[21] to present a range of arguments that we may rightly perceive as radical, if we assume with him that India was roughly at the sort of crossroads at which Europe found itself in the early modern period; and we would only infer that this affinity with the *early* modern radicalism in as *late* a time as the early twentieth century is *anti*modern if we make further highly dubious and complacent deterministic teleological assumptions that Gandhi himself never made. Much more needs to be said on each of the elements in my argument that I have presented here in a very encapsulated form. Yet even in this brief formulation, it should be clear that what Gandhi was analyzing in some detail falls under a certain rubric of changes that Weber describes with his own omnibus term "disenchantment," as do many of the details of Taylor's analysis of the changes wrought in the early modern period. As I have tried to present the details, they cumulatively describe an outlook, one that I summarized in the most general question I attributed to Gandhi, and which breaks down into more detailed and specific questions. Each of these details speak to an increasing *detachment* that characterizes the general outlook, and it is this detachment that Gandhi, I am claiming, saw as flowing from the process of "disenchantment" and desacralization.

However, to return to what I said in my opening remarks, there is something about its entire argument and its conclusions that is bound to prompt misgivings in those who are anxious to find all such arguments backward-looking and outdated. It is fine to see Gandhi as creative for his time of writing, roughly a century ago, but who can deny his irrelevance for our own time, when his ideas will be perceived as nostalgic and even reactionary. This qualm is so naggingly pervasive in commentary on Gandhi that it deserves to be addressed explicitly before closing.

In doing so, I will not speak to Gandhi, in general, but to my specific reading of him in terms of the genealogical dialectic I have drawn briefly in this essay. As in any reading of a dominant figure, I have brushed under the carpet many of his political stances and ideas. I have stressed and developed a line of thought that is undeniably present in his writings, but Gandhi was so diverse, prolific, and instinctive a writer that it would be dishonest to deny that there are also strains in his work (and his actions) that run in directions other than the one

I have presented. I cannot, then, avoid restricting myself to my own reading in responding to this qualm, but I will need to elaborate a little more some structural elements of the reading that should make it at once more clear and more complicated how I see his relevance today without feeling the need to constantly apologize for a nostalgist revivalism of a romanticist thinker with a premodern cast of mind. There is nothing nostalgic about it, so long as the structure of the reading and the argument are properly presented and understood.

So, just to recap how these issues I am about to address go beyond the question of how to read Gandhi that I have addressed so far: I have asked, using a method that I find exemplified illuminatingly in Taylor and using Gandhi's ideas as a guide, "What transformations in the past have landed us where we currently are, conceptually?" I have tried to show that this genealogy often ignores or silences the potential power and significance of dissenting voices in the past against those transformations. And now my question is: "Is the unearthing of those voices (with which Gandhi shares so much) by a counter-genealogy, necessarily an act of genealogical nostalgia?"

To address this question, I want to try and remove a possible misunderstanding of the argument and conclusions I have tried to present. It may be thought that what I have done is present dissenting voices of the past and find relevant for today their anxieties, which in their time, were *anticipatory* of developments they *predicted* would be harmful. And, in turn, it may be thought, now that those developments are deeply entrenched in our outlooks and our societies, that recalling those anxieties cannot retain the particular significance they had in their time, because these outlooks and the structures and institutions they have spawned are not reversible by us. So it will be said: *we* are *not* anticipating and predicting these effects any more, we are amidst them, coping with them, and such coping cannot have realistic aspirations of *reversal* of these tendencies but must seek other forms of containment and constraint.

There is no gainsaying any of this. But the point of the argument was never simply to appeal to the anxieties with a view to restoring either the outlook or the material scenario before the transformations. The use of words like "reversal" in this context can be careless in the presuppositions it makes. Thus, for instance, faced with *disenchant*ment of the sort that Gandhi was analyzing in his criticisms of the "modern" West, and regarding that he had the same premonitions for India as the dissenters in Europe in the early modern period had for Europe, one may think that the point of attending to Gandhi and to these dissenters, as I have done, is to suggest the idea of some sort of "*re*-enchantment." I have no objection to being interpreted as making this suggestion, so long as it is understood that *re*-enchantment today cannot possibly amount to the *revival* of an enchantment that was provided by notions of a sacralized nature, among other things. That is partly why I have tried to present the notion of disenchantment itself along lines that do not *in particular* turn on the loss of sacralized notions but rather in more general terms on the evacuation of value properties in one's conception of the world (including nature) we inhabit.

Talk of "reversal" suggests (1) that there is a *comprehensive* and *global* entrenchment today of developments that the early dissenters were anxiously predicting and wanting to avoid for Europe (and Gandhi was anxiously predicting and wanting to avoid at a much later time for India). And it suggests (2) that as a result of this entrenchment, there is nothing in our subjectivity that is not pervaded by the outlooks that were generated first in the early modern period and gave rise to the dissenters' (and later Gandhi's) anxieties.

Both these presuppositions are quite unjustified. I will start by responding to (2), since it is the more fundamental misunderstanding of the argument and its intention, and it takes more patient argument to repudiate it.

(2)

Having fastened on the period since early modernity in Europe (following to some extent Weber's own focus with the term "disenchantment" on that time and place as significant), I had said that a set of conceptual transformations in that period removed from our collective and public mentality a conception of the world (including nature) we inhabit as containing value properties THAT MAKE NORMATIVE DEMANDS ON US. This, I argued, gave rise to (at any rate, was accompanied by) a certain detachment of outlook that in turn had large effects (at any rate, was accompanied by large effects) on society, political governance, and political economy. That was the more secularized gloss on disenchantment that I was presenting, a secularized counterpart to Weber's rhetoric of disenchantment as desacralization.

Now, my intention in saying this was *not* to deny that ordinary people everywhere still see the world, including nature, as making *normative* demands on them, something that would not be possible if they did not also possess a perceptual phenomenology of *value* in their apprehensions of the world and if the world did not contain perceptible value properties in the way that the early dissenters and later Gandhi insisted on, though in their case, as a result of their *sacralized* understanding of nature. Indeed, I have argued in explicit detail elsewhere (see the essay "Gandhi and Marx" in my book *Secularism, Identity, and Enchantment*,[22]) that we would not even possess the kind of human practical agency we do if the world did not contain value properties to which our agency responded. Thus, I could not possibly be denying that we do, in our everyday agency in fact perceive the world to be shot through with value properties, that is to say, to be 'enchanted', though, of course, in the low-profile sense that in our own time need not require any assumption of sacralization.

But if this is so, a question arises: "What then was the intention in giving the particular genealogy of '*dis*enchantment' that I did, if I am also insisting that our capacity for practical agency to this day requires that there is this form of enchantment?"

Much turns on answering this question adequately. Here, then, is a way to think of it.

In order to make sense of these large disenchanting transformations I presented, even as we (necessarily) retain our quotidian responsive relations to a world suffused with value properties, we need to begin by drawing a distinction between two levels.

The conceptual transformation by which nature came to be conceived as natural resources (along with the other accompanying transformations I mentioned) is one that occurs at a level of *collective and public* understanding, a form of understanding generated by alliances made between powerful forces in society that control governance, political economy, and a slowly emerging and increasingly consciously determined public opinion on these large, collective, and public matters. It is at this level that policy gets shaped and implemented, and though that happens on sites distant from quotidian life, many ordinary people often acquiesce, sometimes even enthusiastically, in these transformative outlooks and policies.

By contrast, there is a level of understanding in these very same people that is and remains *quotidian* in its responses to the world (including nature and human others), often instinctive, but often cultivated too, though cultivated in the habits of *local* forms of solidarity and concern rather than via the inculcation of the wider public, collective understanding I mentioned in the last paragraph, and often implicitly, though mostly unknowingly, at odds with the latter.

We should enter some obvious qualifications here. Though the general contrast and distinctness of these two levels is, as I will try and convey, striking and highly significant, there is no reason to think they are not also often scrambled. So, for instance, it is often the case that there are areas of concern and sympathy shown at the more collective level, but these are formulated in terms that are part of the conceptual vocabulary of the detached outlook that these transformations have wrought—and when pursued at this public level they will surface in various forms of poverty measures, of safety nets for the worse off (broadly welfare and social democratic policy), as well as constraints on pollution of nature via taxes on polluters or the enforcing of "cap and trade" agreements, and so on. Conversely, there is also no doubt sometimes vicious inhumanity that surfaces in the local lives of ordinary people in their instinctive individual everyday responses to one another as well as individual disregard for one's environment. But acknowledging all these qualifiers does not spoil the general point that there have been a set of transformations at the public and collective level, which I have presented via the critique offered by a Gandhi and his early modern antecedents, transformations that are not necessarily echoed in the everyday and local, communal lives of individual responses to nature and to others.

With the distinction between these two levels in place, I want to now invoke a notion familiar to psychologists under the name "the frame problem."[23] The really important point here is that we need not just a distinction between the collective level, on the one hand, and the individual (local) level, on the other, but also, as a result of that distinction we need to register the following: *individual* mentality finds itself in *two quite different frames*. On the one hand, there is the frame of quotidian life, where responses are shaped by one's instincts and locally, communally developed habits, even in metropoles, though obviously there the localities and networks within which the responses are reared will be quite distinct. On the other hand, the individual human mind, unless it has very deliberately and self-consciously resisted it, has also surrendered itself to a different, more collective frame that is dominated by ideas and ideologies that have had a long-standing run since they took hold in the period that I have identified genealogically. And *because they are in two separate frames, these two ways of thinking are insulated from each other and individual subjectivity cannot see the many inconsistencies that may exist between judgments and responses that it makes in the two different frames*. One may show great concern and regard for others and for one's environment in one's everyday individual responses and not see that as broadly inconsistent with the support one gives to outlooks and policies in the other frame within which one thinks and acts.

The idea of such differential framing no doubt has existed throughout history. So it is not as if the *distinction* between two frames emerged only in early modernity. What occurred in early modernity is a significant transformation of *one* frame, a significant transformation of individual mentality as it is shaped by the *public and collective level* of thought, a transformation away from the public and collective outlooks of an earlier period, which were no doubt bad in their own different ways—something that we should acknowledge explicitly even as we delineate, as I have tried to do in this essay, the *distinct* ways in which the collective framework that emerged in early modern Europe was bad. And I am making this point about two frames so as to make clear that there may be a great deal of *continuity* in human mentality in one frame (the frame in which the individual subject makes quotidian responses to the world) even as there are large transformations in the other frame. So, when one is critical today of the outlook and its effects that have developed at the public and collective level, one need *not* be doing so nostalgically from the beliefs and convictions of an *earlier collective* outlook that has been superseded by the transformations at the collective level but rather by the lights available in one's *current quotidian* frame of ordinary individual responses to one another and to our natural environment.

Even if the foregoing analysis has said something very briefly to address the charge that my appeal to the radicalism of the earlier period (and even to someone as late as Gandhi) is an exercise in nostalgia, the question remains about whether this apparatus of differential frames allows us to say anything plausible against the related objection that the only feasible radicalism that is possible today is not what I have presented via my genealogy but, at best, a series of social democratic constraints to be placed on the economic and political structures of capitalist modernity? I believe the apparatus does have something persuasive to say about this question as well.

The focus of a humane and radical politics in our time should seek not merely to put constraints (say, Keynesian constraints), salutary though these constraints might be, on the harmful outcomes of the collective framework we have embraced in the last two or three centuries, but rather also seek to *remove* for us *the boundary between*, what I have called *the two frames* within which our subjectivity engages, making them one single and unified frame. To the extent that this is possible,[24] it may also become possible for one to see the inconsistencies in one's thinking (inconsistencies that were not visible while the two frames were in place) and resolve them in a specific direction—by finding, as I have already suggested, in the resources of one's thinking in the more quotidian frame, the possibilities for criticizing in a more fundamental and radical way, the outlooks developed at the collective level that have shaped our thinking when one's mind thinks within the other frame. Why do I say that the resources in this more quotidian frame might well make for a more fundamental and radical criticism and politics? Because, as I pointed out a little earlier, it is in this frame that our minds have not been contaminated by the public, collective

transformations that I, following Gandhi, have been so critical of. It is in this frame, as I said earlier, that we still possess the sensitivity and responsiveness to the enchantment of the world, to the value properties in the world, including nature, that make the deepest normative demands on us.

So the idea really is this: a politics that is more radical than the social democratic ideal of putting constraints on the runaway effects of our collective outlook and frame must *first* seek to remove the boundary between the collective and the quotidian frames of individual human mentality. If the boundary and the dual frames remain, then such radical politics as we can configure remain limited to the conceptual resources available in the collective and public framework and those, as I said, will be ameliorations conceived in the relatively limited terms of the constraints that come from social democracy. It is when the conceptual resources (available in the more deep-going ideal of an enchanted conception of nature and the ideals of an unalienated agency that it makes possible) that are to be found in our more quotidian frame are brought to bear critically on the collective frame that the most creative possibilities of a radical politics, which is much more *fundamentally* critical of the collective frame, can emerge.

The objections I am responding to are important (and constant) enough that I will risk fretting the reader's patience and repeating in summary the argument against them, which appeals to the "frame" idea. The boundary between the two frames is what keeps the two in place and prevents us from seeing the inconsistency of the judgments and responses we make at the collective and the quotidian levels. Being in two frames, they are insulated from each other, and we cannot detect the inconsistencies between them. But if a politics first brings to our consciousness that we have been locked in two frames and succeeds in removing that boundary and allowing our subjectivity to function in a single, unified frame, it would have, in doing so, brought to our consciousness the inconsistency in our responses and judgments of which we were hitherto unaware. If this happens, there is, as I said, a serious chance that we will be able to remove these inconsistences in a certain direction, seeing in the resources of the quotidian frame the possibilities of radical criticism of the thinking that takes place (and has taken place for some three centuries) in the collective frame. And moreover, if this happens, the criticism will *not* be from the *collective* outlook of some *bygone* period of early dissenters, available only in nostalgic fantasies, but from the resources within the quotidian frame of our mind *in our own time*. And moreover, once we recognize the inconsistencies between judgments and responses we make as a result of removing the boundary that keeps the frames in place, some elements in the collective outlook we have acquiesced in may seem to be *fundamentally and radically* wrong by the lights of our own quotidian thinking today. This shows that we are not only not harking back nostalgically to some *previous* collective outlook but also that we are not restricted to the critical resources of the *collective* outlook in our own time that have been domesticated by the very transformations they aim to criticize, reducing all criticism to merely placing constraints on those transformations.

Now, of course, it is perfectly possible that *some* of these lights or critical resources to be found in the more *quotidian* of our two frames of the present will *coincide* (or cohere) with *some* elements of the *public and collective* frame of the past. That cannot be grounds for indicting us with nostalgia, since these would, given their presence in the everyday responses of ordinary people today, be merely the critical resources we find ourselves with in the *present* to fundamentally resist (rather than merely contain with thought of safety nets and other marginal constraints) what collective assumptions and public policy impose on us. If what were available to us in our everyday responses to the world today did not *at all* coincide, *even in part* with any of the ideas in the collective framework of the past, there would be no possibility for what is called "tradition" to inhere in pockets and interstices of our mentality and help with criticizing our present collective understandings with a view to forging newer and more creative developments of collective thought. This, it seems to me, is to conceive the modern as a tyranny, where one asserts not merely that one is within modernity, which is hardly deniable, but that we must be completely domesticated by it into a complacence that allows no dialectic between tradition and modernity to emerge in a way that gives rise to critical resources for one against the other, in *both* directions. It is this insistence, that *all* criticism that is not to be dismissed as nostalgic will only be *of* tradition *by* modernity, that I am calling a complacence in the dominant outlook of the present. Such a complacence in past times would have prevented or preempted the very changes that are often described, and described with pride, as "the Renaissance," which presumably emerged precisely via a dialectic in which elements of the collective frame of a past classical period inhered as aspects of "tradition" in the responsiveness of individual quotidian agency and talent to the normative demands of the world, to resist some of the collective understanding of the medieval period.

What I must admit, of course, is that it is perfectly possible that once the boundary between the two frames I have identified is removed and inconsistencies in one's thinking are revealed, the deliberations by which the inconsistencies are then resolved might have the opposite effect from the one I am holding out as a possibility—it may have the effect of bringing our individual responses more in line with the large transformations we have wrought and which Gandhi was lamenting. There is no reason to think that there is any inevitability in it happening in one direction or other. But that still does not mean it is not a worthy goal of a radical politics to seek these possibilities of deliberation and to hold out for a possibility that we will find in the instincts and concerns that get their play in our individual responsiveness to the normative demands of others and of the environment critical resources that make us see through the harms of having acquiesced in outlooks that have been formulated at the more collective and public level. As I said, these resources may well be the basis for a more radical politics than one that merely seeks ameliorations of the sort that social democracy does, worthwhile as these latter might be in their own limited terms; and the idea that there is no form of radical politics that is not simply what social democracy offers as a dogma, conjured up by a too quick tendency to convict of nostalgia everyone who seeks such a more radical resistance. What such a radical politics would look like and what it would seek is too large a subject to pursue here. (As I have suggested in another essay in my book *Secularism, Identity, and Enchantment*, to theorize it in fuller terms one would have to reorient the relations between a range of notions such as alienation, liberty, and equality, and link Gandhi's ideas to those of Marx and a range of other dissenting voices in the West that I have briefly presented here.) All I wanted to do in these closing remarks about the effects of there being two frames is to begin to provide a rudimentary conceptual framework and analysis through which it does not seem compulsory for us to think that in finding a radical politics today to be of a piece with dissenting voices in early modern Europe, one is merely indulging in an exercise in nostalgic genealogy.

(1)

Let me close then with a brief response to (1), the first presupposition, which encourages the thought that my genealogy back to early dissent restricts its relevance to an earlier time now superseded by late modernity. This is the presupposition that the outlooks, whose emergence in the early modern period were alarming to the dissenters in Europe in that period, are by now too *comprehensively* entrenched, and so the radical resistance to them offered by the Gandhian ideas I have been expounding is a nostalgic aspiration to reverse a fait accompli.

The question "Is the reach of those outlooks, the reach of this sort of modernity that this genealogy critically analyzed, now really comprehensive?" is, of course, an empirical question. But in assessing the evidence to answer it, one has to use one's judgment about what is so entrenched as to be beyond resistance, what it means for outlooks and the material conditions that they spawn to affect the entire globe's mentalities and economies. Some of this judgment that is needed may have to fight the tendency to think that what holds for Europe and North America today holds for the rest of the world tomorrow—a familiar struggle for those who have resisted and are resisting the intellectual assumptions of a past and present imperialism.

Let me only consider the question in light of the theme of nature and our unalienated relations with it that I have drawn from Gandhi.

Consider the fact that the broad idea of what I have presented as an unalienated relation to nature (even if in secular rather than sacralized terms) is echoed in detail in the indigenous societies of many parts of the Southern world today, from Latin America to Australia, who assume without strain that nature has "rights" that need to be honored and respected. Though "rights" was not initially their term for it, it is now working its way into the language of the legal systems of societies like Bolivia and Ecuador with powerful indigenous actors in the leadership. These are not remote or idle metaphysical principles that reflect out-of-date outlooks, they have had direct policy implications like leaving oil in the ground in Ecuador and ending the mining of uranium in Australia. These are present enough today as alternatives for us to be able to say without any strain of nostalgia that instead of ridiculing it, other so-called advanced and advancing societies who have glibly claimed the comprehensiveness of their own worldview, should take this sensibility seriously and should try to embrace some of it themselves, if they are not to be doomed and drag everyone else to their doom as well. Bolivia takes the lead in this campaign in the global South and is known to have dismissed the posturing in the Copenhagen meeting on the environment a few years ago on the grounds that the naked capital-driven policies of the more powerful governments were insincerely tinkering with the problems rather than asking fundamental questions about the relations between capitalism and the destruction of the environment. To generate alternative fora for policy making, the Bolivian president, Evo Morales, organized a meeting not just of governments and their mandarins, but a massive "summit" with voices from well over a hundred countries and with almost forty thousand people in attendance. Voices from below demanding a variety of detailed antipollution measures and a systematic legal right not restricted to regions but possessed of universal status; a right given to the planet's natural properties that would prevent their further transformation into natural resources. Bolivia is only the leader in all this. It speaks for what is assumed to be right by similar indigenous communities *all over the globe*.

And there is much *theoretical* consolidation of these practical and political efforts in the works For example, Elinor Olstrom, the winner of the Nobel Prize in Economics, and others have shown how water, pastures, forests, fish stocks, were they left in the control of users rather than in the control of capital and states that serve the predatory intent of capital, would have the effect of seriously combating the repeated appeal to the notion of the "tragedy of the commons" to give the impression of the inevitability of the outlook that Gandhi was inveighing against. These voices of traditional societies may lose in the end, but I think it is fair to say that they are more vociferous and more organized now than they have been for a very long time, and that is surely a sign that the reach of that outlook is not comprehensive.

No doubt the possibilities of resistance to the outlook that these efforts and policies offer are still local and regional, and they may well remain so for quite some time. But nothing in the relevance of Gandhi that I am offering asserts that resistance and reversal could either come by a global revolution or overnight. Patience and accumulated effort in such a resistance should be in the service of a bricolage of reversal, and from these angles in which the partial light of reversal comes into view in some places, there is wisdom to be learned for other places in the rest of the world, whose complacence is precisely what this wisdom refuses to adopt. In the success of these more regional efforts there are exemplary sources for growing the resistance, and they owe conceptually and philosophically to local ideals of enchantment, often secular versions of enchantment, but outside the orbit of secular assumptions that emerged in Latin Christendom, though, as I have said, with profound affinities with some of the historically dissenting voices against those assumptions in Latin Christendom itself.

NOTES

1. I had deployed this method in relation to Gandhi and other themes having to do with "occidentalism" before I had read Taylor on this subject, in my essay "Occidentalism, The Very Idea: An Essay on Enchantment and the Enlightenment," *Critical Inquiry* (Spring 2006). But my deployment had none of the tremendous mark of learning and weight of detailed analysis that is found in *A Secular Age*, which I then read with a palpable sense of instruction and solidarity.
2. Anthony J. Parel, ed., *Hind Swaraj* (Cambridge: Cambridge University Press, 1997).
3. In my "Gandhi, Newton, and the Enlightenment," *Social Scientist* 34 (May–June 2006); and "Value, Enchantment, and the Mentality of Democracy: Some

Distant Perspectives from Gandhi," *Economic and Political Weekly* 44, no. 51 (December 2009).

4. "What I object to is the craze for labour-saving machinery. Men went for saving labour, till thousands were without work and thrown on the streets to die of starvation. I want to save time and labour not for a fraction of mankind but for all. I want the concentration of wealth not in the hands of the few, but in the hands of all. Today machinery merely helps a few to ride on the backs of the millions. The impetus is not on philanthropy, or to save labour, but on greed. . . . It is against this constitution of things that I am fighting with all my might . . . The supreme consideration is man" (*Young India*, 13 November 1924).

5. Gandhi's large concern was with the idea of citizens of a *nation-state*, not earlier forms of citizenry such as the polis in ancient Greece, say. In my paper, "Democracy and Disenchantment," *Social Scientist* 37, nos. 11/12 (November–December 2009), I spell out and criticize the role played by the early modern idea of a *social contract* in constructing such a notion of citizenship.

6. Including the lowliest of animals, though that is not a subject I will take up in this essay. A more immediately relevant point is that his stress on the pervasive immanence of divinity is why Gandhi consistently downplayed *moksha* in his understanding of Hinduism.

7. Bauthumley claimed that God was "in all Creatures, Man and Beast, Fish and Fowle, and every green thing, from the highest Cedar to the Ivey on the Wall," as quoted in Norman Cohn, *The Pursuit of the Millennium* (Oxford: Oxford University Press, 1970); and Winstanley said, "God is in all matter" and "The truth is hid in every body," quoted in Christopher Hill, *The World Turned Upside Down: Radical Ideas in the English Revolution* (New York: Penguin, 1984). Such pantheistic and hermeticist ideas are central to the doctrine of a range of radical sects not just in England but also from an even earlier time (since the doctrines of Bruno and Ficino) all over Europe. It is also worth observing that in Europe the later figure of Baruch Spinoza was more influential in politics than some of these earlier Neoplatonists, and he was sometimes an inspiration for the scientific dissenters in England that I have mentioned. Spinoza, too, is well known for having equated divinity with nature, but I do not think that this is properly described as a "pantheism," and it is almost certainly wrong to describe it as "sacralizing" nature. It was too abstract an equation for that. Still, it is interesting to see Jonathan Israel making much of Spinoza's influence on radical groups in Europe in his work *Radical Enlightenment: Philosophy and the Making of Modernity in Europe 1650–1750* (Oxford: Oxford University Press, 2002). The entire work sets out to shift the emphasis from the orthodox liberal influence of someone like Locke to what he calls "Spinozism" and its intellectual sway on a more radical side of the Enlightenment. What is "radical" for Israel, however, is measurably less critical of the orthodox Enlightenment than

the radical groups I am focused on in England. These differences are worth a close study. The channel of radicalism I am appealing to in order to understand Gandhi's radical ideas goes from sects such as the Diggers through the scientific dissenters I have mentioned to figures like Blake and even later to Morris and the nonconformist religious Left ideals of Tawney. Israel seems to be seeking channels that lead to quite different figures such as, say, Condorcet, who have almost no affinities with Gandhian thought. Gandhi apart, even if one were focused just on Europe, there is interesting comparative work to be done here in the intellectual history of the Enlightenment and its legacy for the possibility of a genuinely radical politics. I suspect Israel's historical conception would fall far short of the tradition of radicalism I am seeking.

8. These descriptions occur in the *Opticks*, 1704. For Newton's less public Neoplatonist side see, J. E. McGuire and P. M. Rattansi, "Newton and the 'Pipes of Pan,'" *Notes and Records of the Royal Society of London* 21, no. 2. (December 1966).

9. William Petty, "An Essay Concerning the Multiplication of Mankind," in *The Petty Papers*, vol. 1 (1662) (emphasis added).

10. See the section on "The Cult of the Charkha," in Sabasyachi Bhattacharya, ed., *The Mahatma and the Poet* (New Delhi: National Book Trust, 1997).

11. Dirk J. Struik, ed., Michael Milligan, trans., *The Economic and Philosophical Manuscripts of 1844* (New York: International, 1944), 137.

12. One should not interpret Marx's remarks here about a human element in nature ("Nature becomes Man for him," "the Humanism of Nature," etc.) as presenting a vitalist conception of nature or as nature containing an element of intentionality. That would be to go too far afield from his materialism. It is the rather more sober thought that nature makes normative demands on us. However, even to see nature as making such demands is to see his materialism in a light quite different from rigidly scientific interpretations of Marx. Resistance to this scientism, however, has often led to views that are, in my view, quite implausible. For example, to see intentional elements in nature is implausible for a quite simple reason. Where there is intentionality, we are in a region of phenomena whose elements can be the target of certain forms of criticism. Thus, human intentionality is the sort of phenomenon of which one can say, as we frequently do, such things as: "That is a wrong action to have done, or a wrong belief or even a wrong desire to have." But it makes no sense to say similar things about elements in nature. We do, of course, criticize nature. We may say, "That was a disappointing sunset," but that is not the form of criticism that addresses itself to intentional elements. The inappropriateness of the more conceptually weighted (by "conceptually" I mean to suggest concepts having to do with moral psychology) criticisms, when it comes to nature, is something of a proof that it is quite extravagant to propose that nature is suffused with intentional properties over and above value properties that make normative demands on us.

The term "demands" in respect of nature making normative demands on us should not, therefore, be taken too literally. These are not demands coming from an intentional subject or subjects, nor does Marx intend to say they are, in his rhetoric of "Nature becomes Man for him" and the "Humanism of Nature."

13. I am focusing on England particularly because the alliances that I mention between scientific bodies and commercial interests and established Protestantism were first most explicitly formulated in England as a result of the Royal Society's openly commercial and religious links, both in the body of its membership, as well as in its self-understanding, as exemplified, for instance, in Boyle's own instructions with which he set up the lectures bearing his name. I should also explain not only my focus on England but my emphasis on Newton rather than earlier figures who were well-known antecedents to some of these metaphysical ideologies. The reason I do not take up Bacon or Descartes and Galileo on the continent is because it was not till the late seventeenth century that bodies like the Royal Society made the worldly alliances that exploited this desacralized metaphysics in the ways I have outlined, citing the authority of their immediate contemporary and hero, *Newton*, in doing so. Perhaps the first to have pointed out the role of Newtonianism in the rise of capitalism is the Soviet scientist and historian of science Boris Hessen in his address "The Social and Economic Roots of Newton's Principia" to the Second International Congress of the History of Science in 1931 in London. The claims in that address are remarkable for their simplicity and their attribution of intentions to Newton himself. It is far more plausible to see it as what Margaret Jacob calls the "culture of Newtonianism," a mandarin phenomenon in which the Royal Society was the most active agent. See M. Jacob, *Newton and the Culture of Newtonianism* (Amherst, N.Y.: Humanity, 1994). Still, there is no doubt that the Hessen thesis was a great mobilizer in this direction in the cultural history of science.

14. Gerard Winstanley, *The Breaking of the Day of God* (1648). Available in electronic reproduction by the Early English Books Online Text Creation Partnership (Ann Arbor: University of Michigan, 1999).

15. That is why the opposition to Neoplatonist and pantheistic ideas took on the entire rhetoric of *absconditus* or safekeeping. This rhetoric is essential to the providentialist turn. It adds considerably and very specifically to the more general idea of a transcendent God. The idea of a transcendent rather than immanent, pantheistic conception of God was, of course, by no means an innovation of the seventeenth century nor of this emerging metaphysical doctrine around the idea of a *Deus absconditus*. But it began to have a quite new and enhanced meaning, as well as urgency, in this time in the Royal Society in England and other parts of Europe that resisted Neoplatonism as well as Spinoza's immanentist and pantheist ideas, an urgency in which older ideas of transcendence were given entirely new motivations of a desire to put God in "safekeeping,"

that is, put him away from an availability to the ordinary perceptions of all who inhabited his earth that his immanence would provide, since that was a metaphysical and religious basis for "enthusiasm." And it is for this reason that these explanations of motion and all the familiar Newtonian images of a "clock winder" were invoked by the scientific establishment, who had made open alliances with worldly interests, thus making the transcendent conception into a providentialist ideology of far wider significance than a mere metaphysical interpretation of the new science.

16. Gandhi too writes scathingly in a number of places of the antidemocratic tendency in law and medicine as institutionalized in the West along very similar lines, just as he writes by contrast about the democratizing possibilities in Bhakti ideals.
17. Norbert Elias, *The Civilizing Process* (Oxford: Blackwell, 2000).
18. V. D. Savarkar, *Hindutva* (New Delhi: Hindi Sahitya Sadan, 2003). I had heard Ashis Nandy give a brief but shrewd and convincing reading of this work along these modernist lines in a lecture on the trial of Gandhi's assassin a few years ago. For a denial of the view that Nehru's ideas of the nation amounted to something Western and Westphalian, but rather viewing it as what I called Archimedean, see my "Two Concepts of Secularism: Reason, Modernity, and Archimedean Ideal," *Economic and Political Weekly* 29, no. 28 (July 1994).
19. I will not trace here the further morphing I had mentioned earlier of the notion of "knowledges to live by" into the idea of an "expertise to rule by" that followed these ideas of citizenship. There is a large and nuanced story to be told of the loss of engagement and an elevation of detachment in the study of human society that came from seeing the world, including nature, as brute, such that it could no longer make any normative demands on us that prompted our engagement. All agency and engagement was relegated by this move to our subjectivity, not to subjectivity *responding* to the demands of a value-laden material and natural environment. As the passage from Marx I cited earlier makes clear, Marx's ideas of an unalienated life are very much part of (and a specific sophistication of) a picture in which our subjectivity is in responsive sync to the normative demands of a material and natural world, a world that, if it can make such demands on us, can be described (as I have elsewhere done) as possessed of a "secular enchantment," a secular counterpart, that is, to Bhakti and Neoplatonist ideals. The democratization that this makes possible is what thwarts or might help thwart the passage from the "knowledges to live by" (which the world, including nature so conceived, provides to all who live in it) to the pervasive dominance we see of the "expertise to rule by." I realize these remarks are far too cryptic to convey substance. They are elaborated at much greater length in the papers I mention in note 3, among others.

20. For an elaboration of this form of determinism, see, among several other papers by him, Prabhat Patnaik, "Socialism and the Peasantry," presented at an Alam Khundmiri Foundation Conference on the Radical Enlightenment and subsequently published in *Social Scientist* 37, nos. 11/12 (November–December 2009). These papers and their argument are convincing to me. But they leave my argument untouched for the reason I gave earlier in the text.
21. It was perverse of Gandhi to describe himself as a *sanatani,* or orthodox Hindu. By any measure of orthodoxy, Gandhi's Hinduism is a very maverick mix, about as far from orthodoxy as it is possible to be. I am stressing the Bhakti elements, which are, of course, well-known to be remote from orthodoxy. But even Gandhi's Vaishnavism, owing to the sant-poets of Gujarat such as Narsin Mehta, and his mother's early influence on him, are far removed from Hindu orthodoxy. In fact many elements in it are quite continuous with the Bhakti elements I appeal to in my argument.
22. *Secularism, Identity, and Enchantment,* (Cambridge: Harvard University Press, 2014).
23. In the essay "Occidentalism, the Very Idea: An Essay on the Enlightenment, Enchantment, and the Mentality of Democracy," in my book, *Secularism, Identity, and Enchantment,* I put the notion of frames to use in a quite different context, one of studying certain forms of seeming irrationality, and in that context, I trace the origin of the notion to Freud's methodology for studying irrationality.
24. "What sort of politics in our time makes it possible to remove the boundary between these frames and allow us a single frame for our subjectivity?" is a question I address in the closing pages of my essay "What is Is Disenchantment?" on Charles Taylor's book *A Secular Age* in Michael Warner, Craig Calhoun, and Jonathan Antwerpen, eds., *Varieties of Secularism,* ed. Michael Warner, Craig Calhoun, and Jonathan Antwerpen (Cambridge: Harvard University Press, 2009).

10

A SECULAR AGE OUTSIDE LATIN CHRISTENDOM
CHARLES TAYLOR RESPONDS

Charles Taylor

Perhaps it might help to sharpen some points that emerge from this interesting collection of essays, or at least to bring them more clearly into focus, if I comment on the descriptions they offer of their respective periods and regions. I'll try to do this by contrasting them with the basically North Atlantic trajectory to a secular age, as I understand this.

SUDIPTA KAVIRAJ

Sudipta Kaviraj raises the issue, at several points in his paper, why the existence of religious difference with intense rivalry and intellectual polemic didn't lead to a general decline of religion. One might expect this kind of conflictual, sometimes even violent behavior, to discredit all the parties.

> We can hypothesize that in the long history of religious life there are stages when interreligious conflict threatens to undermine the whole basis of religious life itself, when the observing popular audience might lose faith not in one but in all religions. But this is a *possibility*, not a necessity; given the complex architecture of historical conditions, these occasions might also pass without that possibility being taken in the direction of popular disenchantment.

I would argue that intense conflict of itself didn't lead to a decline in the West either. The period roughly from 1500 to 1700 in Europe saw great confessional conflict, the banning of "heretical" confessions, forced emigration, even armed clashes, but it was nevertheless an age of great religious fervor. All this didn't offer a persuasive argument for the abandonment of the religious forms in dispute until an alternative social imaginary came on the scene that would open the possibility of living outside these forms.

I try to describe this emerging alternative in terms of the construction of an "immanent frame" (IF). One stage in this construction was the development of the modern theory of society, from Hugo Grotius, as constituted by individuals and based on the norm of mutual benefit; another stage, building on the first, was the outlook I describe as "providential deism." The fullness of the IF comes when the new economic, social, educational, and political disciplines and practices end up entrenching a new social imaginary that projects our human social condition as the intersection of impersonal, this-worldly orders: cosmic (the universe understood in the terms of post-Galilean natural science), political (the modern state with a historically chosen constitution), and moral (universal human rights and equality).

In the sixteenth century, most Europeans saw themselves facing at death the alternative of eternal salvation or damnation. The stark drama of this predicament could be softened by a confidence that as good Christians we are on the right track or by the hope that one would be rescued through the intercession of Mary and the saints or by the prayers of one's family. But for most people it couldn't be wished away. In the circumstances, it is understandable that one couldn't regard with total indifference the issue between salvation coming by faith alone or also through good works, however disruptive the dispute was proving to be.

For a similar reason, the existence of strong intellectual arguments against religious beliefs, rituals, or norms will not lead of itself to a general decline of religion. Epicureans in ancient Greece and Rome, *nastikas* like the Carvakas in ancient India, produced such arguments, but they failed to change the social imaginaries of their time. The intellectual "subtraction story" of modern secularization, that science rendered religion incredible, is historically false. The argument from science against religion only comes strongly into play after the IF starts to emerge. For Newton and Boyle, the law-governed universe was one of their principal arguing points in favor of a belief in a benevolent creator.

Of course, modern natural science plays a big role in the story of modern secularity, because its projection of an impersonal cosmic order is a key component of the contemporary IF. But that is because science in our day is more than a set of beliefs held by a minority of experts; science, intertwined with technology, has become a major institution of modern society.

Against this background, Sudipta's account of developments in nineteenth and twentieth century Bengal is very revelatory. Élite experiments in partly Western-derived religious forms, and even in atheist humanism, just produced a disconnect with the social and religious imaginary of the majority. This imaginary evolved, but largely outside the influence of these élites. The new religious and antireligious forms often appeared alien, an unacceptable implant from another civilization. Even many

> Bengali intellectuals, including the most militant modernists, often condemned European modernity as egotistic, materialist, unrestrained, and prone to collective violence. Bhudev Mukhopdhayay produced the first systematic and forceful critique of European modernity, with a powerful message that Indians should not learn anything from them except modern science and political economy. Bankimchandra rejected what he saw as excessive individualism in utilitarian doctrines, and eventually also in positivism, though he was initially drawn to both.

What was lacking was a change in the social forms and practices that would have been hospitable to an imaginary of an immanent frame. Of course, globalization, urbanization, the greater penetration of markets may produce something like this change. However, it is not likely to bring about a carbon copy of Western society but perhaps something more like a mutation of the religious that Sudipta describes in the contemporary forms of Durga Puja.

CLAUDIO LOMNITZ

Claudio has very well set out the problems and aporiai connected to my use of the term "Latin Christendom." In fact, my story only really claims to cover the North Atlantic area and the settler societies emanating from it (United States, Canada, Australia, New Zealand). The reason for speaking of "Latin" Christendom was twofold: first, it at least established a boundary to the East, over against the Orthodox world, as well as the Islamicate; but second, because the religious dynamic was very different in the Christendom centered on Rome than it was in that which related to Constantinople. Different relations of church and state were intertwined with different impulses to reform.

But the dynamic I'm describing only worked out in the way I describe it in the northern tier. One can argue that it doesn't fit the development of Italy very well, at least until relatively recently, partly because of a lack of strong independent and nonecclesiastical states. And it certainly doesn't fit the Iberian states and their overseas possessions. Indeed, very important reservations would have to be registered about my whole account, even in its selected core areas. There are a lot of different stories to be told, and some of them get a much less full hearing than others. Various Lutheran trajectories fall into this category.

I really see *A Secular Age* as a first attempt to sketch out the issues and very much in need of amendment and complementation. And some of the necessary amendment and filling out of the picture is taking place in this book, notably in Claudio's paper.

But the irony stands: Iberia was one of the earliest, most assimilated parts of the Roman Empire of the West, which was the heartland of Latin Christendom, and so the term jars when we leave Iberia out of the picture, as I was forced to do, because of my limitations.

But Claudio has cast a great deal of light on why the drive to reform, which was very alive in Spain at roughly the time of the Protestant Reformation (think of the religious orders, think of the reforms of Cardinal Ximinez), took a rather different direction both in Iberia and in Latin America. The way in which the distinction of Old and New Christians, inherited from the original religious diversity of the peninsula, and its suppression through forced conversions, played out very differently in the Spanish Empire as the basis of a caste system between Creoles and Indians, and obviously had a crucial role in the way Latin American societies evolved.

Again, the gendering of the opposition Catholic/secular obviously has parallels to European Catholic societies. One can think of Third Republic radicals whose wives were Catholic; or Enrico Berlinguer, the Italian communist leader, whose wife also openly practiced her religion. But what is extremely suggestive is that what we tend to see as two very different ways of being human—the individual, buffered, secular self on one hand, and the embedded, porous, open-to-enchantment self on the other—could be lived as roles that can be assumed or cast off depending on the situation.

In addition, the way that multiple strands of religious or nonreligious identification—Catholic, Liberal, secular—overlap and crisscross with different conservative, radical, and revolutionary political stances in Mexico, while it has some analogies to European Catholic societies (and to Quebec), obviously exhibits a quite different type of secularity, which deserves its own sui generis theoretical account. Claudio's paper offers important elements for this account.

PETER VAN DER VEER

Peter van der Veer's paper is as usual very alive to the interspaces between the different Axial civilizations and the borrowings and rejections that take place when they come in contact. Looking at China and the West at different periods and seeing what transpires between them when they come in contact is obviously a very fruitful approach, one that I wish I had taken more advantage of.

I would like to clarify a little what I have said about the immanent/transcendent dyad, and the Western split between the two. In a great many societies and civilizations, both pre- and post-Axial, there is a distinction between things and agencies that are constantly encountered in everyday life and "higher" realities and agencies (spirits, moral forces, numinous powers) that impinge powerfully at some times and places. This distinction between higher and lower is often talked about in terms of immanent/transcendent. Perhaps our use the word "transcendent" depends on how exalted the higher powers are seen to be. But this distinction between higher and lower is what we can call the immanent/transcendent dyad.

The *split* is something different. In almost all cases in which we can speak of the dyad, events in the immanent realm are not seen as fully understandable or explicable without reference to powers of the higher realm. This is true even of the foundational philosophical outlooks of Western civilization. For Plato and Aristotle, the shape of events in our ordinary world is to be explained by the Ideas, which are beyond space and time, and the operation of the Ideas by God (Aristotle) or the Idea of the Good (Plato).

But in Latin Christendom the two sides of the dyad were driven apart, first by a theological attempt to distinguish clearly the workings of Nature and Grace; and then, building on this, by developing a view of a "watertight" immanent sphere, whose workings could be explained without reference to any causal powers outside it. The first important facet of this was the impersonal order of the universe as laid out by Newton and others, governed by natural law. Of course, one could (and Newton did) argue that this universe pointed to a benevolent creator, but it tended to make less and less credible the idea that this creator intervened in the ongoing system he had set up.

This was the basis for a view of what I'm calling a watertight immanent sphere. It is immanent, because it arises in a civilization that recognizes a strong dyad, and it comes about by pleading the self-sufficiency of the lower term. A set of laws applying to this immanent level becomes wholly sufficient to explain what happens down here. This notion of impersonal order is then complemented by others to bring on the social imaginary of the immanent sphere.

This produces a radical concept of the secular that allows for (though it doesn't make necessary) an affirmation that this sphere is all there is. If a secular age is one wherein everyone makes this affirmation, then nowhere, certainly not Europe, is in a secular age. But if it means rather that an age and place shares broadly the IF social imaginary, then Europe (and North America in general) qualifies today.

But this is a minor footnote to the big discussion of how to find the concepts to understand the differences and interinfluences between China and other Axial civilizations, and I am following Peter's work both here and elsewhere, with growing interest and dawning insight, which in turn provoke rising enthusiasm.

RAJEEV BHARGAVA

Rajeev's question about the existence or not of an Indian secular age in past millennia brings us to the heart of the issues we're trying to clarify in this volume. When we take a term used to analyze one civilization and time and apply it to another, the useful question may not be "Is this move right?," but rather "What in our understanding of the term has to change if we are to make sense of the transfer?"

I want to react to Rajeev's paper by looking at two of the terms (or in one case a cluster of terms) that he takes from *A Secular Age* and examining what needs to be adjusted in the tacit understanding they trail behind them, often unnoticed. I suppose I will be speaking often, but not exclusively, of the tacit understanding behind my use of these terms.

First, I want to look at "exclusive humanism." Rajeev wants to apply this term to, for instance, practitioners of Vedic ritual, who saw this as virtually coercing the gods to yield certain goods, and to (at least some) Buddhists and Jains, as well as to others in the last millennium B.C.E. But for me, and perhaps most Westerners today, this term would normally be understood (I put this in the conditional, because it is hardly a term in common use) in relation to what I've called "the immanent frame" (also not a term in common use). Now, the IF is a term that I think captures an important part of the modern Western imaginary. The "immanent" domain that it posits excludes not just gods but also any mode of existence beyond death. When Kant wants to demonstrate what he takes to be the crucial conditions of morality, he mentions not only freedom but God and immortality.

I know that nirvana is an enormously difficult concept to tie down, but it seems to me that Buddhists and Jains and others already transgress this boundary in proposing their soteriologies.

But this is not a critique of Rajeev's claim; rather it is an invitation to grasp what underlies these two different understandings of the term. Why do God and what we might call "transmortality" get lumped together as a matter of course in much Western thinking, whereas the lines are drawn differently in other civilizations?

Maybe part of the answer to this question emerges when we look at the other term, or cluster of terms, that Rajeev analyses here around the secular as a common space that can encourage mutual understanding and permits relatively easy movement between different religious positions. In his discussion of the three conditions for this secularity—the theological, social, and political—a crucial factor is the relative disarticulation of different facets of what we think of as religious life. So as he points out, a choice between different soteriologies doesn't dictate the form of communal ritual in which one engages.

But it is a crucial fact about faiths founded on the "Mosaic distinction" that they tend to a certain "bundling," so that the choice of soteriology (the Torah, or Jesus Christ, or the revelation of Muhammad) dictates the religious community (people of Israel, church, or *umma*), and also what rituals are licit and illicit; and these boundaries have often been closely guarded.

This makes for a striking distinction between Christendoms and Islamic societies on one hand, and those descended from other Axial turns, on the other. Westerners are often astonished to see Japanese holding Shinto rituals for newborns, but getting married in a Christian ceremony, and then buried with a Buddhist ritual.

This absence of "Mosaic bundling" is one of the great sources of misunderstanding of other religions among Westerners. It even affects our definition of religion and hence utterly confuses us (Westerners) when we look at the Chinese scene. But once we get beyond it, we can see why God and immortality don't necessarily go together, and perhaps we can get some greater insight into what Rajeev has described as the ancient Indian secular age. And all that is grist to our mill in this volume.

ALFRED STEPAN

Al Stepan's paper continues the powerful arguments he has been making for a number of years, whose main thrust can be summed up in three basic theses: (1) Secularist or *laïque* régimes, which can assure equal and peaceful coexistence in a context of religious diversity, must no longer be conceived simply in terms of models drawn from the Western experience. (2) An adequate secularist régime, can be defined in terms of what Stepan calls the "twin tolerations," or two basic principles: (a) government or state should not be dominated by any one outlook, religious or antireligious, and (b) there should be maximum freedom or religious expression and practice consistent with requirement (a). (3) There are many roads to a régime meeting condition (2), and each society has to draw on its own traditions and moral outlook, as well as its own earlier precedents (what Al calls their "usable past"), to devise their own solution to the problem.

I heartily agree with these theses and have found Al's work tremendously useful and stimulating, particularly in his offering facts and arguments to counter the reflexes of unreflecting Islamophobia that tend to recur in our Western societies and are frequently encouraged by xenophobic movements and political parties.

He also sees clearly that there is no purely political solution, and certainly not a military one, to the problem of how to create political forms based on the twin tolerations in the Arab and Islamic worlds. A big part of the job has to be done by civil society contacts, discussions, and negotiations, since the developments of the twentieth century have left an immense legacy of fear and distrust between Islamist movements and those of a more secular and diversity-friendly bent. Islamist movements themselves have been responsible for much of this, but the actions of authoritarian secularist governments in the Arab world and Turkey have also envenomed the situation. The good news is that there is a growing recognition on both sides that this mutual fear is sterile and can lead to no peaceful, democratic solution, and that some reconciliation is a vital necessity.

The evolution of Turkey, and now Tunisia, gives reason for hope as well as possible models to follow, even though the Arab Spring is elsewhere either stymied or in trouble, with the future of Egypt uncertain and that of Syria even more tragically in the hazards.

Fortunately, Al's work, either on his own or with Juan Linz, has greatly clarified what the conditions are for a successful transition to a democracy based on the twin tolerations, and laid out the steps which have to be taken and which offer the basis for a "road map," to use this much-abused phrase through the confusing and conflictual terrain of the Arab uprisings.

SOULEYMANE BACHIR DIAGNE

Bachir's paper directly addresses the issue that Al makes central, of finding an alternative form of secularism adapted to non-Western societies. One of the cherished dogmas that circulate in the West is that what Bachir calls "accommodation" between different religious and philosophical views can only come about if we create a special, neutral space between all religions. This is especially strong in the discussion of *laïcité* in France, where one hears of "les espaces de la République," which are supposed to be free from religious symbols. But similar ideas surface in the United States, as we can see in John Rawls's proposal (later withdrawn) that public discussion should be carried on in an idiom free from religious references.

Bachir's account of Islam in West Africa, and specifically in Senegal, shows a quite different model. This is one in which the integrity of the spiritual life requires a certain wariness of too great an identification with the state. The conditions of genuine piety require that one be able to take a certain distance from political power, and thus the claim of a state to be "Islamic" must be treated with a certain skeptical reserve.

In a political context in which religious life is carried on in Sufi brotherhoods, and in which a plural number of these coexist in the same political space, we have the condition for a quite different *laïcité* than the one offered by the French paradigm. This is not to say that French *laïcité* cannot be interpreted in an open fashion that steers away from attempts to marginalize religion and is respectful of religious freedom. We see this kind of régime defended in the work of

Jean Baubérot, whom Bachir quotes. But the original idea behind the French form is nevertheless rather different from the one we find, for instance, in Senegal.

In this latter case, the driving ideal is not so much one of neutrality between and freedom from religions; it is rather powered by an ideal of the proper spiritual path. This means that it can gladly accommodate recognition of different religious communities, can even celebrate their existence in society, without threatening the states neutrality or evenhandedness.

In some respects, it is more like the original American separation, which started as the First Amendment refusal of an established church on the federal level. This was seen as a measure to protect religious freedom. But what was thus protected was still often an established church at the state level.

What Bachir's paper shows is that the most powerful force defending religious freedom and equality may not come from outside religion; it may be a certain deeply felt understanding of piety. The understanding that Bachir is talking from is deeply opposed to "Islamism," understood as the doctrine that Islam offers a paradigm for the state superior to all others and more or less obligatory for Muslims. The whole world has an interest in how this difference will ultimately be resolved in the Islamic world.

Meanwhile it is intellectually liberating to see that there are other possible bases for a diverse and egalitarian democratic society. It is clear that the attempt to build a world in which such democracies can thrive and coexist depends on our ability to recognize and cherish this plurality of outlooks, which include the Indian secularism of which Rajeev has discovered some of the deeper roots in the ancient secular age, as well as Bachir's Sufi-derived régime of accommodation, and others that Western scholars have yet to identify.

ABDULLAHI AHMED AN-NA'IM

Abdullahi's essay is fully engaged in this project of defining an alternative foundation for a diverse and democratic society and, in his case as in Bachir's, one founded on his fundamental commitment as a Muslim. Such a society requires a kind of secularism, but this kind doesn't consist in an attempt to sideline religion or preclude the presentation of religiously based reasons in public debate. Rather, it requires the neutrality of the state between different religious and philosophical worldviews.

> Since citizens who are not religious or do not organize to lobby the state as religious communities are entitled to equal respect for their views and interests, the state and its organs must not fall under the control of one religious community, however large its number may be.

Abdullahi holds that he can, indeed must, subscribe to this principle as a Muslim, because state indentification with any religion would infringe a fundamental liberty that each human being has. For him this is an essential principle of Islam, and it rules out the possibility of an Islamic state under one common definition of this term: that is, a state which would coercively apply a certain definition of the sharia. The duty of a Muslim is to live according to the sharia to the best of his or her understanding: "Being a Muslim is founded on the strict individual responsibility of each and every Muslim to know and comply with what is required of him or her by sharia." A Muslim state on the usual interpretation confiscates the right to do this.

Abdullahi believes that this understanding of an Islamic-inspired secularism is resisted because of the dominance in postcolonial society of the long hegemonic outlook of Western philosophy. He sees a sign of this in the widespread acceptance in Muslim societies of a view of secularism defined by its aim to exclude or sideline religion. It is under this definition that secularism is so often rejected in these societies.

But Abdullahi might agree with me that the scope of this Western influence goes beyond the definition of secularism. As he points out, the last few centuries have seen a radical narrowing of acceptable forms of Muslim life. The domination of the Sudan under Turco-Egyptian rule in the nineteenth century imposed a legalistic conception of Islam "contrary to the preceding community-based Sufi Islam of sub-Saharan Africa." Various Salafist movements have intensified this legalist and

Sufi-unfriendly trend. But this has become particularly significant in tandem with the Western-derived understanding of the modern state, founded on some universally accepted philosophy that binds all citizens.

This meant that Muslim-inspired resisters to colonial rule could easily conclude that the principle of liberated postcolonial states could and should be Islam itself. And this was pushed further by Islamist movements like the Muslim Brotherhood, who saw Islam as answering the same questions that liberalism, socialism, and communism proposed to settle, this time according to the correct, divinely endorsed formula.

This turn threatened a drastic reduction in acceptable intra-Islamic diversity wherever an Islamist régime came to power. As indeed, we saw in Shi'ite form in the Iranian Revolution and continue to see in a Sunni form in Pakistan. This basic understanding of what an Islamic state might look like is still bedeviling the aftermath of the Arab Spring in Egypt and Tunisia and, of course, hovers in the background of the Syrian civil war.

One could indeed argue that there is no way out of the present impasse in a society like Egypt, other than the spread of a conception of secularism on the lines that Abdullahi proposes. And this does indeed require what he calls an "indigenous self-liberation," not only from the unthinking acceptance of Western categories but also from the dangerous temptations of Islam as a militant ideology in which neither God nor human freedom seems to play a major role.

AKEEL BILGRAMI

Here again, there is a striking continuity with the contribution just discussed. Akeel is vitally concerned, in his reading of Gandhi, with the vital need for resistance to a hegemonic view. But neither he nor Gandhi see this simply as the view of the West. It was the view supported and imposed by the colonial powers, which were Western. It was and is the view still hegemonic in the West, but it is not the only outlook that has arisen there, and one can find the elements of an antidote in earlier Western traditions, as well as in those arising in Indian civilization.

Seen from this point of view, Gandhi's arguments in *Hind Swaraj* could be understood as essentially antimodern, wherever the mode of (industrial, capitalist globalized) life which we now live in arises, and not at all as essentially "Indian" versus "Western."

And when we survey the changes Gandhi was resisting, in the formulation Akeel offers, we can see that this resistance finds echoes in certain strands of radical thought in our time. Four transformations are singled out: (1) "How and when did we transform the concept of nature into the concept of natural resources?" (2) "How and when did we transform the concept of human beings (the inhabitants of nature) into the concept of citizens (3) and the concept of people into the concept of populations?" (4) "How did we transform the concept of *knowledges to live by* into the concept of *an expertise to rule by*?"

Number (1) reminds us of Martin Heidegger; (3) and (4) call to mind Michel Foucault. Number (2) may seem unexceptionable; indeed, one of our cherished values in democracy is that of citizenship. But as we follow the argument we can see that Akeel is mainly attacking here the modern state, justified as the common instrument of the homogeneous nation, and hence a standing threat to the diversity of the forms of life that continue to arise spontaneously in this inhospitable environment. Number (2) is thus linked to (4), mechanisms of control, and drives the kind of homogenizing of identities parallel to that which, as we saw, underlies Islamism in the Muslim world.

Akeel is here calling for a very radical form of Abdullahi's "indigenous self-liberation," radical in the sense that it cuts into the very bases of the world economy and state system we now live in (or under). So much so that our first reaction may well be despair, granted that this critique speaks to us at all (as I confess it does to me).

But two things speak against immediately writing it off as impractical. The first is that these lines of criticism do have a deep and wide appeal. They speak to immense numbers of people in our world, even those who shortly after being moved by them will dismiss them as incapable of leading to effective practical action. The second point is that the stances toward nature, control of the environment, economic growth, and bureaucratic mastery of collective human action that this critique pillories are likely to get us (human beings in general) into a host of terrible troubles if they continue to dominate our lives. For that if for no other reason, we have a strong motive to understand better what these transitions have consisted in, and what could perhaps reverse them or inflect them in new directions.

CONTRIBUTORS

DR. ABDULLAHI AHMED AN-NA'IM is Charles Howard Candler Professor of Law, and Associated Professor in Emory College of Arts and Sciences of Emory University, and Senior Fellow of the Center for the Study of Law and Religion. An-Na'im is the author of *What Is an American Muslim?* (2014); *Muslims and Global Justice* (2011); *Islam and the Secular State* (2008); *African Constitutionalism and the Role of Islam* (2006); and *Toward an Islamic Reformation: Civil Liberties, Human Rights and International Law* (1990). His edited books include *Human Rights Under African Constitutions* (2003); *Islamic Family Law in a Changing World: A Global Resource Book* (2002); *Cultural Transformation and Human Rights in Africa* (2002); and *Human Rights in Cross-Cultural Perspectives: Quest for Consensus* (1992). He has also published more than 70 articles and book chapters on human rights, constitutionalism and Islam, and politics in African and Islamic countries. An-Na'im's research projects include women's access to, and control over, land in seven African countries; a global study of Islamic Family Law; and a fellowship program in Islam and Human Rights. The archives of the website of each of the three projects remains accessible (though no longer updated or revised) at: https://scholarblogs.emory.edu/aannaim/project-archive/.

RAJEEV BHARGAVA is the director of the Institute of Indian Thought at the Centre for the Study of Developing Societies (CSDS) in Delhi, where he served as the Director from 2007 to 2014. He has also been a professor at the Centre for Political Studies at Jawaharlal Nehru University, New Delhi (1980–2005), Bhargava's publications include *Individualism in Social Science* (1992), *What Is Political Theory and Why Do We Need It?* (2010), and *The Promise of India's Secular Democracy* (2010). His edited books include *Secularism and Its Critics* (1998).

AKEEL BILGRAMI is the Sidney Morgenbesser Professor of Philosophy at Columbia University, where he is also a professor on the Committee on Global Thought and the Director of the South Asian Institute. His publications include the books *Belief and Meaning* (1992), *Self-Knowledge and Resentment* (2006), *Democratic Culture* (2012), *and Secularism, Identity and Enchantment* (2014). He is due to publish two short books in the near future: *What Is a Muslim?* and *Gandhi's Integrity*. His long-term future work is on the relations between agency, value, and practical reason.

SOULEYMANE BACHIR DIAGNE is a professor of French and Philosophy at Columbia University. He also taught for many years at Cheikh Anta Diop University, Dakar (Senegal) and Northwestern University. His book *Bergson postcolonial. L'élan vital dans la pensée de Senghor et de Mohamed Iqbal* was awarded the Dagnan-Bouveret prize by the French Academy of Moral and Political Sciences for 2011. He also received the Edouard Glissant Prize for his work in 2011.

SUDIPTA KAVIRAJ is a professor of Indian politics and intellectual history at Columbia University. He also taught for many years at SOAS, London University, and Jawaharlal Nehru University in New Delhi. He has been a fellow of St. Antony's College, Oxford, and a visiting professor at the University of California, Berkeley, the University of Chicago, and Sciences Po in Paris. He is the author of *The Unhappy Consciousness: Bankimchandra Chattopadhyay and the Formation of Indian Nationalist Discourse* (1995), *The Imaginary Institution of India: Politics and Ideas* (2010), *Trajectories of the Indian State* (2010), *Enchantment of Democracy and India* (2011), *The Invention of Private Life* (2015), and co-editor with Sunil Khilnani, *Civil Society: History and Possibilities* (2001).

CLAUDIO LOMNITZ is the Campbell Family Professor of Anthropology at Columbia University. He is the author of *Death and the Idea of Mexico* (Zone Books); *Deep Mexico, Silent Mexico: An Anthropology of Nationalism;* and *Exits from the Labyrinth: Culture and Ideology in the Mexican Space.* His most recent book, *The Return of Comrade Ricardo Flores Magón* (Zone Books, 2014), is about exile, ideology, and revolution.

ALFRED STEPAN is the Wallace Sayre Professor of Government at Columbia University, the founding director of the Center for the Study of Democracy, Toleration, and Religion (CDTR), and the co-director of the Institute for Religion, Culture, and Public Life (IRCPL). He has authored and edited a large number of books, including *Arguing Comparative Politics* (Oxford University Press, 2001), and, co-authored with Juan Linz and Yogendra Yadav, *Democracy in Multinational Societies: India and Other Polities* (Johns Hopkins University Press, 2010). In 2012 he was the recipient of the Karl Deutsch Award of the International Political Science Association.

CHARLES TAYLOR is professor emeritus of philosophy at McGill University. His recent publications include *Modern Social Imaginaries* (2004), *A Secular Age* (2007), and (with Jocelyn Maclure) *Secularism and Freedom of Conscience* (2012).

PETER VAN DER VEER is director at the Max Planck Institute for the Study of Religious and Ethnic Diversity and Distinguished University Professor at Utrecht University. He works on the comparative study of religion and nationalism in India and China. He is the author and editor of many books, most recently *The Modern Spirit of Asia* (Princeton, 2014), *Handbook of Religion in Asian Cities* (California, 2015), and *The Value of Comparison* (Duke, 2016).

INDEX

Abhinavagupta, 147
absconditus (safekeeping), 243n15
absolutism, 105, 107, 136
Abu Bakr, 32–33
Abul Fazl, 153–54, 182n43
accommodation, 41–42, 150–53, 155, 255–56
Acquaviva, Rudolfo, 183n62
Action Française, 21
Advaita, 168
advanced and advancing societies, 239
African Muslims, 51–52, 53, 64
Āgamaḍambara (Bhatta), 143, 144, 179n14
agency, 191, 192, 195
agribusiness, 221
Akbar (Mughal emperor), 9, 25, 26n6, 153–56, 182n43, 190
AKP. *See* Justice and Democracy Party
Algeria, 65, 84, 93
Ali (caliph), 29, 33
Alliance Française, 128
almaamiyya, 37
Ammar, Rachid, 87
Amnesty International, 83
amratva (immortality), 192
Amun-Re, 202

anarchism, 110, 114
Anaximander, 18
ancestor worship, 168
Andalucía, Spain, 79
Anderson, Lisa, 96n27
Anglicanism, 220, 222
Anglo-Egyptian Condominium, 55
Annales rationalism, 78
Anṣār (Helpers), 31, 32
anticlericalism, 110, 114
antimodernism, of Gandhi, 215–17
anti-Semitism, 99, 203
"Appel de Tunis (Call from Tunis)," 88–89
Arabic Thought in the Liberal Age: 1798–1939 (Hourani), 80
Arab-Muslim military conquest, 53
Arab Spring, 78, 80, 85, 88, 254–55, 258
Argentina, 106
Argumentative Indian, The (Sen), 26n6
Aristotle, 18, 251
Asad, Talal, 119
Asian Muslims, 51–52, 53, 64
asocial Buddhism, 195
Asoka, 25, 190, 205–7, 212n49, 213n50
Assmann, Jan, 10, 201, 203, 208
āstikas, 139–41

Atatürk, Mustapha Kemal, 23, 34, 76–77
atheism, 4, 6, 144
atmapasandavraddhi, 207
Augustine, 7
Australia, 98, 239, 249
authoritarian secularist modernization, 81–84
Axial Age, 117, 118–20, 144, 250
Axial revolution, 10–13
Al Azhar, 29

Bacon, Francis, 243n13
Badayuni, 153–56
Bailey, Greg, 195
Bakhtin, Mikhail, 174
Bamba, Ahmadu, 39–40, 44n25
Barani, Ziauddin, 150, 181n40
battle of Valmy, 14
Baubérot, Jean, 41, 256
Bauthumley, Jacob, 219, 241n7
belief (*pramāṇa*), 139
Bell, Daniel, 128
Ben Achour Commission (Fulfillment of Revolutionary Goals, Political Reform, and Democratic Transition), 90–91
Ben Ali, 78, 81–84, 88–89, 91, 95n23
Benavente, Toribio "Motolinía," 102
Bennabi, Malek, 65
Bentley, Richard, 220
Berlinguer, Enrico, 250
bhaavshuddhi, 207
Bhagavatgītā, 145
Bhakti, 182n45, 219, 221, 223, 225, 226
Bhargava, Rajeev, 138, 252–53
Bhatta, Jayanta, 143, 179n14
bhulna (forgetting), 182n47
Bilgrami, Akeel, 165, 231, 237, 240n1, 245n23, 258–60
blood purity (*limpieza de sangre*), 101, 104
Boko Haram, 42
Bolivia, 98, 239
Bose, J. C., 163
Bourguiba, Habib, 77–78, 81–84, 88

Boyle, Robert, 243n13, 248
Boyle Lectures, 222
Brahmans, 192, 193, 195, 198, 206
Brahmos, 13, 169, 184n82; modern religions and, 166–67; reforms, 162–66
Brazil, 76, 80, 106, 109
Britain, 55, 160. *See also* England
British Council, 128
Brown, Nathan J., 81
Brumairianism, 86, 87, 95n24
Buddha, 10, 12, 195
Buddhism, 9, 64, 118, 125–27, 129, 132, 149, 198; asocial, 195; Chan-Buddhism, 121; churches and, 204–5; exclusive humanism and, 252; Hinayana, 141; in India, 141–42, 144, 146–47; nirvana and, 253
buffered self, 109, 114
bundling, 253

Caillois, Roger, 4
Caitanya, 148
Caitanyacaritāmṛta, 147
caliphate, 29, 30
Calles, Plutarco Elías, 114
"Call from Tunis (Appel de Tunis)," 88–89
Canada, 98, 249
capital, 227, 240
capitalism, 63, 64, 115, 227, 239
Carranza, Venustiano, 114
Carrithers, M., 195
Cārvākas, 139–41, 179nn13–14, 180n17, 199, 247
Casanova, Giacomo, 178n1
castes (*jati*), 24
castes (*varna*), 142, 145
caste system, 101–2, 103, 162
caste wars (*guerras de castas*), 112
Catholicism, 9, 22, 64, 99, 121, 131, 223, 250; in France, 21, 26n2; in Mexico, 105; national identity and, 106; peasant community and, 109–11; toleration of, 4, 7

Catholic Party, 107–8, 113–14
CCP. *See* Chinese Communist Party
ceerno, 38
Central Africa, 72n9
Central Asia, 53
certainty, 71
Ceylon, 205
Chan-Buddhism, 121
Chatterjee, Bankim Chandra, 161, 163, 185n97
Chattopadhyay, Bankimchandra, 170, 171
Chattopadhyay, Saratchandra, 172
El Chebbi, Ahmed Nejib, 93
Chiapas revolt (1712), 112
Chile, 76, 88
China, 8–9, 12, 25, 124, 190; Cultural Revolution in, 23–24; modernizing movements in, 13; popular cults in, 10; *wu* in, 26n10. *See also* Confucianism
Chinese Communist Party (CCP), 128–29, 132
Chinese Rites Controversy, 121
Christendom, 253; Eastern, 13. *See also* Latin Christendom
Christian Democratic Party, 88
Christianity, 7, 39, 46, 62–63, 65, 191; Axial revolution and, 10; as communal religion, 200; disenchantment and, 15; Hinduism and, 161; hyper-Christians, 102; in Iberian Peninsula, 99–100; moral ideals of, 155; New, 101–2, 103; Old, 101–2, 103; popular, 103; Primitive, 104; ritual and, 11; sainthood and, 3; shamanism and, 126; in United States, 21–22; as universalistic, 123. *See also specific denominations*
Christianization, 64
Chulalongkorn (king), 125
citizenship, 35, 49, 244n19
civic engagement, 50
civic reason, 70, 71
civility, 208, 224–25
civilization, 46, 59

civil-military relations hypothesis, of twin tolerations, 85, 87
civil rights movement, 1
civil society, 84
Cixi (dowager empress), 125
Clarke, Samuel, 220
class, 52, 215, 219. *See also* caste system; middle class
Collection of All Philosophic Schools (Sarvadarśanasaṃgraha) (Mādhavācarya), 141, 179n13
collective mentality, 233, 236
Collins, Anthony, 220
colonialism, 13, 37, 48–54, 65, 158–59, 225; education and, 52; in France, 38–39; in India, 159–61; Sufism and, 40–41
Columbian Exhibition, 126
Common Era, 195, 197
common ground, 66
communal religion, 200
Communist Party, 173
communitarianism, 128
Confucianism, 8–9, 117–18; Axial Age and, 118–20; conclusion to, 131–32; imperial interactions and, 122–27; Jesuits and, 120–22, 133n7; in nineteenth century, 122–27; in present day, 127–31; in seventeenth century, 120–22; in sixteenth century, 120–22
Confucius Institutes, 128
Confucius Temple, 128
Conservative Party, 107, 108, 115
constituent assembly, 90–91
Constitution, of Mexico (1917), 107
Constitution, of Tunisia (1861), 80
constitutionalism, 49–51, 68
constitutional rights, 64
constraints, 234–35
consultation (*shura*), 31–32
las contentas (the happy ones), 108, 115
Cooper, Frederick, 53
coordinated protests, 74n46
cosmos, 18, 191

Council of Trent, 102
Counter-Reformation, 102, 121, 131
"Covenant of Social Peace," 80
Creoles, 250
cruelty, 224–25
Crusades, 203
Cuba, 106
Cultural Revolution, 23–24, 129
cultural secularism (secularism 3), 105, 108, 114, 115

Dabistan-i-Mazahib, 155, 181n36, 184n76
DaMatta, Roberto, 109
Dan Fodio, Uthman, 39
Daniel, Jean, 87
Daoism, 9, 121, 124, 126–27, 129, 132, 133n18
Das, Jibanananda, 186n111
daśāvatāra myth, 152
decolonization, 48–54, 65
deep decolonization, 65
democracy, 136; social, 237; twin tolerations and, 76–77
democratization, 76
Derozio, 161
Descartes, René, 16, 243n13
determinism, 227
deva (god), 195
devādideva, 145
dhamma, 206–8
Diagne, Souleymane Bachir, 255–56
Díaz, Carmelita, 108
Díaz, Porfirio, 108, 109, 112
difference, sociology of, 147–48
diffused religion, 131
Diggers, 165, 221
Din-i-Ilahi, 153, 156
Diouf, Abdou, 42
disciplines, 15, 16–17, 19
disembedding, 11, 15, 17, 132
disenchantment (*Entzauberung*), 16, 19, 142, 152, 157–58, 168, 231; Christianity and, 15; Gandhi and, 228, 230; India and, 24, 141
dissent, 216–18, 220, 222–23

Dissenters, 222–24
doctor's coup, 83
doctrinal conflict: in India, 143–49; Islam and, 181n37
Dodds, E. R., 209
Dominicans, 100, 121, 131
double fear, 95n23
Dumont, Fernand, 44n19
Durga (deity), 171
Durga Pūjā (festival), 173–75, 248
Durkheim, Émile, 175, 193
Dutt, Michael Madhusudan, 162

early religions, 188, 191–201
Eastern Christendom, 13
Economic and Philosophical Manuscripts of 1844, The (Marx), 221–22
Ecuador, 239
education: colonial, 52; in Tunisia, 79
egalitarianism, 221
Egypt, 80, 90, 93, 190, 202, 255, 258; Anglo-Egyptian Condominium, 55; Islamism in, 23; Muslim Brotherhood in, 86–87; twin tolerations and, 84–86
"18 October Coalition for Rights and Freedoms in Tunisia, The," 89
Eighteenth Brumaire, 85
Eisenstadt, S. N., 118–19
electoral system, 91
Elias, Norbert, 224
eliteness, 165
elites, 24, 52, 167, 185n95, 191, 227, 248; Christianity and, 100; Hinduism and, 160–61, 168; intellectual, 118, 148; Islamic, 149; Mexican, 108; modernist, 168–69; in reflexive society, 14
elites' theory, 196
England, 17, 21, 105, 159, 216–17, 223, 243n13
Enlightenment, 54, 163, 191, 224, 241n7
Ennahda (Renaissance Party), 83, 86, 89, 91–93, 96n32
enthusiasm, 5, 6, 166–67, 222
Entzauberung. *See* disenchantment

environment, 239
Epicureanism, 195–96, 247
equality, 238; of citizenship, 14; of women, 81, 88–89
Escalante, Fernando, 115
essentialization, 203
ethical secularism, 138–39
ethics, 140; of self-realization, 201
ethnic cleansing, 101
etymology, 63
European Union (EU), 20
exclusive humanism, 77–78, 81–82, 194–96, 198–99
exclusive monotheism, 203

Faidherbe (governor), 41
Falun Gong, 24
Family of the Prophet, The (*Nabībaṃśa*), 152
fanaticism, 5, 6
Al Farābī, Abu Nasr, 34–35
fear, 60–61; double, 95n23
feasts, ritual, 193
feeding the gods, 11
Filali-Ansari, Abdou, 30
filial piety (*xiao*), 128–29
Filiu, Jean-Pierre, 80
First Amendment, 21, 256
folk religions, 133n18
forced emigration, 247
forgetting (*bhulna*), 182n47
Foucault, Michel, 102, 259
frame problem, 233–34, 235, 245n23
France, 5, 76, 80, 93, 159; absolutism, 105, 107; Bamba and, 44n25; Catholicism in, 21, 26n2; colonialism, 38–39; *laïcité* and, 5–6, 25, 26nn1–2, 41, 42, 77, 88, 255; laic Republic and, 41
Franciscans, 100, 121, 131
Frazer, James, 16
Frederick the Great, 5
free elections, 83, 86
French Protectorate, 80
French Revolution, 5, 14, 95n24
Freud, Sigmund, 245n23

Fulfillment of Revolutionary Goals, Political Reform, and Democratic Transition (Ben Achour Commission), 90–91
fully accomplished human being (*insān kāmil*), 35
fundamental rights, 49
al Fūtiyu, Umar, 37, 39–40
Fuuta Tooro, 37

Galileo, 243n13
Gambetta, Léon, 26n2
Gandhi, Mahatma, 1, 49, 55, 61, 69, 165, 259; antimodernism of, 215–17; civility and, 225; disenchantment and, 228, 230; Hinduism and, 241n6, 245n21; majoritarianism and, 226; Marx and, 238; modern science and, 217–19; nation-state and, 241n5; nature and, 219–22; occidentalism and, 240n1; radicalism of, 215–16, 226, 242n7
Garza, Catarino, 113
Gaudiya, 148
geographic locations, renaming of, 72n9
Germany, 89, 105
Ghannouchi, Rachid, 83–84, 86–87, 89, 96n27
Girardot, Norman, 125
global community (*umma*), 23, 31–32, 48
globalization, 60, 248
Glorious Revolution (1688), 224
Gobir, 39
god (*deva*), 195
God (*Shangdi*), 125–26
"Gods of Greece, The" (Schiller), 16
Goethe Institute, 128
Gombrich, Richard, 192, 194, 199–200, 205
Gonda, Jan, 180n25
Gora (Tagore, R.), 185n97, 185n99
governance, 50, 224, 232; self-governance, 71
gravity, 220
Greco-Roman tradition, 189

Greece, 118, 139, 199, 209–10, 247; Axial revolution in, 10–13; Epicureanism in, 195–96; rationalism, 78
Gregory VII, 7
Grotius, Hugo, 17, 247
Guerra, François Xavier, 115
guerras de castas (caste wars), 112
guojiao (national religion), 132
Gutiérrez, Eulalio, 114

Haddad, Tahar, 81, 88
happy ones (*las contentas*), 108, 115
Hapsburg, Maximilian von, 107
hard secularism, 76
Hayy ibn Yaqzān (ibn Tufayl), 36
Hebrew Bible, 11
Hebrew society, 10–11
Heidegger, Martin, 259
Helpers (*Ansâr*), 31, 32
Heraclitus, 18
Hessen, Boris, 243*n*13
heterodoxy (*xie*), 120
Hildebrandine reforms, 7
Hinayana Buddhism, 141
Hindi language, 152
Hind Swaraj (Gandhi), 216–17, 259
Hindu College, 161
Hinduism, 13, 49, 63, 118, 147, 170, 184*n*86; Brahmos reforms and, 162–66; Christianity and, 161; as communal religion, 200; elites and, 160–61, 168; Gandhi and, 241*n*6, 245*n*21; Islam and, 149, 151, 153–54, 181*n*26; moral ideals of, 155; Mosaic, 203; Sufism and, 151; Vedic, 141–45, 149, 252
Hindutva, 20, 25, 226
historical language, 147
historical materialism, 227
historical-sociological theory, 157
Hölderlin, Friedrich, 15
Holland, 159
Holyoake, George Jacob, 63
Hourani, Albert, 80
Hu Jintao, 128

humanism, exclusive, 77–78, 81–82, 194–96, 198–99
human rights, 49, 60, 64, 68
hyper-Christians, 102, 104

Iberian Peninsula, 99–100, 249
Ibero-America, 97–98, 109, 114
Ibn Bājjah, 34–36
Ibn Khaldun, 29, 78–79
ibn Tufayl, Abu Bakr, 36
ideal state, 34
identity: equal citizenship and, 14; national, 20–21, 106
idolatry (*shirk*), 11, 12, 61, 103
IF. *See* immanent frame
ijtihad (juridical reasoning), 68–69
illegitimate rule (*xie*), 120
Iltutmish (emperor), 150, 156
imagination, 59
imagined citizens, 115
immanent frame (IF), 114, 137, 139–43, 247–48, 252
Immigrants (*Muhajjirûn*), 31, 32
immortality (*amratva*), 192
imperialism, 61; Confucianism and, 122–27; European, 37
inclusive monotheism, 202
India, 9, 12–14, 25, 53, 76, 98, 124, 188–91, 247; accommodation in, 150–53; Akbar's court and, 153–56; Brahmos reforms in, 162–66; collective in, 172–77; colonial policy in, 159–61; Confucianism and, 117; disenchantment in, 24, 141; doctrinal conflict in, 143–49; early religions in, 188, 190, 191–201; individualism in, 170–72; modernity in, 137–38, 156–59, 161–62; modern religion in, 166–67; native religion in, 159–61; in nineteenth century, 156–59; political condition in, 205–11; premodern religious beliefs in, 139–43; religious change in, 156–59; religious diversity in, 149–50; religious transcendence in, 177–78; secular transcendence in,

177–78; skepticism in, 143–49; social condition in, 204–5; theological condition in, 201–4; traditional religiosity in, 167–70
Indian Congress Party, 55
indigenous religions, 62, 65
indigenous self-liberation, 48–49, 51–53, 54–61, 62–67, 258–59
individualism, 170–72, 173; possessive, 109, 223
individual mentality, 233, 235
Indo-European tribes, 17
Indonesia, 76
insān kāmil (fully accomplished human being), 35
institutionalization, 47
intellectual elites, 118, 148
interest on loans (*riba*), 70
intolerance, regulation of, 100
Iqbal, Muhammad, 36
Iran, 23, 118
Iranian Revolution, 20, 83, 258
Ireland, 20
irrationality, 245n23
Ishwara (prayer), 197
Islam, 2, 8, 9, 13, 63, 191, 253, 255, 257; accommodation and, 41–42; African Muslims, 51–52, 53, 64; Asian Muslims, 51–52, 53, 64; Axial revolution and, 10; caliphate and, 29, 30; Christianization of, 64; civilization and, 46; colonization and, 48–54; as communal religion, 200; decolonization and, 48–54; doctrinal disputes and, 181n37; Hinduism and, 149, 151, 153–54, 181n26; in Iberian Peninsula, 99, 101; indigenous self-liberation and, 54–61; institutionalization and, 47; neutrality and, 45; perfect state and, 34–35; petrifaction and, 36; pluralism and, 31, 34; religious authority and, 47; ritual and, 11; secular state and, 67–72; Shia, 32, 48, 64, 149, 181n37, 258; Sunni, 32–33, 48, 64, 149, 181n37, 258; tribal law and, 31–32; in Tunisia, 79–80, 82–83; in Turkey, 23; wars of apostasy and, 33; in West Africa, 37–39. *See also* Sufism
Islam and the Foundations of Political Power (Razik), 29
Islam and the Secular State (An-Na'im), 30
Islamic Salvation Front, 83
Islamic state, 30–32, 73n18
Islamism, 20, 42, 56, 83–84, 92, 256; in Egypt, 23; propaganda and, 30
Islamization, 37–38
Islamophobia, 99
Israel, 10, 118
Israel, Jonathan, 241n7
Īśvara-Pratyabhijñā-Vimarśinī (Abhinavagupta), 147, 180n27
Italy, 106, 249
Izala, 44n27

Jacobins, 106, 107, 110–11, 114
Jahangir (emperor), 155
Jainism, 144, 154, 195, 198, 206, 252–53; lay community and, 196; *paddhatis* and, 146; Vedic Hinduism and, 141
Jamison, S. W., 194
Japan, 25, 126, 127, 205
Jaspers, Karl, 118–19
jati (castes), 24
Jayadeva, 147
Jebali, Hamadi, 87
Jesuits, 104, 105, 117, 120–22, 131, 133n7
Jesus, 155, 253
jihad (religious war), 37, 39, 56
Joseph II, 5
Juárez, Benito, 113
Judaism, 12, 22, 99, 101, 155, 191
Judeo-Christian tradition, 189
juridical reasoning (*ijtihad*), 68–69
Justice and Democracy Party (AKP), 86, 89

Kabir, 151–52
Kali (deity), 168
Kane, Ousmane, 44n27

kāngalī bhojan, 174
Kangxi (emperor), 121
Kang Youwei, 127, 132
Kant, Immanuel, 252
kapalikas, 148, 155
karma, 195–96
Kasbah One, 89
Kashmir, 143, 144, 152
Kaulas, 148, 155
Kaviraj, Sudipta, 14, 246–48
Kemalist Turkey, 23
Keynesian constraints, 234
Khalji, Alauddin, 181n40
Khayr al-Din (Khéréddine), 80, 81, 88
Khusrau, Amir, 151
King, Martin Luther, Jr., 1
kinship structures, 129
knowledges to live by, 219, 244n19
Koran. See Qur'an
Krsna (deity), 155, 202
kshatriyas, 192, 198

ladino, 104
laïcité, 5–6, 25, 26nn1–2, 41, 42, 77, 88, 255
laic Republic, 41
Lake Victoria, 72n9
Lange, Oskar, 227
language, 66; European, 51–52, 63; Hindi, 152; historical, 147
Lapidus, Ira, 53
Las Casas, Bartolomé de, 102
Latin America, 97, 98, 239, 249. See also specific countries
Latin Christendom, 2, 3, 4, 47, 138, 240, 249, 251; Confucianism and, 117; in Iberian Peninsula, 100; Jesuits and, 131; missing factors and, 77; reform and, 12, 102; Spanish America and, 104, 115; Taylor and, 97, 100, 102, 104, 136
laypersons, 196–97
Legge, James, 124–26
legitimate rule (zheng), 120
Leibniz, Gottfried Wilhelm von, 122
levée en masse, 14
Liberal Party, 107–8, 115

Liberal Spirit of the Koran, The (Thaalibi), 95n15
liberation (mokśa), 143, 145, 180n27, 241n6
limpieza de sangre (blood purity), 101, 104
Linz, Juan J., 92, 93, 255
literacy, 106
Locke, John, 4, 6, 17, 241n7
Lomnitz, Claudio, 249–50
London Missionary Society, 124
Lord of Heaven, 120–21
Lutheranism, 249

Mabbett, Ian, 195
MacCulloch, Diarmaid, 79
Macina Empire, 40
Madan, T. N., 63, 185n91
Madero, Francisco I., 107, 113
Mādhavacārya, 141, 179n13
magic (Zauber), 15–16
magic realism, 16
Magón, Enrique Flores, 114
Magón, Ricardo, 114
Mahabharata, 153
Mahdist state, 54–55
Maitreya, 122
majoritarianism, 226
Mali, 38, 42
Mandate of Heaven, 120, 122
mangalācarana, 147
marabouts, 38, 43n16
margas, 199, 205
marquees (pandals), 175–76
Martí, José, 98
Martínez, María Elena, 104
Marx, Karl, 219, 221–22, 244n19; Gandhi and, 238; nature and, 242n12
Marxism, 9, 128, 159, 169, 171, 227; Brahmos and, 164; Indian philosophy and, 141
Mary, Virgin, 112
mass mobilization, 13–14
Masuzawa, Tomoko, 123
materialism: historical, 227; unethical, 59
material progress, 46
Maududi, Abul A'la, 30

Maurras, Charles, 21
Mauss, Marcel, 109
Mayan revolt, 112
Mecca, 28, 41, 56
Medina, 31, 32, 56
Meghnādbadhkāvya (Dutt), 162
Mehta, Narsin, 245n21
Mesopotamia, 190
metaphors, 125–26
metaphysical outlook, 217, 218, 221
metaphysics, 38–39
methods of proper worship (*paddhatis*), 146
Mexican Revolution, 108, 113–14
Mexico, 97–98, 250; Catholicism in, 105; conclusion to, 114–16; ecclesiastical council of, 103; illustrative developments in, 111–14; in nineteenth century, 106–9; peasant community in, 109–11
Mexico City riots (1892), 113
middle class, 110, 174–75; Catholicism and, 109; in Mexico, 115; revolts and, 112
military campaigns, 150
millenarian-style revolts, 112
missing factors, 77
mobilization: mass, 13–14; national, 20
modernity, 7, 9, 13, 54, 65, 178n6; frame problem and, 233; in India, 137–38, 156–59, 161–62; tradition and, 236–37
modernization, 77, 160; authoritarian secularist, 81–84
modern science, 217–19
Mogul Empire, 79
mokṣa (liberation), 143, 145, 180n27, 241n6
monotheism, 12–13, 197; exclusive, 203; inclusive, 202
monster castes, 24
Moore, Thomas, 102
Moors, 99, 101
moral choice, 58, 61
moral economy, 18
morale indépendante, 5, 6
Morales, Evo, 239
morality, 7

Mosaic distinction, 203–4, 208, 253
Mosaic Hinduism, 203
Moses, 155
Motolinía (Toribio Benavente), 102
Muawiyya, 29
Mubarak, Hosni, 90
Mughal Dynasty, 122, 155, 184n76
Muhajjirûn (Immigrants), 31, 32
Muhammad (prophet), 28, 32–33, 68, 253
Mukhopadhyay, Bhudev, 163–64, 168, 171
Müller, Friedrich Max, 124–25
Muridiyya, 39
Muslim Brotherhood, 86–87, 258
Muslim Modernity in Postcolonial Nigeria: A Study of the Society for the Removal of Innovation and the Reinstatement of Tradition (Kane), 44n27
Muslims. *See* Islam

Nabībaṃśa (The Family of the Prophet), 152
An-Naʿim, Abdullahi Ahmed, 30, 256–58
Nandy, Ashis, 9, 185n91, 244n18
Napoleon Bonaparte, 95n24
Napoleon III, 107
nāstikas, 139
national identity, 20–21, 106
nationalism, 136, 225, 226
national mobilization, 20
National Reform Association, 22
national religion (*guojiao*), 132
nation-state, 20, 52, 54, 226, 241n5
native memory, 51, 72n9
natural law, 18, 251
natural philosophers, 220
natural science, 248
nature, 218, 219–22, 231, 238; desacralization of, 220, 223; Marx and, 242n12; pollution of, 232, 239
Nehru, Jawaharlal, 24, 160, 185n91, 190, 226
Neoplatonism, 219, 226, 241n7, 243n15, 244n19; of Newton, 220; Winstanley and, 223
Netherlands, 223
neutrality, 45, 71, 256

New Christians, 101–2, 103
New Spain, 103
Newton, Isaac, 218–20, 248, 251
Newtonianism, 243n13
Newtonian universe, 16
New Zealand, 98, 249
Nibbana (nirvana), 200, 253
Nigeria, 39, 40, 42
Nīlāmbaras, 144, 180n25
nirvana (Nibbana), 200, 253
nonviolent civil disobedience, 1
normative demands, 231
North Africa, 53
nostalgia, 234, 239
Notre femme dans la Legislation Muselmane et dans la Societé (Haddad), 81
Nouvel Observateur, Le, 87
nova effect, 144, 169, 198
Novalis, 16
Numeiri, Gaafar, 55–57

Obregón, Álvaro, 114
"Occidentalism, The Very Idea: An Essay on Enchantment and the Enlightenment" (Bilgrami), 240n1, 245n23
Old Christians, 101–2, 103
Olstrom, Elinor, 239
ontological subordination, of gods, 202
Opium War (1839–1842), 122
Orange Revolution, 1
Orientalism, 147, 183n65
Orozco, Pascual, 114
orthodoxy (*zheng*), 120
Ottoman Empire, 54–55, 79, 80
Oxford University, 124

paddhatis (methods of proper worship), 146
paganism, 11, 39
Pakistan, 258
Palestine, 189, 190
pandals (marquees), 175–76
pantheism, 220, 241n7, 243n15
Paramhansa, Ramakrishna, 167–68

pasandas, 206–7
Pascal, Blaise, 104
Pax Gallica, 40
peasant community, 109–11
Peng Guanyu, 126, 127
perfect state, 34–35
Pericles, 35
Petty, William, 220, 221
Phakir, Lālan, 152
piety, 4, 6; filial, 128–29
Pinochet, Augusto, 88
Plato, 4, 19, 32, 34, 251
Platonism, 8, 18. *See also* Neoplatonism
pluralism, 25, 31, 34, 69
Poland, 20
political condition, in India, 205–11
political economy, 215, 219, 232
political secularism (secularism 1), 105, 108, 115, 138–39, 190
political society hypothesis, of twin tolerations, 85, 87–91
Pollock, Sheldon, 208, 210
polytheism, 202
popular Christianity, 103
porous self, 109
possessive individualism, 109, 223
pramāṇa (belief), 139
Pratyabhijñā, 145, 180n26
pratyakṣa (sensory perception), 139
premodern religious beliefs, 139–43
Primitive Christianity, 104
Primus Apostolus, 122
Priya-darshi (king), 213n50
Problems of Democratic Transition and Consolidation: Southern Europe, South America, and Post-Communist Europe (Linz and Stepan), 92
Progressive Democratic Party, 93
Protestantism, 9, 64, 104, 113, 131, 223, 243n13, 249; anticlerical leaders and, 114; Brahmos and, 163; Confucianism and, 123, 125; First Amendment and, 21; peasant community and, 110–11; Reformation and, 77, 101; Spanish America and, 105; Taylor and, 121

providential deism, 163, 247
pūjās, 173, 176
puruṣa, 145–46

Qadiriyya, 38–39, 42
al Qādir Jīlānī, Abd, 38
Qing Empire, 117, 121, 126, 127
Qingmingjie (grave sweeping festival), 129
Qubadu, Muhammad, 81
Quiroga, Vasco de, 102
Qur'an, 56, 68, 95n15; 3:159, 31; 4:59, 30–31; 4:79–80, 47; 5:105, 47; 30:6–7, 59; 41:46, 47; 42:38, 31–32; 53:36–42, 47; 61:2–3, 60
Quraysh tribe, 32
Qutb, Sayyid, 30

Radical Enlightenment: Philosophy and the Making of Modernity in Europe 1650–1750 (Israel), 241n7
radicalism, 171, 215–16, 217, 226, 228, 234, 242n7
Raghavan, V., 180n22
Rājā, Hāsan, 152
Rama (deity), 155, 202
rasa theory, 180n22
rāshidūn (rightly guided), 33
rationalism, 78, 155, 170
rationalization, 158–59
Rawls, John, 8, 76, 77, 255
Razik, Ali Abdel, 29
reason, 36; civic, 70, 71; juridical, 68–69; secular, 66–67
reciprocal toleration, 138
reciprocity, 194
Redfield, Robert, 118
re-enchantment, 230
reflexive society, 14, 24, 25
Reformation, 77, 101, 122, 203, 223, 249; Counter-Reformation, 102, 121, 131
Reformation, The (MacCulloch), 79
reforms: Brahmos, 162–66; Hildebrandine, 7; Latin Christendom and, 12, 102; in Spanish America, 101–4
regulation of intolerance, 100

reincarnation, 140
relativity, of secularism, 62–67
Religion of India (Weber), 136
Religions of China: Confucianism and Taoism Described and Compared with Christianity (Legge), 126
religious diversity, 149–50, 249
religious hypothesis, of twin tolerations, 85, 86–87
religious virtuosi, 12
religious war (*jihad*), 37, 39, 56
remembering (*yād ānā*), 182n47
Renaissance Party (Ennahda), 83, 86, 89, 91–93, 96n32
Renan, Ernest, 124
Renou, Louis, 196
Republic, The (Plato), 19
Republican Party, 55
republican revolutions, 105
Rerum Novarum, 110
Revolution of Tuxtepec, 113
riba (interest on loans), 70
Ricci, Matteo, 120
rightly guided (*rāshidūn*), 33
rights, 225–26; civil rights movement, 1; constitutional, 64; fundamental, 49; human, 49, 60, 64, 68
Rig Veda, 125, 191–201
Rilke, Rainer Maria, 16
ritual, 7, 11–13, 23, 192–93, 210
ritual prayer (*salāt*), 33
Robinson, David, 40–41
Rodó, José Enrique, 98
Roy, Himanshu, 63
Roy, Olivier, 30
Roy, Ram Mohan, 161, 162, 164, 170, 184n74
Royal Society, 220, 222, 243n13, 243n15
Russia, 106

Saad ibn Abī Waqqās, 28–29, 34, 36, 40–41, 43
Sacred Books of China, 124
Sacred Books of the East, 124, 125
Sadiki College, 79, 81, 83

Sáenz, Aaron, 114
safekeeping (*absconditus*), 243*n*15
sahajiyas, 148, 155
Saivism, 143, 144–45, 147, 148
Saktaism, 145, 146, 148, 171
Salafism, 42, 44*n*27, 257
salāt (ritual prayer), 33
samyama (self-restraint), 207
sangha, 204–5
Saraswati (deity), 185*n*93
Sarvadarśanasaṃgraha (*Collection of All Philosophic Schools*) (Mādhavācarya), 141, 179*n*13
Sastri, Sibnath, 167, 184*n*79
sati (widow burning), 160
Saudi Arabia, 80
Savarkar, Vinayak Damodar, 20, 226
SCAF. *See* Supreme Command of the Armed Forces
Scandinavia, 21
Schiller, Friedrich, 16
Schipper, Kristofer, 133*n*18
School of Military Sciences, 79, 81
science, 59, 60, 73*n*26; modern, 217–19; natural, 248; social, 135–36
scientism, 242*n*12
Scottish Enlightenment, 163
Second International Congress of the History of Science, 243*n*13
Second Message of Islam, The (Taha), 56
Secular Age, A (Taylor), 76, 97, 135–37, 157, 188, 191, 199; Bhargava and, 252; Gandhi and, 215
secular enchantment, 244*n*19
Secularism, Identity, and Enchantment (Bilgrami), 231, 237, 245*n*23
secularism 1 (political secularism), 105, 108, 115, 138–39, 190
secularism 2 (societal secularism), 108, 115
secularism 3 (cultural secularism), 105, 108, 114, 115
secularization, 1, 2, 64, 112, 137, 138
secular reason, 66–67

secular state, 67–72
self-governance, 71
self-liberation. *See* indigenous self-liberation
self-preservation, 58–59, 61
self-realization, ethic of, 201
self-restraint (*samyama*), 207
Sen, Amartya, 26*n*6
Sen, Keshub Chandra, 166–67
Senegal, 37–38, 40, 42, 76, 255–56
Senghor, Léopold Sédar, 42
Señor de las Misericordias, El, 112
sensory perception (*pratyakṣa*), 139
September Laws, 57
seriñ, 38
shamanism (*wu*), 26*n*10, 126–27
Shame and Necessity (Williams), 209
Shangdi (God), 125–26
sharia, 47, 55, 68, 69, 70
shaykhs, 38, 41
Shia Islam, 32, 48, 64, 149, 181*n*37, 258
shirk (idolatry), 11, 12, 61, 103
Shramanas, 198
shura (consultation), 31–32
Siam, 125
Siecle de Louis XIV (Voltaire), 133*n*7
sinarquistas, 99
Singapore, 130
Singh, Man, 154
Sinha, Kaliprasanna, 187*n*117
Siva (deity), 145, 146
skepticism, in India, 143–49
slavery, 80
Smith, Cantwell, 204, 205
Smith, Vincent, 183*n*65
"Social and Economic Roots of Newton's Principia, The" (Hessen), 243*n*13
social condition, in India, 204–5
social constitution, 149
social democracy, 237
social imaginary, 209
socialism, 110, 114
Socialist Party, 88
social order, 3, 6, 17, 19, 25
social organization, 13–14, 17

social practice, 172
social science, 135–36
societal secularism (secularism 2), 108, 115
socioeconomic bases of empire, 53
sociology, of difference, 147–48
Socrates, 10, 195
Sokoto Caliphate, 39
Somadatta, 180n26
Son of Heaven, 120, 122
soteriologies, 200, 206, 253
souls, transmigration of, 164
South Africa, 98
Spain, 53, 76, 106, 249–50; Andalucía, 79; New Spain, 103
Spanish America, 98–101, 115; reform in, 101–4; secularism problem in, 105–6. *See also specific countries*
Spinoza, Baruch, 241n7, 243n15
spontaneity, of capital, 227
Stepan, Alfred, 92, 93, 254–55
Stietencron, Heinrich von, 147
Story, Joseph, 21
subtraction stories, 170, 247
Sudan, 54–55, 56–57, 257
Sufism, 29, 34, 54, 156, 255, 257–58; accommodation and, 150–53; colonialism and, 40–41; European imperialism and, 37; musical lyrics and, 182n45; toleration and, 151; in Tunisia, 78–79; in West Africa, 38
Sunni Islam, 32–33, 48, 64, 149, 181n37, 258
superstition, 5, 6, 9, 15
Supreme Command of the Armed Forces (SCAF), 90
Supreme Court, of United States, 21–22
Śvetāśvatara Upaniṣad, 145
Sy, Malick, 40
symbols, 125–26
Syria, 255, 258

Tagore, Abanindranath, 186n105
Tagore, Debendranath, 167, 170
Tagore, Rabindranath, 164, 170, 172, 173, 185n97, 185n99
Taha, Mahmoud Mohamed, 46, 48–49; indigenous self-liberation and, 54–61; secular state and, 67–72
Taji, Zaheen Shah, 151
Talking Cross, 112
Tambiah, Stanley Jeyaraja, 118
Taoism. *See* Daoism
Taoist Body, The (Schipper), 133n18
Tattvabodhinā Patrikā (journal), 163
tax (*zakāt*), 33
Taylor, Charles, 36, 108, 135–38, 196, 197, 199, 203, 209, 228–29; buffered self and, 109; Confucianism and, 117, 119, 121; early religion and, 191–92; elites and, 185n95; exclusive humanism and, 76, 82, 194–96; Gandhi and, 215; hyper-Christians and, 102, 104; Ibero-America and, 98; Latin Christendom and, 97, 100, 102, 104, 136; nova effect and, 169, 198; porous self and, 109; providential deism and, 163; religious change and, 156–58; secular reason and, 66–67. *See also Secular Age, A*
technology, 60, 176
Thaalibi, Sheik, 95n15
Thailand, 12
theological condition, in India, 201–4
Thiong'o, Ngugi wa, 72n9
Third Republic, 5, 250
Thirty Years' War, 63
Tianzhu Shiyi (Ricci), 120
at-Tijānī, Abul Abbass Ahmad, 38
Tijaniyya, 38–40, 42
Toland, John, 220, 222
toleration, 156; of atheists, 4, 6; of Catholics, 4, 7; reciprocal, 138; Sufism and, 151. *See also* twin tolerations
Torah, 253
tradition, 236–37
traditional religiosity, in India, 167–70
tragedy of the commons, 240
transcendence, 177–78
translatability, 201
transmigration of souls, 164

transmortality, 253
tribal law, 31–32
Tsinghua University, 128
Tunisia, 77–78, 92–93, 254, 258; authoritarian secularist modernization in, 81–84; twin tolerations and, 78–81, 84–91
Turkey, 20, 23, 26n2, 76–77, 86, 89, 254
Tu Weiming, 128
twin tolerations, 76–77, 78–81, 254; civil-military relations hypothesis of, 85, 87; political society hypothesis of, 85, 87–91; re-emergence of, 84–91; religious hypothesis of, 85, 86–87

Umar (caliph), 33
umma (global community), 23, 31–32, 48
unethical materialism, 59
United States, 8, 98, 105, 115, 249, 255–56; Christianity in, 21–22; founding of, 5; Mexico and, 107; slavery in, 80
Université de Tunis, 82
Upaniṣads, 145, 168, 196
urbanization, 248
Uruguay, 83, 106
usable past, 77, 78–81, 254
Uthman (caliph), 33
utopia, 32, 34, 49, 102, 104

Vaisnavism, 144–46, 148, 167, 171, 245n21
Valmy, battle of, 14
Vāmācāra, 148
van der Veer, Peter, 26n10, 250–52
varna (castes), 142, 145
Vasconcelos, José, 98
Vedic Brahmanism, 206
Vedic Hinduism, 141–45, 149, 252
Velvet Revolution, 1
Venezuela, 106
Vicarius Christi, 122
Victoria (queen), 125
Victoria Falls, 72n9
Victorian evolutionism, 123

village worship, 173
Villarreal, Antonio, 114
Villismo, 14
Virgin Mary, 112
Visnu (god), 145, 147, 202
Vivekananda, 168, 170
Voltaire, 133n7

Wahhabism, 13
Wang Tao, 125
Wārjābī, 37
wars of apostasy, 33
Weber, Max, 121, 136, 158, 164, 170, 228, 230; disenchantment and, 15, 152, 157; rationalization of religion and, 118; religious virtuosi and, 12
West Africa, 37–39, 42, 255
Westphalian ideal, 225, 226
widow burning (*sati*), 160
Williams, Bernard, 209
Winstanley, Gerard, 219, 223
Witzel, M., 194, 210
women, 81, 82–83, 88–89, 91, 96n32
Wordsworth, William, 15, 16
World Parliament of Religions, 126
world religions, 123
World War I, 98
wu (shamanism), 26n10, 126–27

xiao (filial piety), 128–29
xie (heterodoxy, illegitimate rule), 120
Ximinez (Cardinal), 249

yād ānā (remembering), 182n47
Yang, C. K., 131
Yusuf Ali, Abdullah, 31, 32

zakāt (tax), 33
Zapatistas, 114
Zauber (magic), 15–16
Zaytuna Mosque, 80
Zeitouna University, 79, 81, 82, 83
zheng (orthodoxy, legitimate rule), 120

RELIGION, CULTURE, AND PUBLIC LIFE

Series Editor: Karen Barkey

After Pluralism: Reimagining Religious Engagement,
edited by Courtney Bender and Pamela E. Klassen

Religion and International Relations Theory,
edited by Jack Snyder

Religion in America: A Political History,
Denis Lacorne

Democracy, Islam, and Secularism in Turkey,
edited by Ahmet T. Kuru and Alfred Stepan

Refiguring the Spiritual: Beuys, Barney, Turrell, Goldsworthy,
Mark C. Taylor

Tolerance, Democracy, and Sufis in Senegal,
edited by Mamadou Diouf

*Rewiring the Real: In Conversation with William Gaddis, Richard Powers,
Mark Danielewski, and Don DeLillo*,
Mark C. Taylor

Democracy and Islam in Indonesia, edited by
Mirjam Künkler and Alfred Stepan

Religion, the Secular, and the Politics of Sexual Difference, edited by
Linell E. Cady and Tracy Fessenden

Boundaries of Toleration, edited by
Alfred Stepan and Charles Taylor

Recovering Place: Reflections on Stone Hill,
Mark C. Taylor

Blood: A Critique of Christianity, Gil Anidjar

*Choreographies of Shared Sacred Sites: Religion, Politics,
and Conflict Resolution*, edited by
Elazar Barkan and Karen Barkey

Beyond Individualism: The Challenge of Inclusive Communities,
George Rupp

Love and Forgiveness for a More Just World,
edited by Hent de Vries and Nils F. Schott

GPSR Authorized Representative: Easy Access System Europe, Mustamäe tee 50, 10621 Tallinn, Estonia, gpsr.requests@easproject.com

www.ingramcontent.com/pod-product-compliance
Lightning Source LLC
Chambersburg PA
CBHW021938290426
44108CB00012B/880